NORIA MABASA

DAVID KRUT PUBLISHING

Published by David Krut Publishing with funding from
The French Institute of South Africa (IFAS)
Pro Helvetia – Arts Council of Switzerland
The Swiss Agency for Development and Cooperation
The Royal Netherlands Embassy
The National Arts Council of South Africa (NAC)

Advisory Committee: Nessa Leibhammer, Santu Mofokeng, Brenda Schmahman,
Sarah Tabane, Kiren Thathiah

Editor: Karen Press

Design and layout: Welma Odendaal

David Krut Publishing Co-ordinator: Bettina Schultz

Translations: French – Catherine Lauga du Plessis
Dutch – Loes Nas

Reproduction: Bell-Roberts

Printing: Mega Print cc

Set in Photina MT and News Gothic

DAVID KRUT PUBLISHING CC
P O Box 892, Houghton 2041,
Johannesburg, South Africa

bettina@taxiartbooks.com

www.taxiartbooks.com

www.davidkrut.com

ISBN 0-9584496-5-1

Photographs: Unless otherwise stated, photography is by Merwelene van der Merwe, Mukondeni Fine Arts Gallery.

Cover photograph: Sasa Kralj/Trace Images

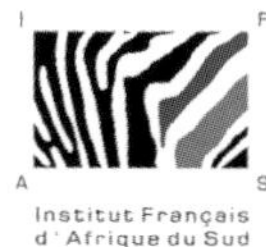
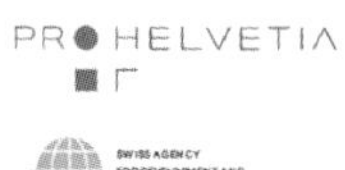
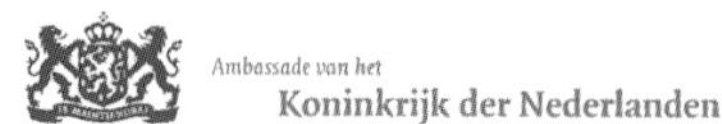
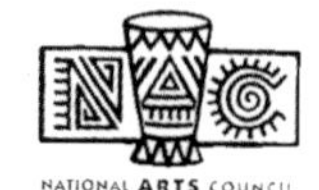
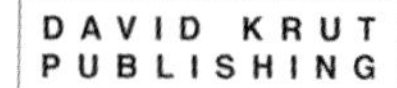

CONTENTS

ART AND LIFE

" I was born in Xigalo Village, 1938. That year there was a big initiation school for girls, *Tshikumbana*, where you sit in the bush for six months and you cannot go home. The day I was born was very special, my mother gave birth to me and on the same day my sister had a son, Matumba, and the chief's wife gave birth to Makone, the future Chief Kutama. "

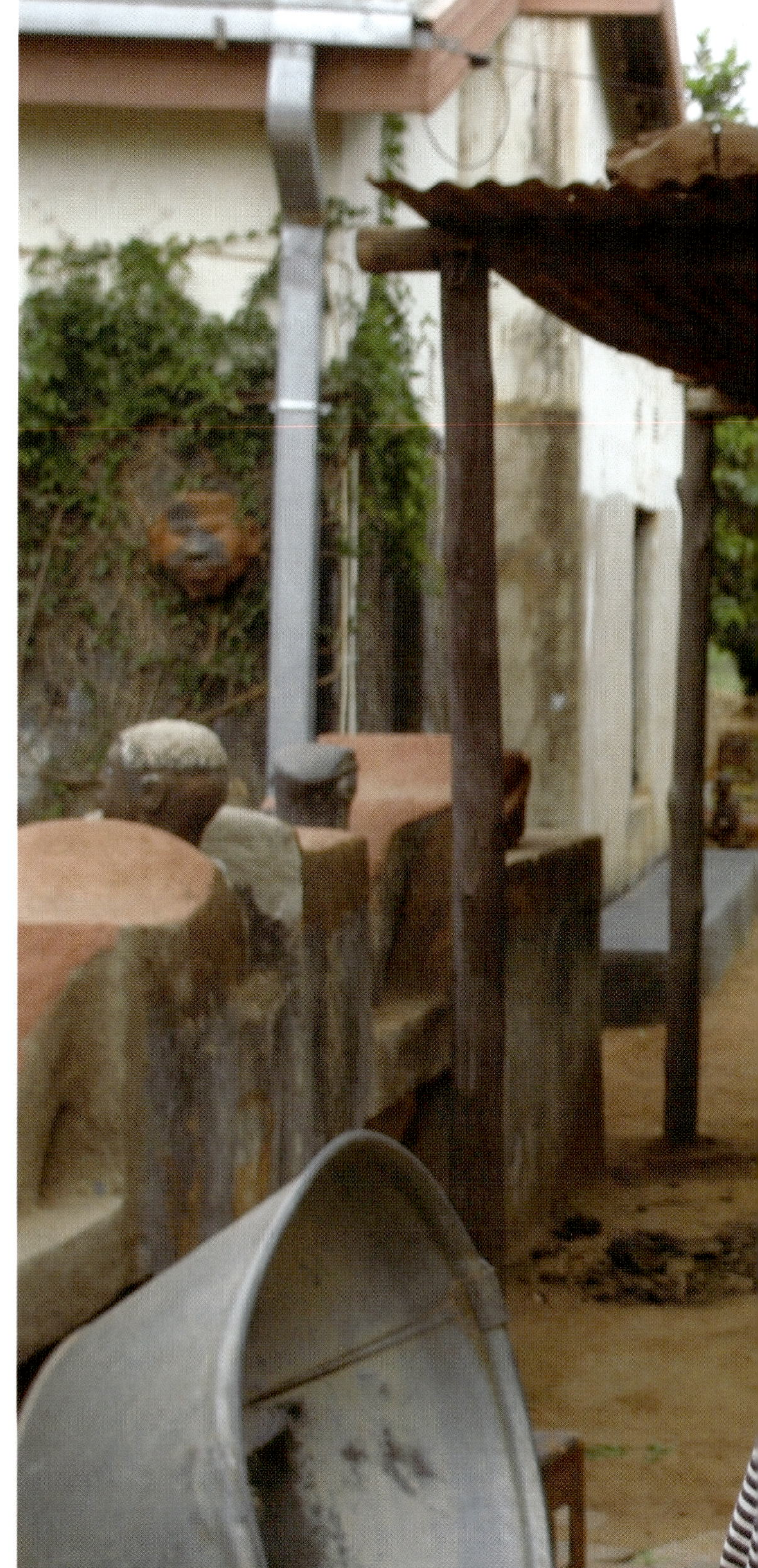

Pages 4–7:
Noria Mabasa at her homestead in Tshino village, Vuwani, in Limpopo Province, where she was visited by photographer Merwelene van der Merwe in November 2002.

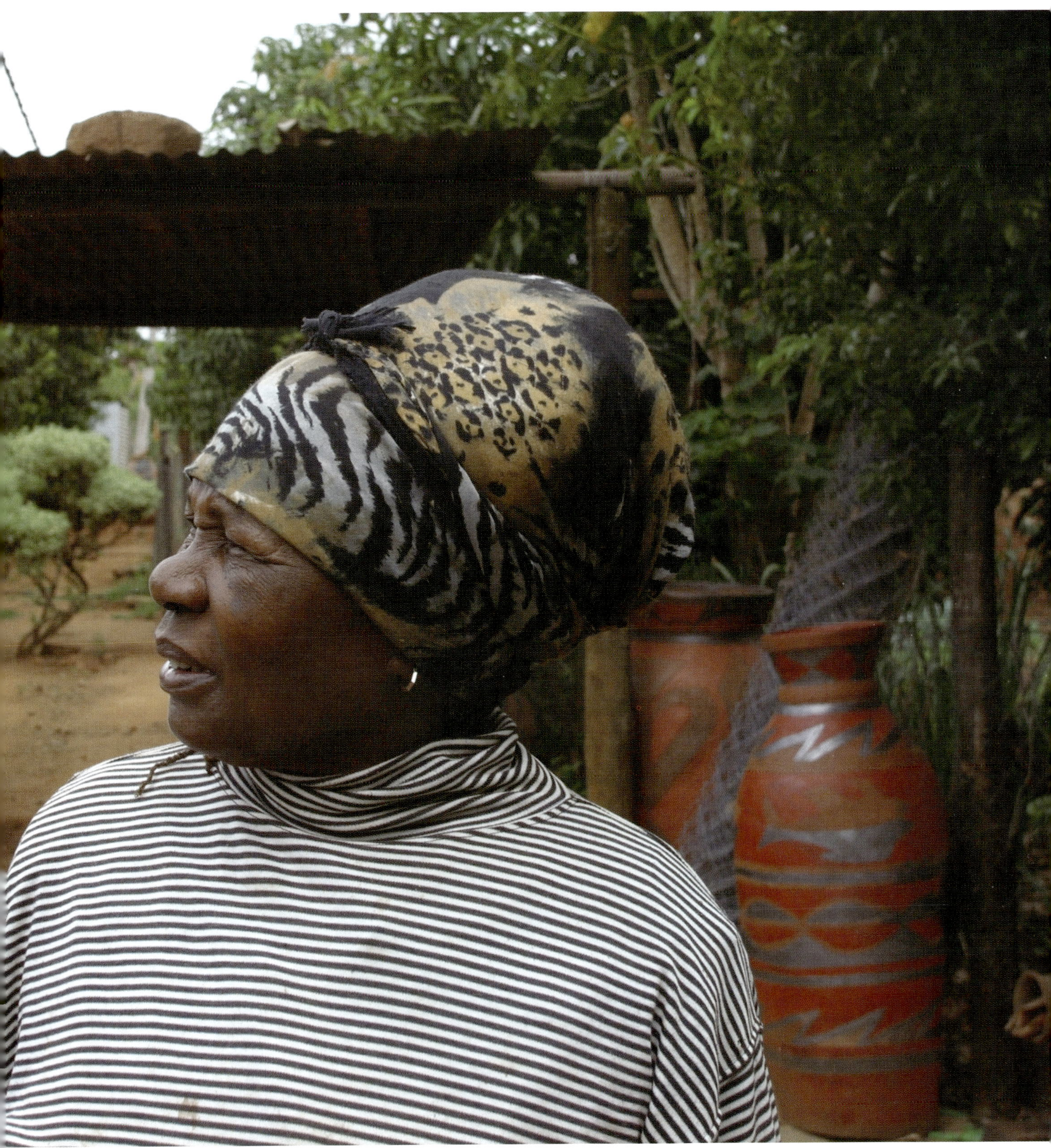

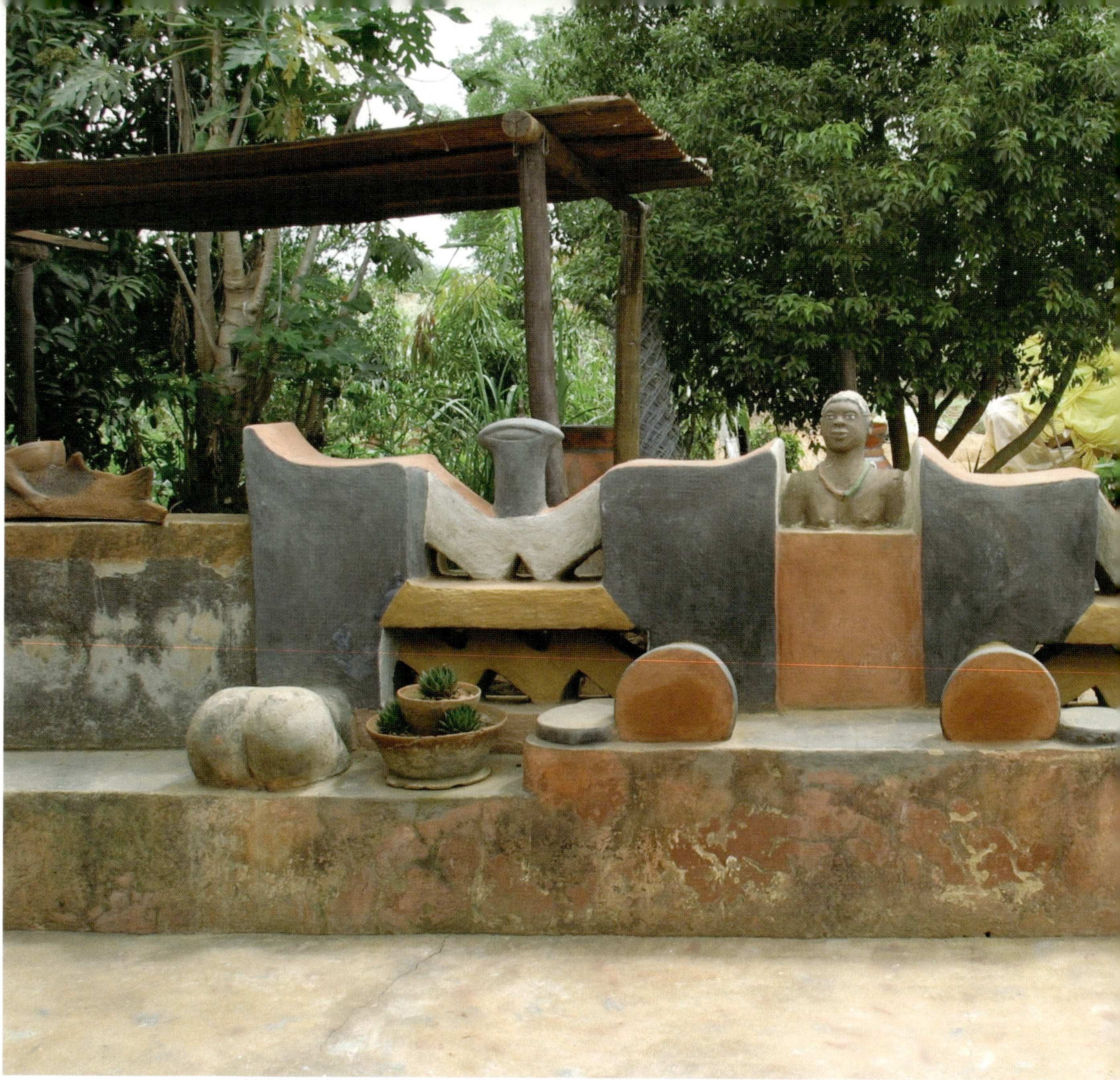

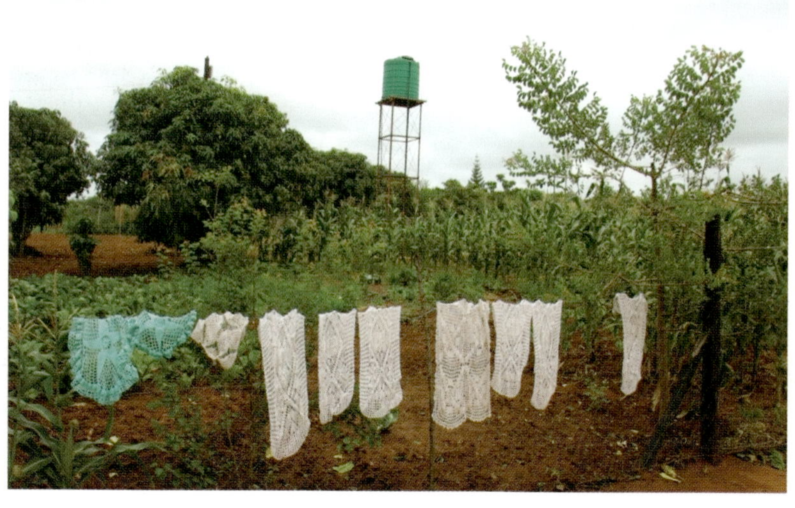

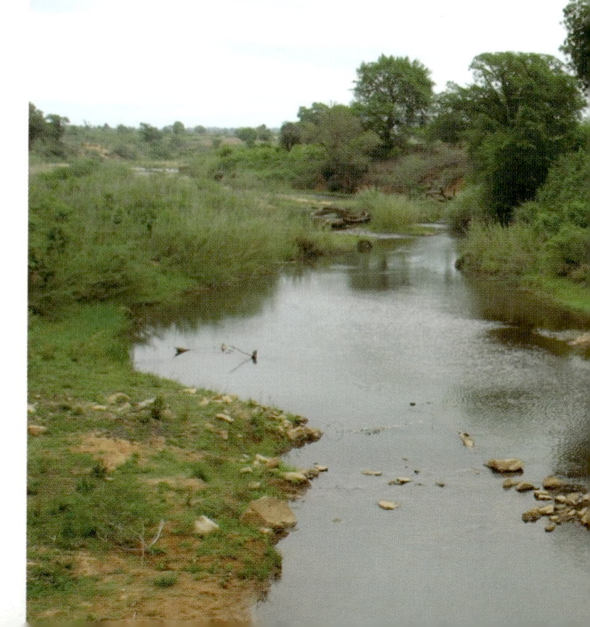

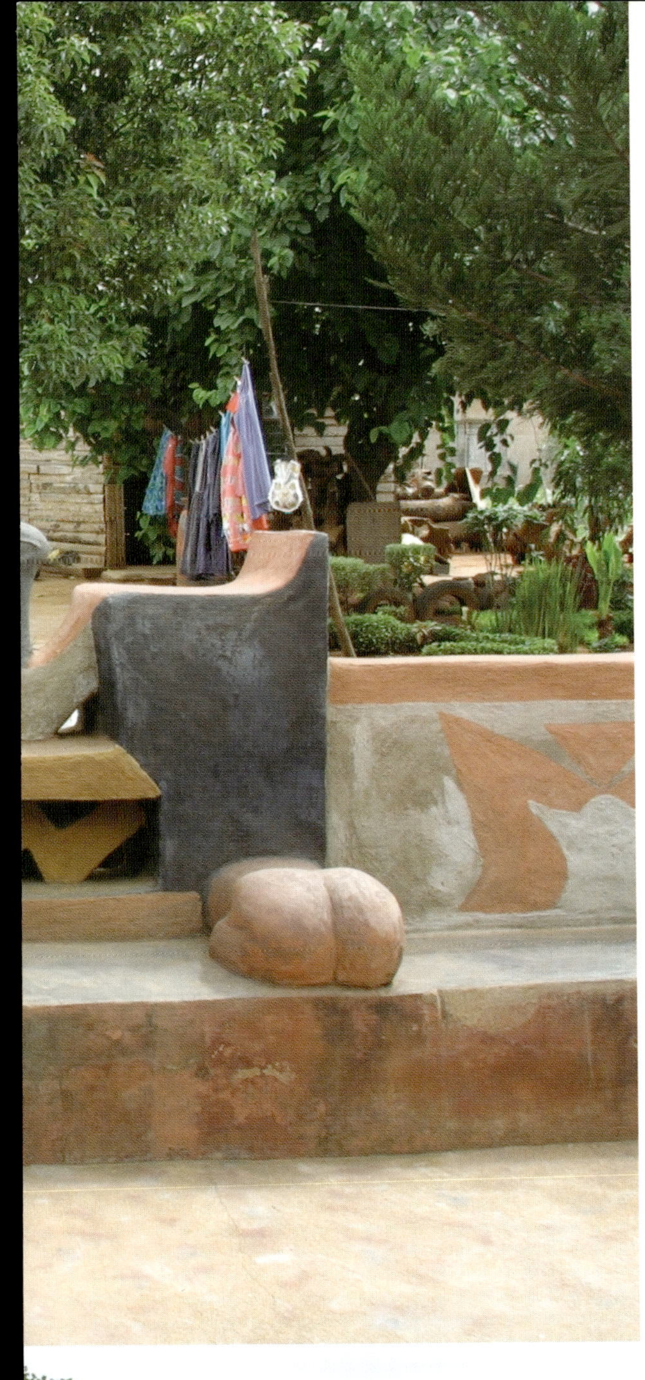

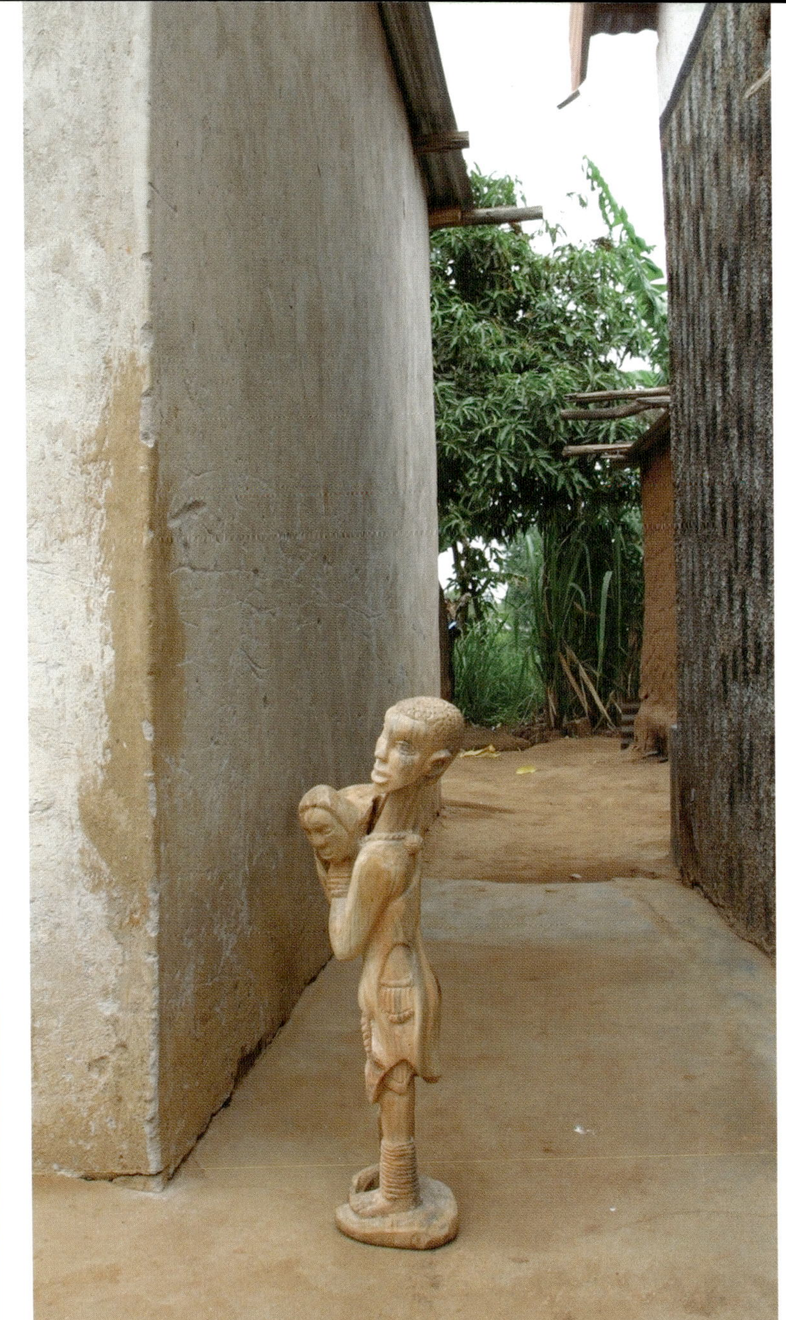

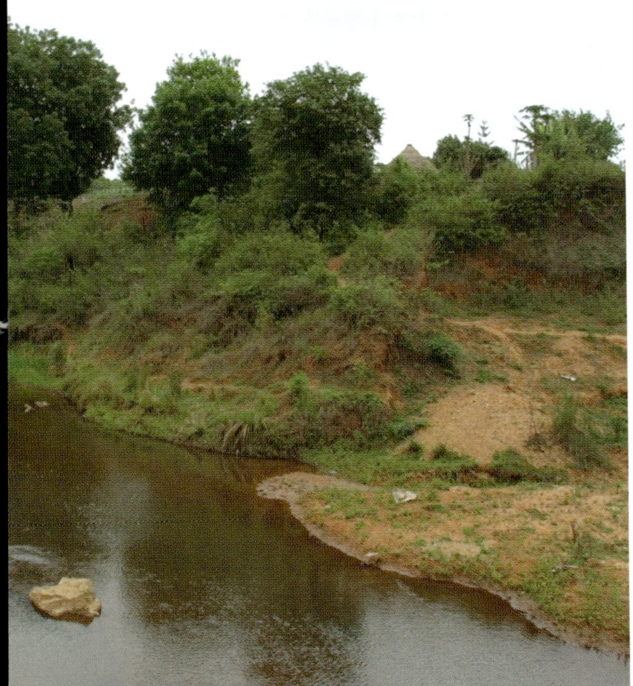

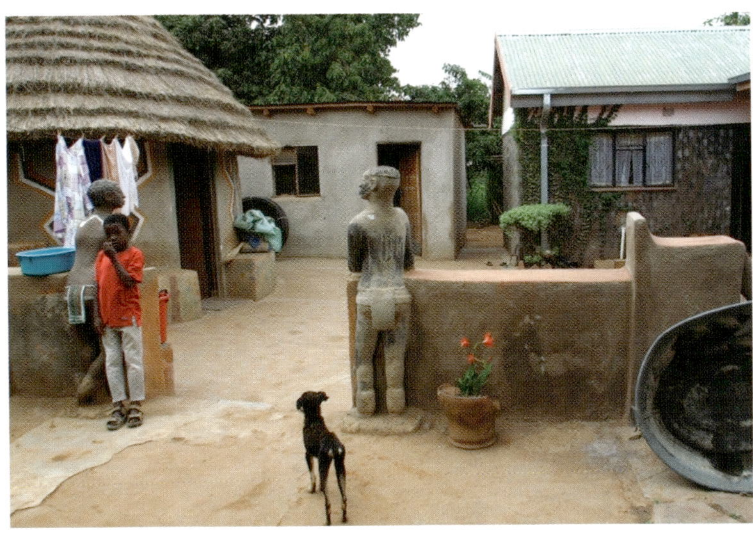

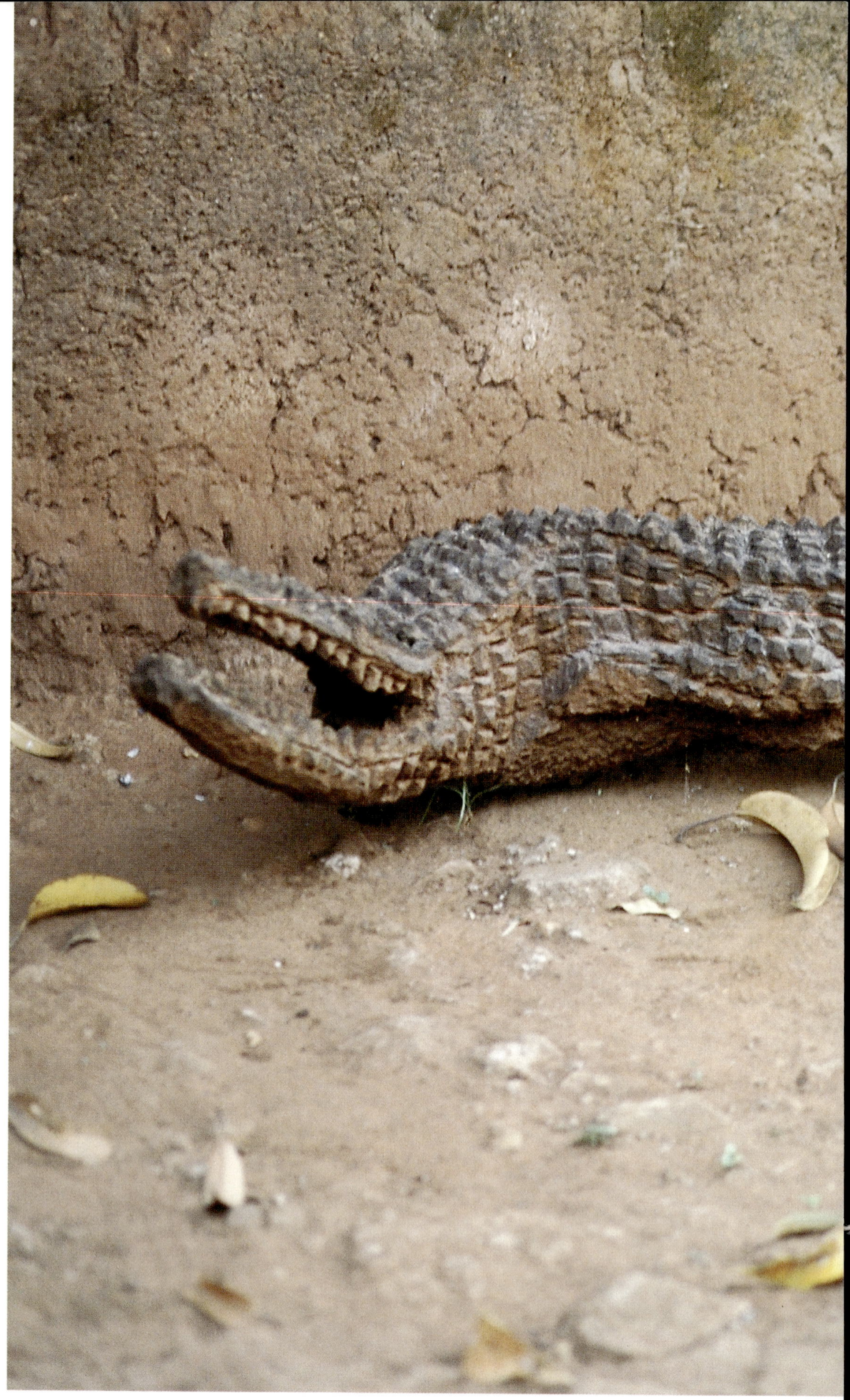

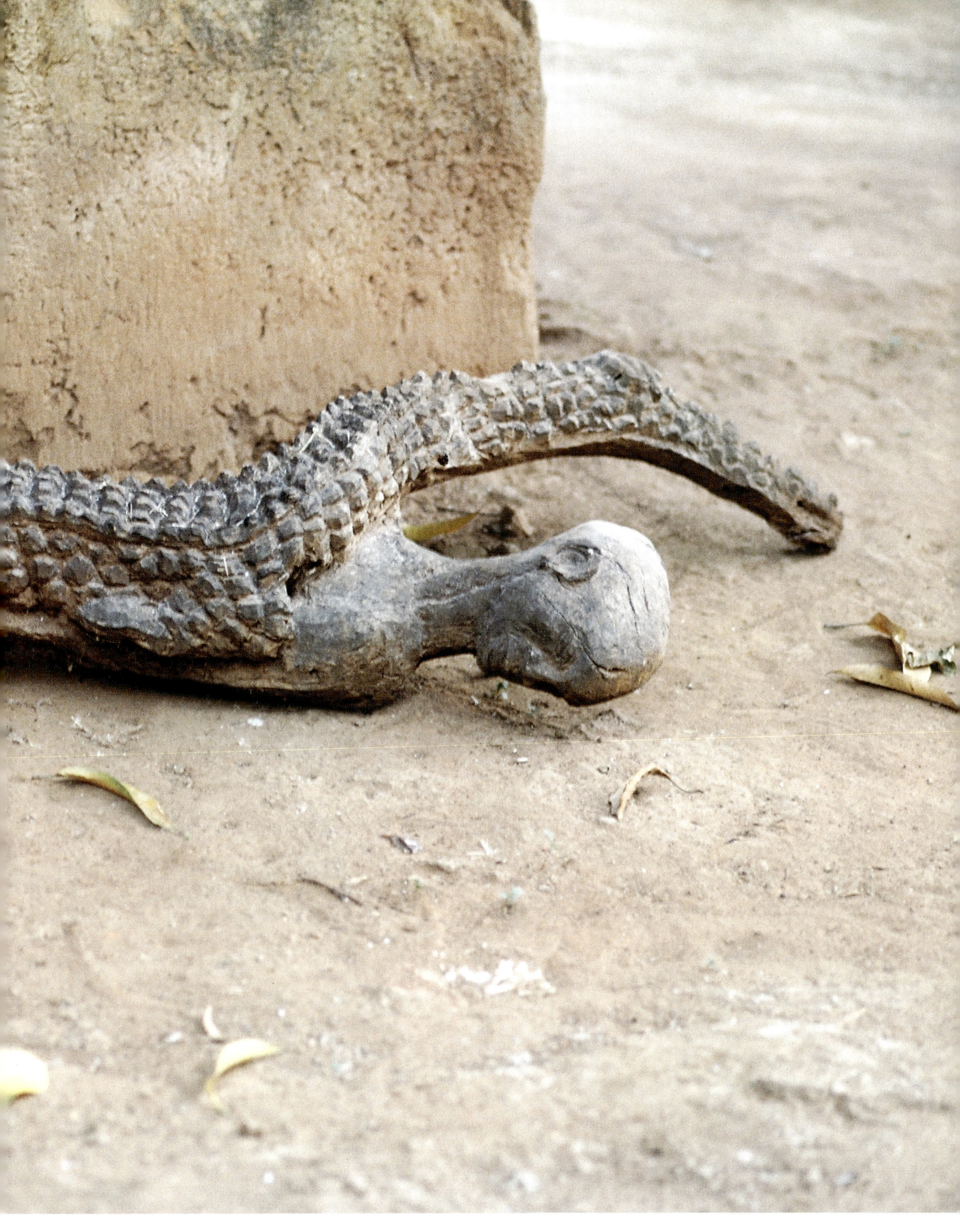

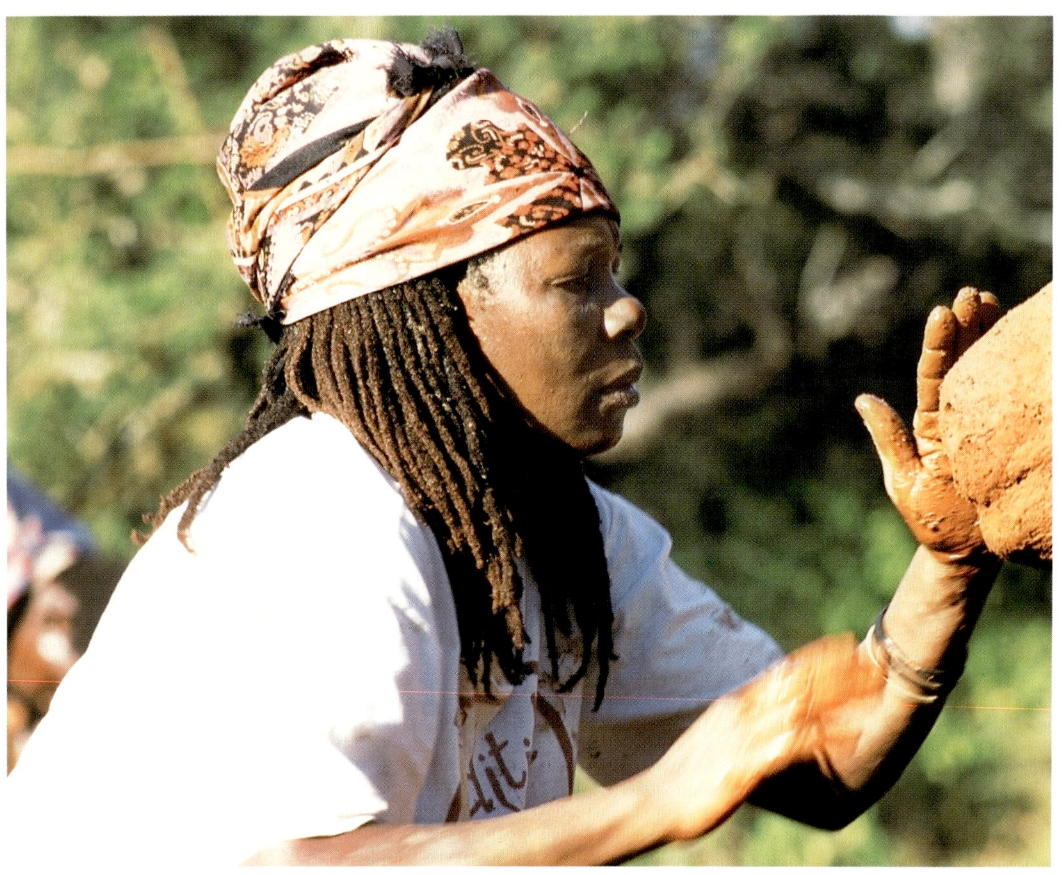

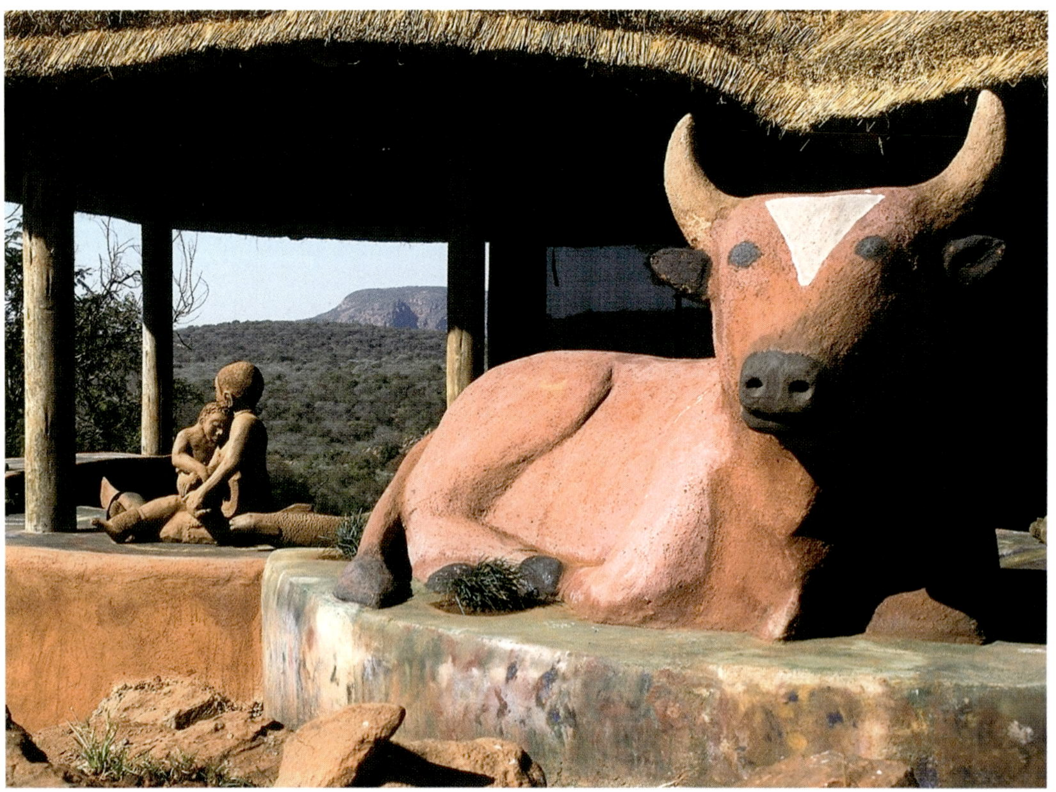

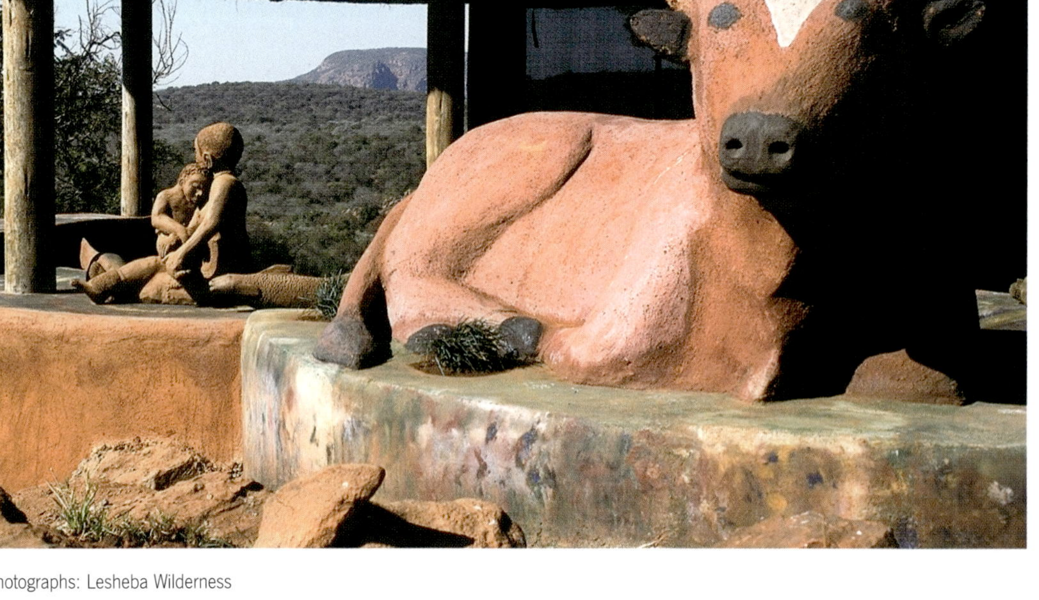

Photographs: Lesheba Wilderness

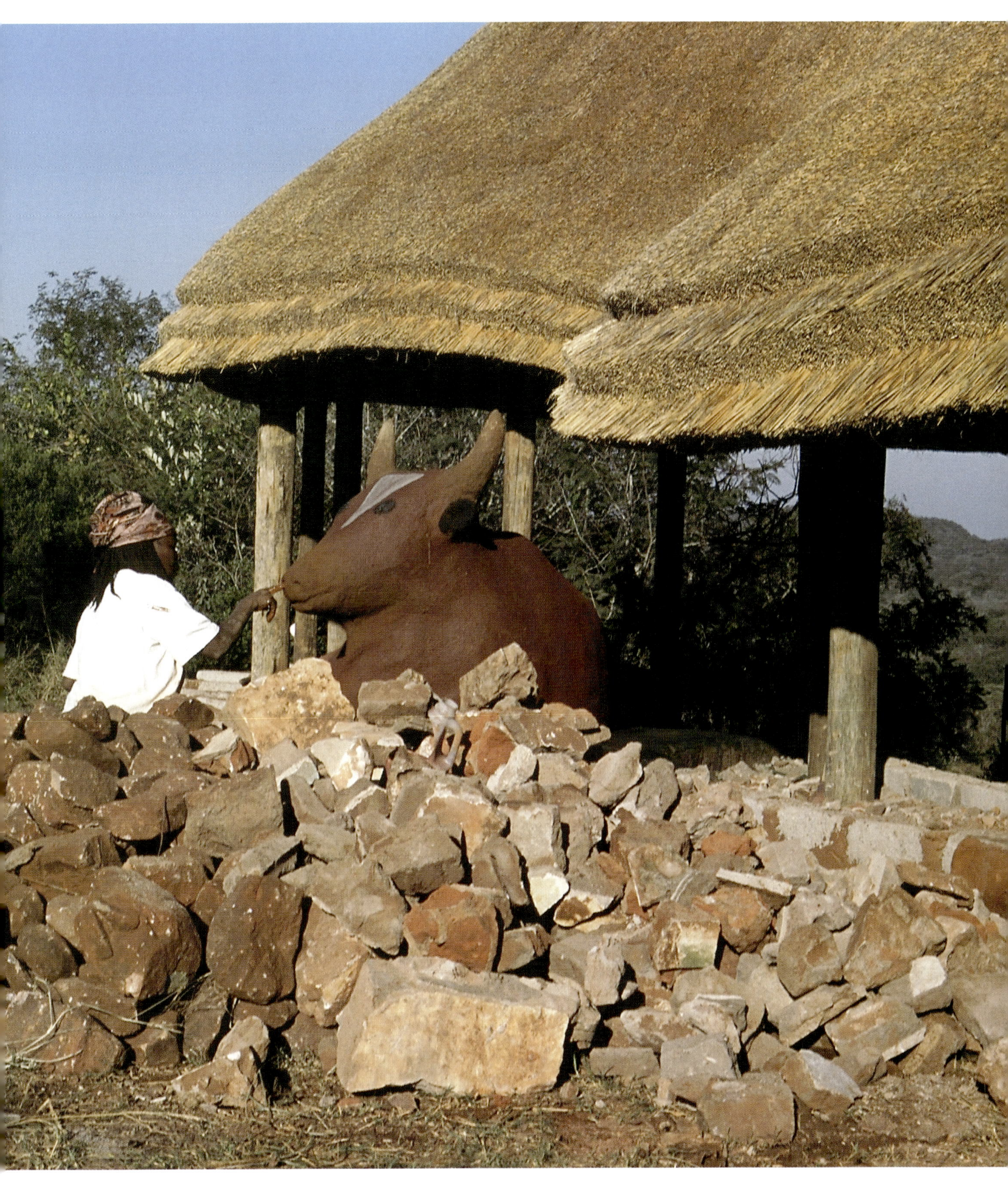

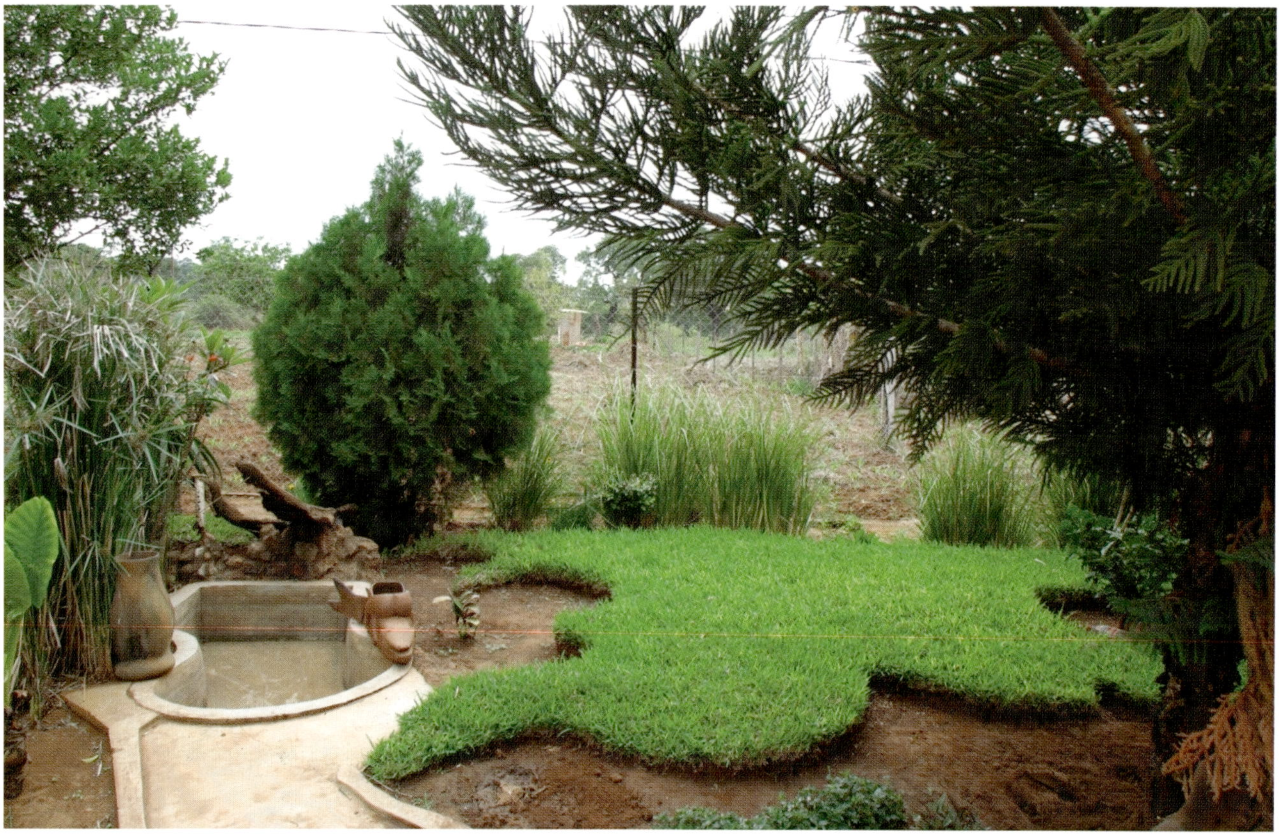

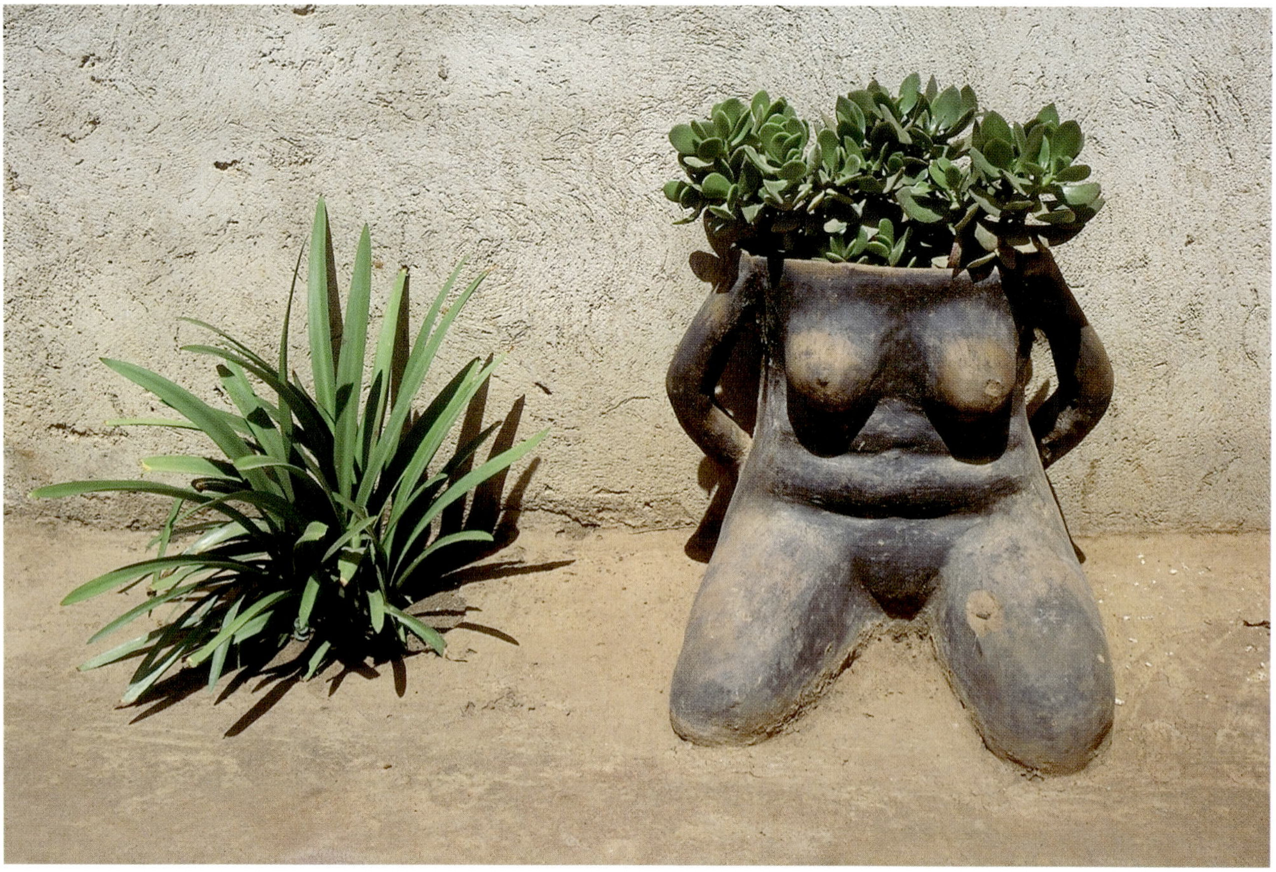

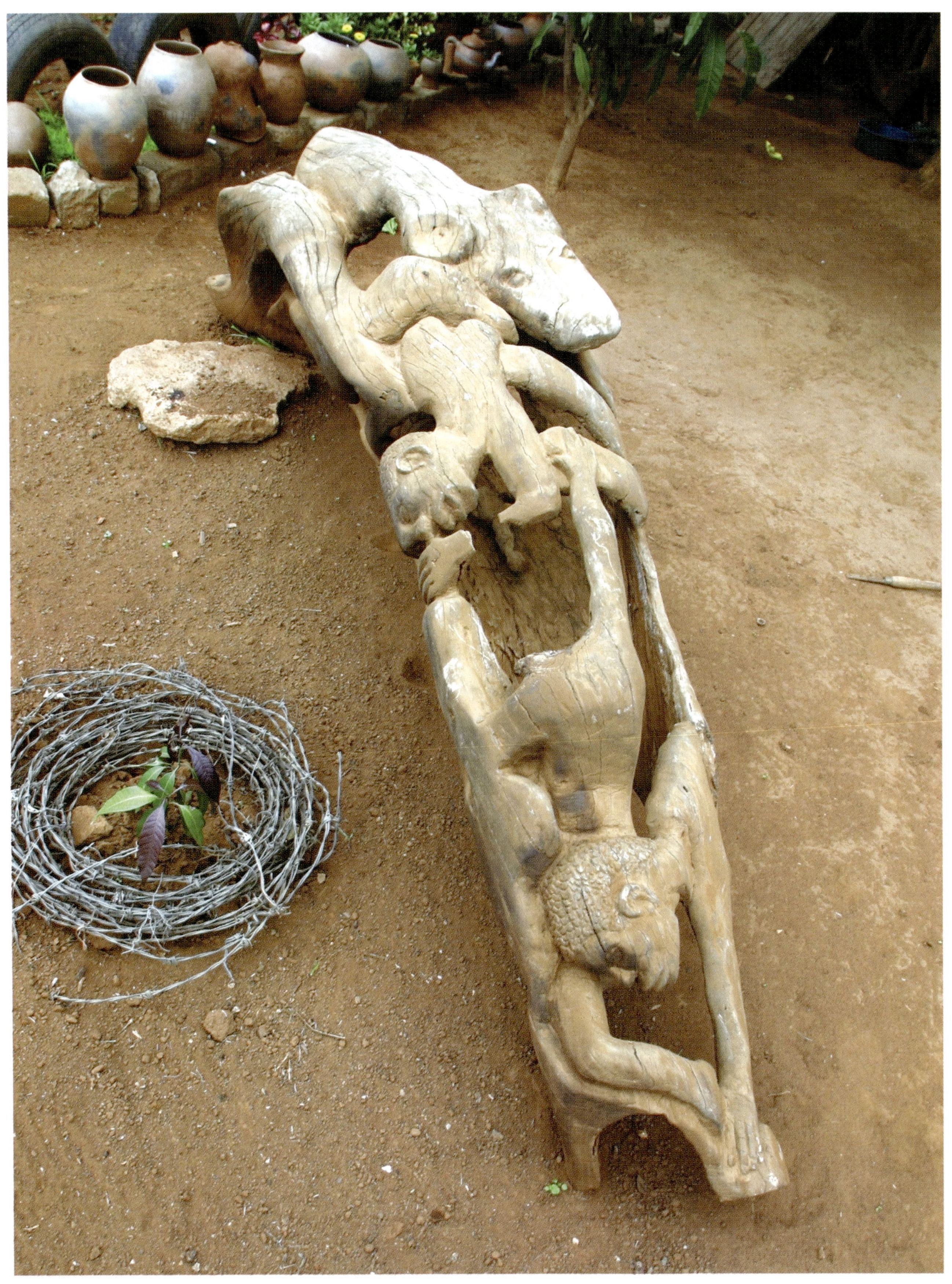

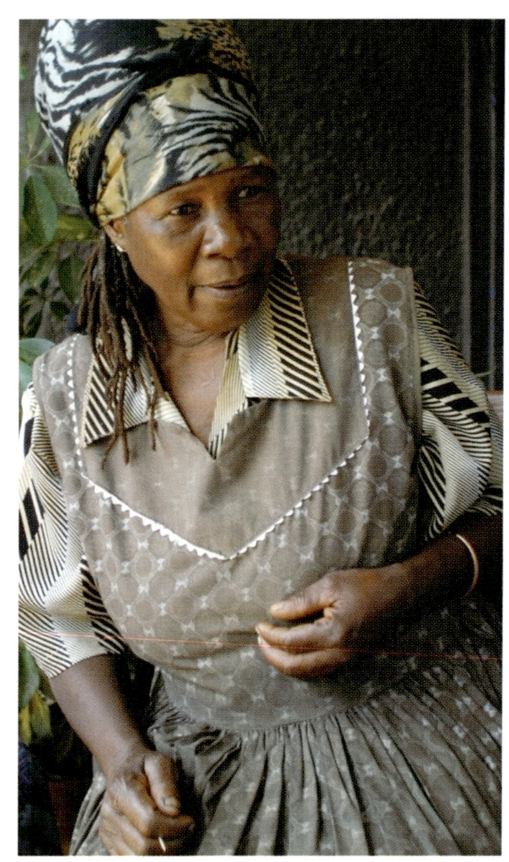 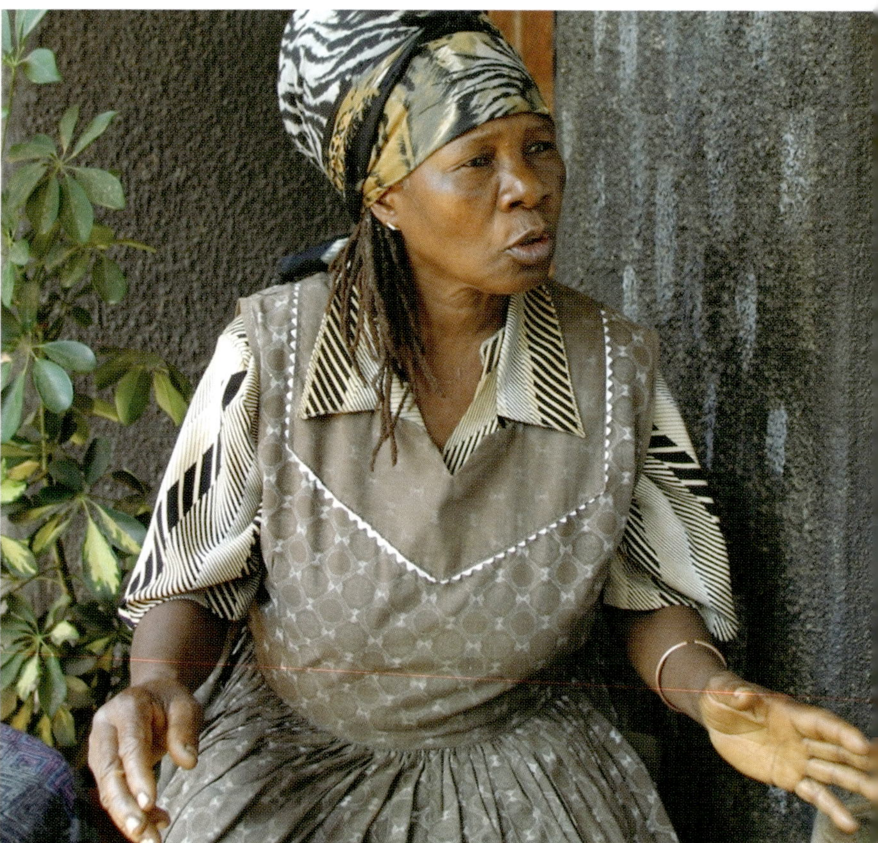

JOURNEY TO

An interview with Noria Mabasa

In June 2002 Kathryn Straughan interviewed Noria Mabasa about the genesis and growth of her commitment to sculpture as her life's work, and the ways in which she has located her art in relation to the cultural traditions of Venda society.

What follows is a record of these conversations.

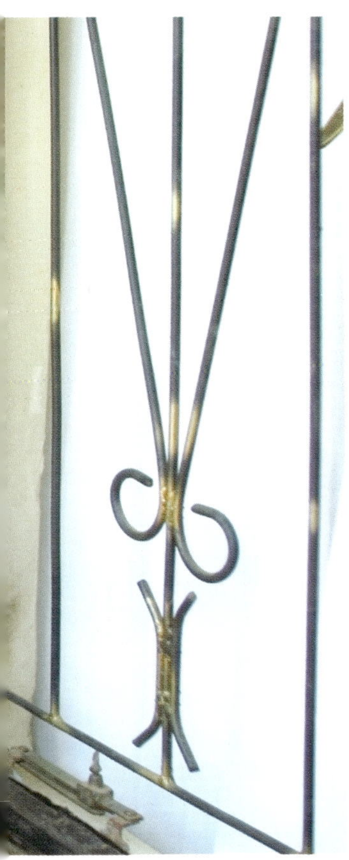

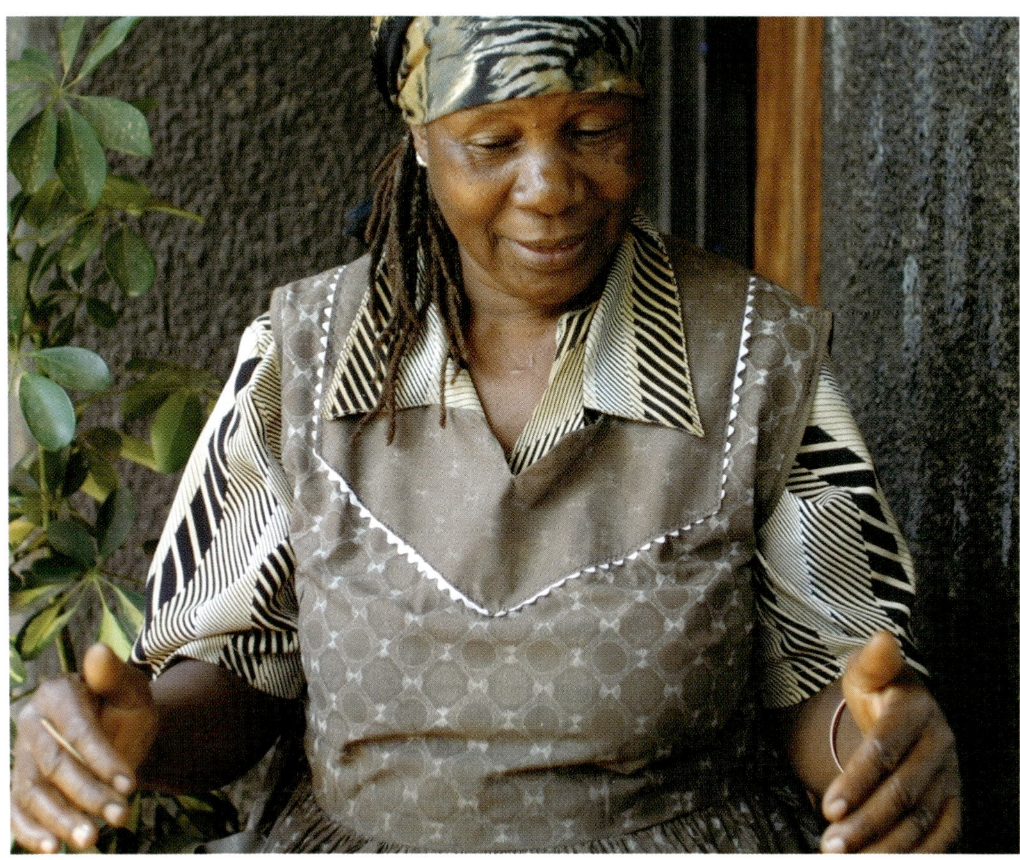

VENDA

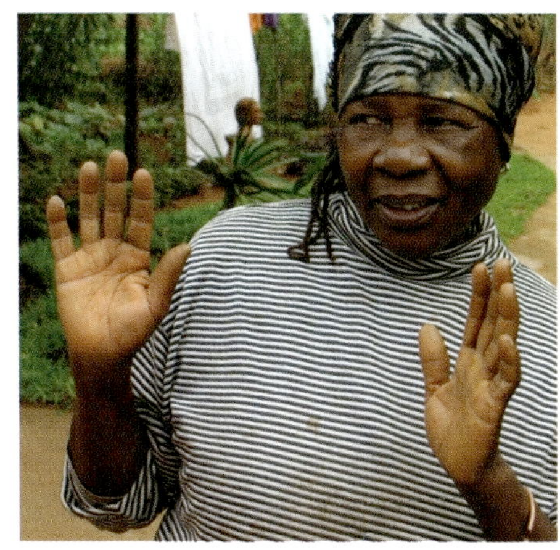

"If I start to work with clay or wood, I don't see anything. Then as I start it comes to me here [points at her head] and then it's coming and coming and I don't know how, but it is wonderful and the piece becomes something ..."

NORIA MABASA'S home is in Venda, a region in the north-eastern part of South Africa where most of the inhabitants live in the valleys between high, mist-shrouded mountains. They have many tales and legends about their people and their origins, as well as about the land itself. Noria lives in the village of Tshino which, like other villages in the region, is filled with housing settlements (*midi*) where each home is surrounded by hedges and low mud walls. Huts are thatched and some are painted with traditional designs. The chief (*khasi*) of the village has his home on the highest ground, with his wives and family living just below him. The rest of the villagers occupy the surrounding lower areas. In Venda society the household group (*mudi*) comprises either a single family or a collection of families, usually belonging to the same clan. The inhabitants of the *mudi* live together in a closely arranged collection of huts, each with its own surrounding courtyard (*muta*). Each individual household is known as a *khoro*. The traditional round houses in Tshino are interspersed with modern brick houses.

People mill around – women with babies tied to their backs with colourful blankets, men sitting in the shade of trees, smoking tobacco and drinking homemade *marula* beer, mongrel dogs slinking between legs searching for scraps and chickens scratching and pecking at the ground.

A large rust-coloured metal gate, flanked by two sculptured pillars, and a high fence, unusual in this rural setting, surround the property where Noria lives and works. Her open-air 'studio' lies beneath an old mulberry tree where *Union Buildings*, her latest work, stands covered with yellow plastic sheets. Other large works in progress can be seen lying around. Surrounding the studio area are her maize fields, orchards and vegetable garden.

On the banks of the Luvuvhu River, where women wash their clothes on the rocks and children splash in the water, Noria has built her home. Her property is a fusion of traditional Venda culture and Western influence. Round thatched huts painted with customary designs and a conventional rectangular house with metal frame windows surround a central courtyard. A low wall, stained with red oxide and intricately decorated with throne-like seats and clay statues, encircles this area. One of the huts functions as a bed-and-breakfast facility and another as a workshop where she stores and creates her clay pieces. There is also a small tin-roofed gallery and shop outside the complex, where Noria keeps a selection of her works and beadwork that her daughter produces. She and her family

Entrance to Noria Mabasa's homestead, November 2002.

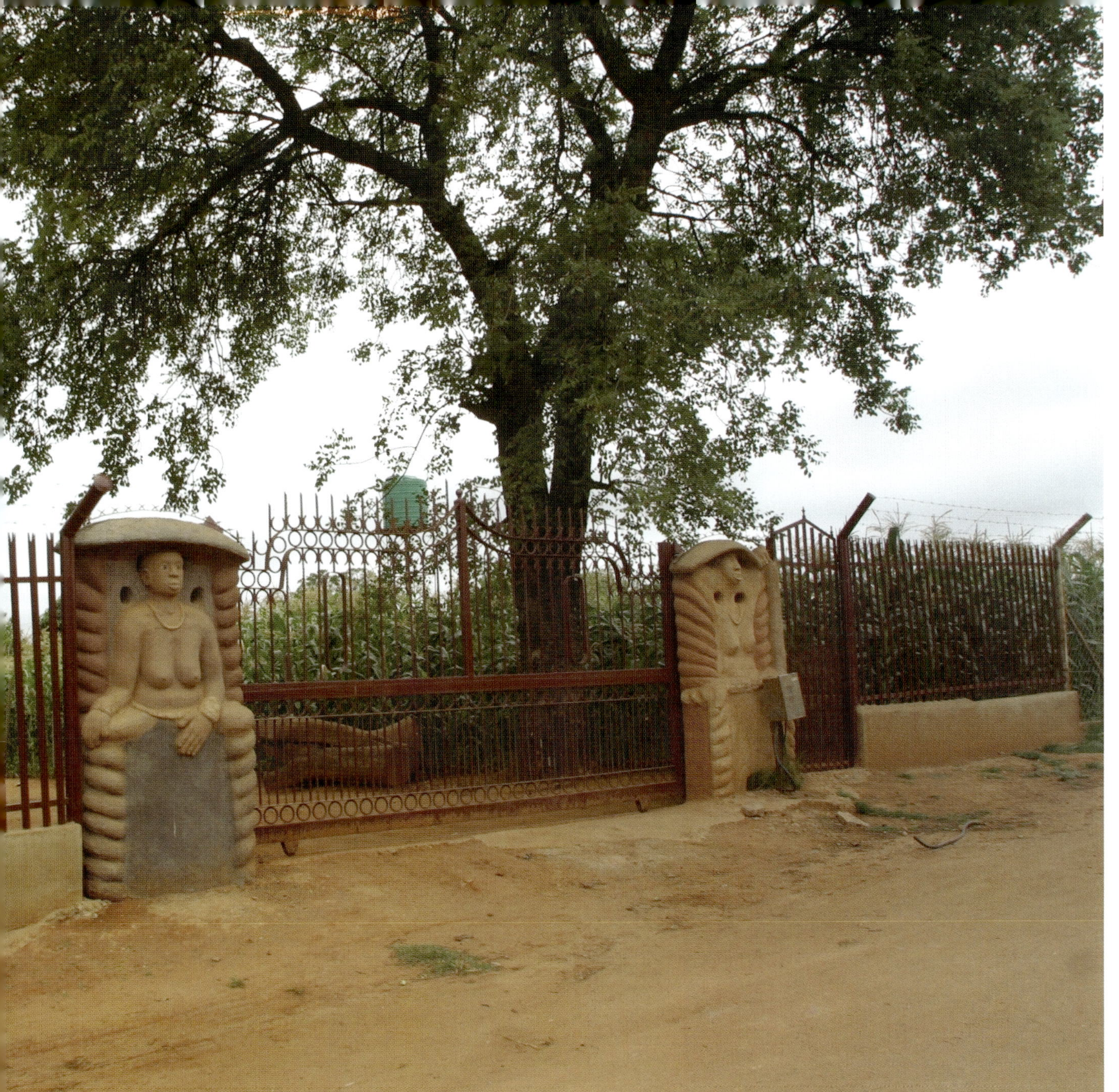

live in the Western-style house which has running water and electricity – luxuries in this community.

Two clay figures, one male and one female, stand at the entrance to the courtyard. Noria recreates these bas-relief sculptures on an annual basis. Her art is everywhere. Nubile maidens lie down in the position of respect, vha a losha, sacred crocodiles bask in the sun, lions keep watch and pot plant holders in the shape of the female body are filled with succulents. This is her domestic space, the centre of her private life. It is this setting that nourishes Noria, the beautiful dreadlocked mother, grandmother, carver, potter and teacher. When people see her works they are surprised by her humility and her joy in the reaction her pieces inspire, for she too is astonished by what she has made.

Noria makes a big impact on those who meet her for the first time. She has not cut her hair since 1989 and wears it long, with the top covered by a scarf or woollen hat. In a dream she was told that every time she cut her hair, she cut her creativity. She says, 'If I cut my hair, art is gone and I get sick ...'

In order to understand Noria's sculptures one needs to hear her tell of where she comes from, as her culture and spiritual beliefs are paramount in her works. She never attended formal school and has not learnt to read or write, except for her name, which she marks on her works. She has also had no art training.

Noria Muelelwa (meaning 'to remember') Luvhimbi was born on 10 May 1938 in Tshigalo Village, in the Ramukhumba district in the north of what was then known as the Transvaal.[1] She was the third child born to Makhado Samuel Luvhimbi and Ntho Martha Rathivhunwane. She has two sisters, Mwanero Josephina and Muketwa Johannah, and a younger brother, Ditebele Phineas.

Noria grew up in Tshigalo Village. Her duties as a young child included looking after the family's goats, cows, donkeys, sheep and chickens. It was unusual for the daughters in a family to tend to the animals, but because there were not many sons in this large extended family, the girls were expected to help. Noria's father was a wealthy man, not in monetary terms but in the terms of animals and crops. He was much older than Noria's mother and had eighteen wives. Each wife produced three or four children. Noria explains how the children would form small groups of about ten who ate together. She says they were forced to eat quickly so as to make sure they got food before the other children came to take it away from them.

In 1952 Noria, aged fourteen, went to live in White City, a section of Soweto, Johannesburg. The wife of one of her brothers had given birth to a child and had become blind. Noria went to help the new mother. She did all the washing, cleaning and cooking and took care of the infant. After a year had passed, the wife's eyesight returned and Noria went to live with a cousin in Alexandra, in the northern part of Johannesburg.

DREAMS AND VISIONS

It was in Johannesburg that Noria's dreams, which play such a major role in her life, first began. In one dream she recalls her father telling her that when the stars came out that night she was to bring water to his grave in Giyani. She refused because her father was long dead, but the dream kept recurring until she went to her brother and asked that he help her return home. However, her brother did not trust in the dream as Noria did, and would not give her any money.

During her stay in Alexandra she met an older man, Jim Mabasa, a Shangaan. The two fell in love and Jim requested Noria's brother's permission to marry her. In December 1955 Noria and Jim returned to Venda where they were married and went to live at Hamutsha, which is now called Vuwani. Noria, who had spoken Shangaan her whole life, now began to speak Venda. Although raised speaking only Shangaan, her ancestry is VhaVenda and she regards herself as a MuVenda. In 1958 Noria and Jim's first child, Sikane Joyce Mabasa, was born, followed by Bomane Edward Mabasa in 1960.

Throughout this time in her life the dreams persisted. Her visions were sometimes prophetic: in one she saw that a neighbour's one twin would die and in another she was able to see a letter written to a friend. She could see the colour of the paper and could tell who had sent it. These prophecies disturbed her and she felt weighed down by the responsibilities they presented. She was a young wife with two young children and she did not wish to have these powers. In 1965 she had a dream in which an old lady appeared to her and showed her that she must begin working with clay. At that time there were no women that she knew of who made clay figures, and yet here was this vision telling her to sculpt.

Noria ignored the dreams but gradually she began to get sick. Her whole body ached and she was weak all the time. No doctor could tell her what was wrong and as the dreams continued, so her health deteriorated. Jim disowned her and sent her and their children back to live with her family in Tshigalo. Noria had no house, no means of supporting her children and no food. However, she was relieved to be able to get away from Jim, who had become an abusive husband.

1. Detail of clay seat at Mabasa's homestead.

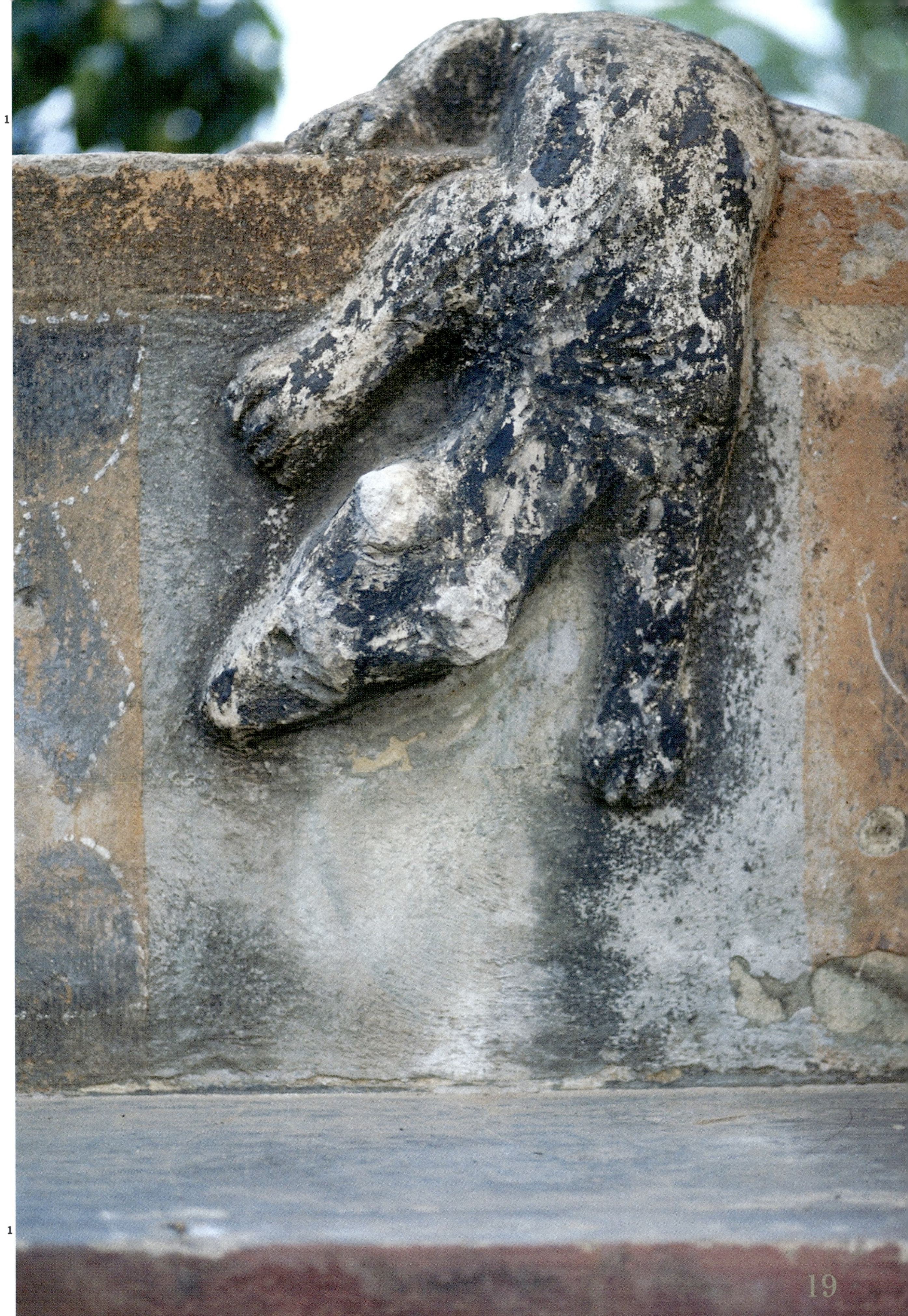
1

From 1965 to 1967 Noria stayed with one of her brothers in Tshigalo. Finally in 1967 her family helped her to build a small room next to her brother's house. Her mother, her daughter Joyce and her sister fetched water from far away to make the bricks from soil and dung. Her family gave Noria and her children some blankets but were unable to offer her much more in the way of items such as clothes. Noria, Joyce and Edward slept on the floor by a small fire to keep warm. Noria recalls how she used to take the leftovers from the homemade malt beer, usually given to chickens and pigs, which she and the children would eat. She was too poor even to afford maize meal (a staple food in South Africa) for her family. She was so sick that Joyce and her mother had to help wash and feed her. Throughout this trying time Noria remained ill, and continued to have dreams of the old woman. Her family, desperate to help her, went to a *nyanga* (traditional healer).

When she slept, the old woman whom she now calls 'Tshidzeuli', meaning 'chewing the cud' or 'remembering nicely', returned in her dreams. This old lady, ravaged by leprosy, had badly damaged hands with few fingers, no nose and parts of her mouth missing. She wore animal hides, had very black skin, short black hair, exposed hanging breasts and was very old and wrinkled. The appearance of this woman so terrified Noria that she was afraid to sleep.

One day the old lady spoke to her and said, 'You do not understand because I am teaching you and you are not listening.'

When Noria woke up, her tongue was hanging out and she couldn't draw it back into her mouth. She started crying, and her mother wrapped a cloth around her face. Together they went to the *nyanga*. The healer took a blade and made some cuts near Noria's cheek and ear and put some medicine in her ear, but nothing helped. Joyce was very distressed and decided that they should go to the church[2] for a drumming ceremony, in which the ancestors are called upon.

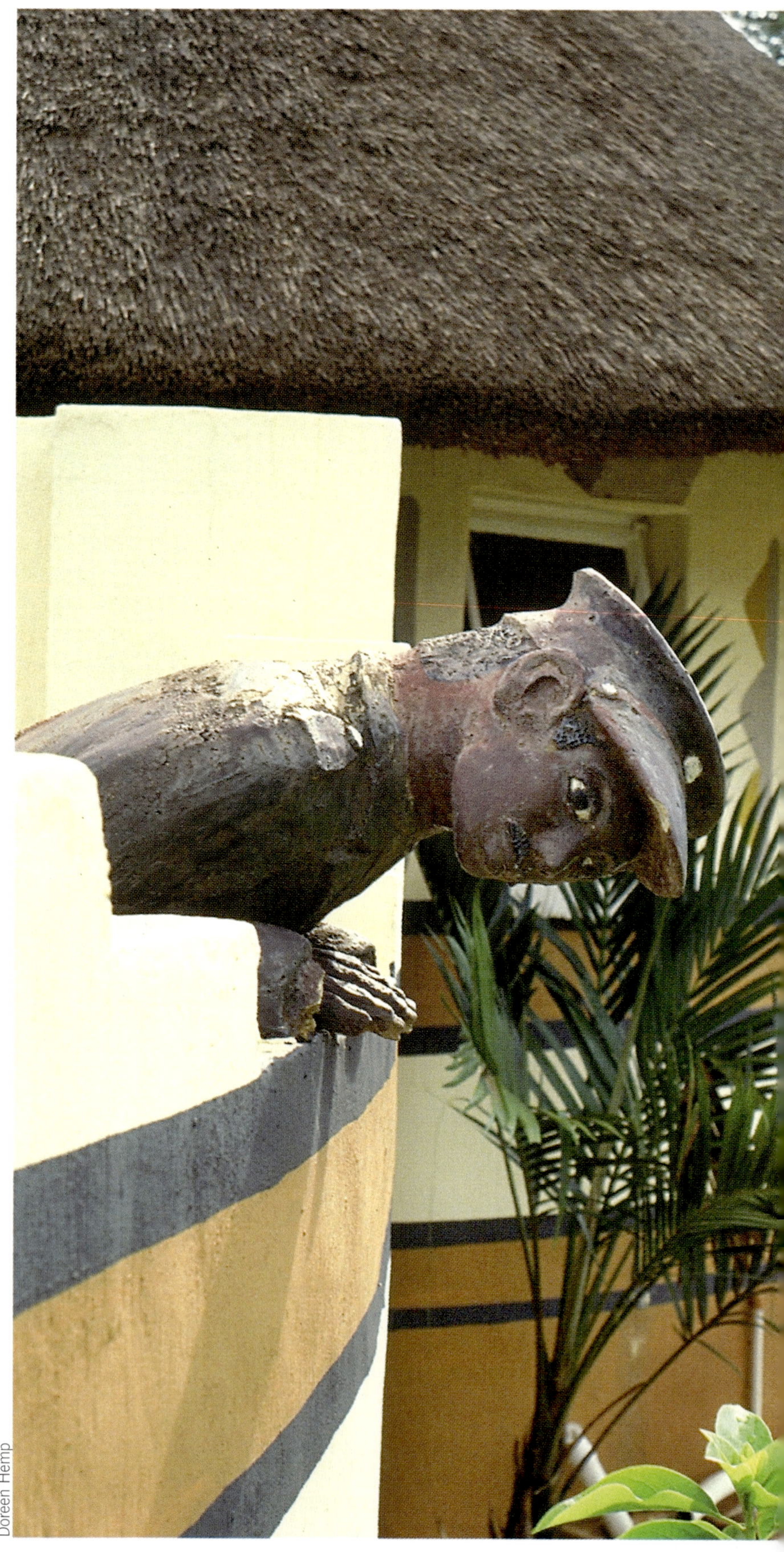

At the church there was a man who had come from Johannesburg, who was said to have healing powers. When he saw Noria he removed the cloth from her face and told Joyce to fetch some ash from the fire. He put the ash in a cup with some water and started praying and touching Noria on her head. When he did this, her tongue went back in but was not straight. Noria found it difficult to breathe. The man then bottled some ash water and told her to drink it. She was to take it home and drink from it frequently. Every night Noria returned to the church to pray and within a week she had recovered.

Then one night she dreamed of her father. She was standing next to him, waist deep in a pool of water. He called out 'Muelelwa' (Noria's Venda name) and asked, 'Why, when the old lady is giving you a lesson to be rich, do you say no?' Noria shrugged and turned away. Then she awoke, scared and shaking. Before she had turned away in her dream, her father had hit her on the shoulder with some reeds. She trembled. The old lady and her father were both gone from her dream, but she couldn't return to sleep. The shaking carried on for a week, then again on the Friday her father came back and shouted, 'Muelelwa, wake up now! Go to Muthewana (Noria's sister) and tell her that you must go and pray to the ancestors.'

Noria woke up and her terrible fear was gone. It was the middle of the night but she ran to her sister's house to tell her of the dream. At first Muthewana would not believe her, but she went to fetch one of their younger sisters. Together the three women went to Noria's brother's house where the plant of the ancestors, the *wame (Boophane disticha –* bushman poison bulb), grew. They fetched the calabash and water, called the family and went to sit by the *wame*. The three sisters each took some water and all placed some on the *wame* plant at the same time. Noria's shaking stopped and the women returned home. In the morning Noria told Joyce and Edward about her dream and asked Joyce to fetch some clay from the river. Together they stamped the clay and made a fire in the house and that evening, Noria began to sculpt a clay figure by the light of the fire. Her first piece was very small, a figure of a woman. Immediately she began to feel better. That night she produced three figures and the next day three or four more. This carried on for a few days until she began gathering wood and grass and made a pit in her yard. Within that first week, Noria had fired her first batch of clay pieces.

Early one morning, Noria was working when she broke a small figurine. She dropped off to sleep and the old lady appeared in a dream and showed her how to make larger figures. Noria awoke and began to work. In no time at all she had created a much larger sculpture. However, she was uncertain about where she should try to sell it. She wrapped it up and went to Vuwani police station. At the time there were only two white men stationed at Vuwani, one of whom was the commissioner, a passionate art collector. When he saw Noria's piece he immediately bought it for ten rands. Noria was overjoyed, After having sold a batch of small figurines before for 50c each, she now knew she could earn a living from her art.

In 1976, Avashoni Mainganye, a fellow artist, came to Noria and offered her an exhibition at the Venda Sun Hotel. All her works were sold and Mainganye took photographs of them to the Goodman Gallery in Johannesburg. Noria also began working for Ditike, a craft shop that had been established near Thohoyandou, the capital of the Venda homeland, by the Venda Development Corporation.

Noria received a letter from the Goodman Gallery requesting figures of soldiers and police. She produced approximately 200 pieces over a period of three months. She painted the figures using grey and green enamel paints. The Goodman Gallery took all the pieces, as well as some other male figures that Noria had made. Her career had begun.

The demand for Noria's work increased dramatically when her scupltures were included in two exhibitions in Johannesburg: *Tributaries* at the Africana Museum in Progress in 1985, and a subsequent solo exhibition at the Goodman Gallery in 1986.

2. Detail of wall at Ditike.

CLAY

Working with clay in rural conditions is extremely challenging. Noria goes to a special area near her home where she digs the clay from the river bank. It is heavy work, requiring the help of young men whom she employs to assist her. She is very particular about the clay she chooses: it needs to be the right texture, colour and consistency. She likes black clay best; when fired, it turns a reddish brown. Once the clay is collected, Noria covers it with plastic and leaves it for a day or two. She then takes a long, heavy wooden club and pounds the clay. Then the clay is kneaded and sculpted. She uses the coil method when making her clay artworks. She has no potting wheel, specialized tools, chemical glazes or electric kiln. Everything is done in the traditional way. The pieces are left to dry slowly under blankets or plastic sheeting. During the drying process, Noria stains the sculptures with *luvhundi* (red ochre soil) and graphite.

The firing process is a big event. A large area of earth is dug out to form a huge but shallow depression. A thin layer of stones lines the bottom, with wood placed on top. The sculptures are then carefully arranged and covered with a thick layer of straw-like grass. Noria often uses corrugated iron on the edge of the fire to reflect and generate greater heat. The fire is kept burning for a long period of time. It can take an entire day to fire a batch.

WOOD

In 1976, Noria had a dream. 'I was sleeping in the morning. I saw the Luvuvhu River below my house. I saw a large piece of wood caught under the bridge. I asked someone, "Is it yours?" She answered, "No, there is no wood."'

When she awoke, Noria went down to the river and to her amazement, there was the wood she had seen in her dream. Inspired,

The firing process ... Mabasa at work.

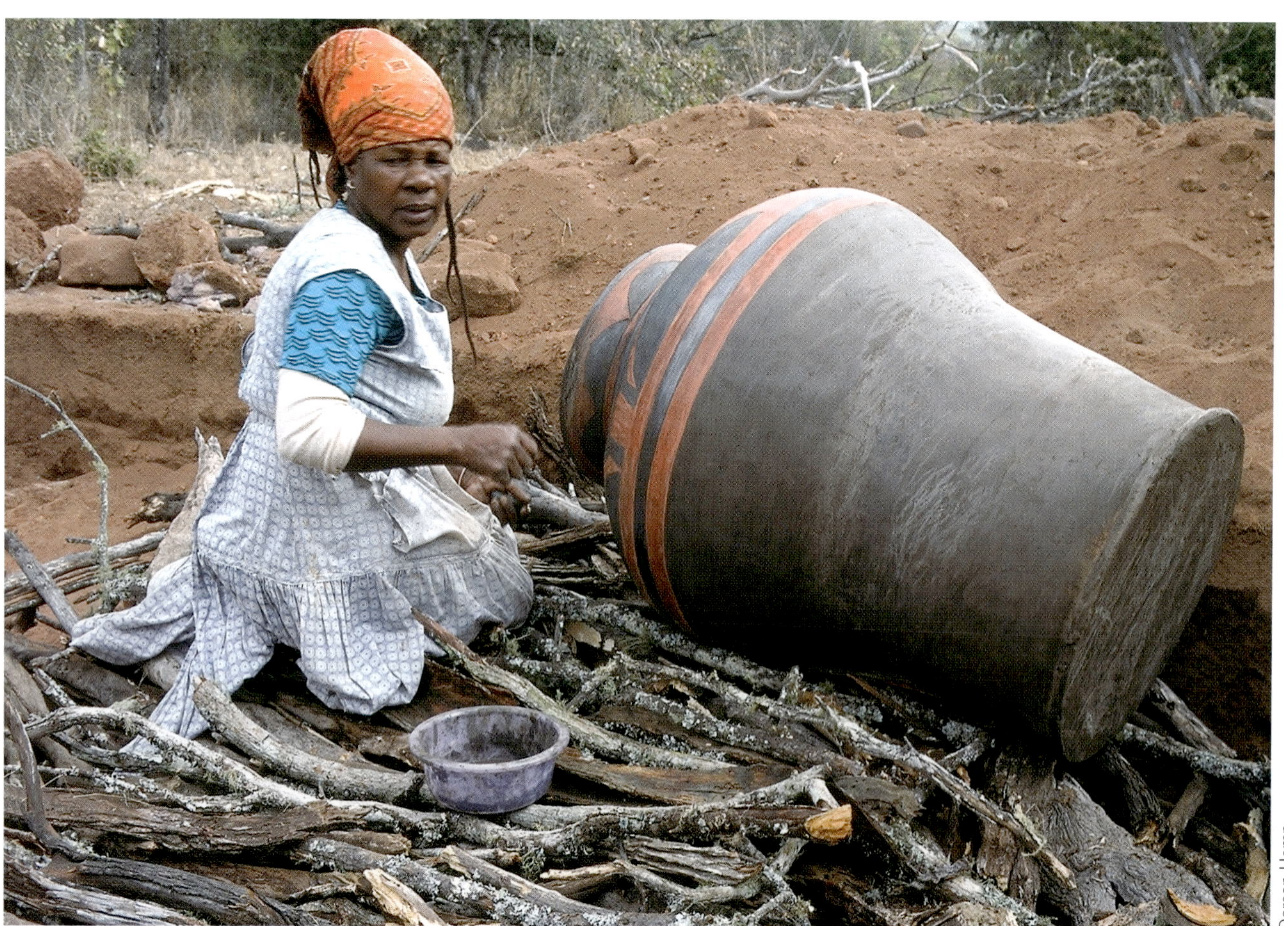

Doreen Hemp

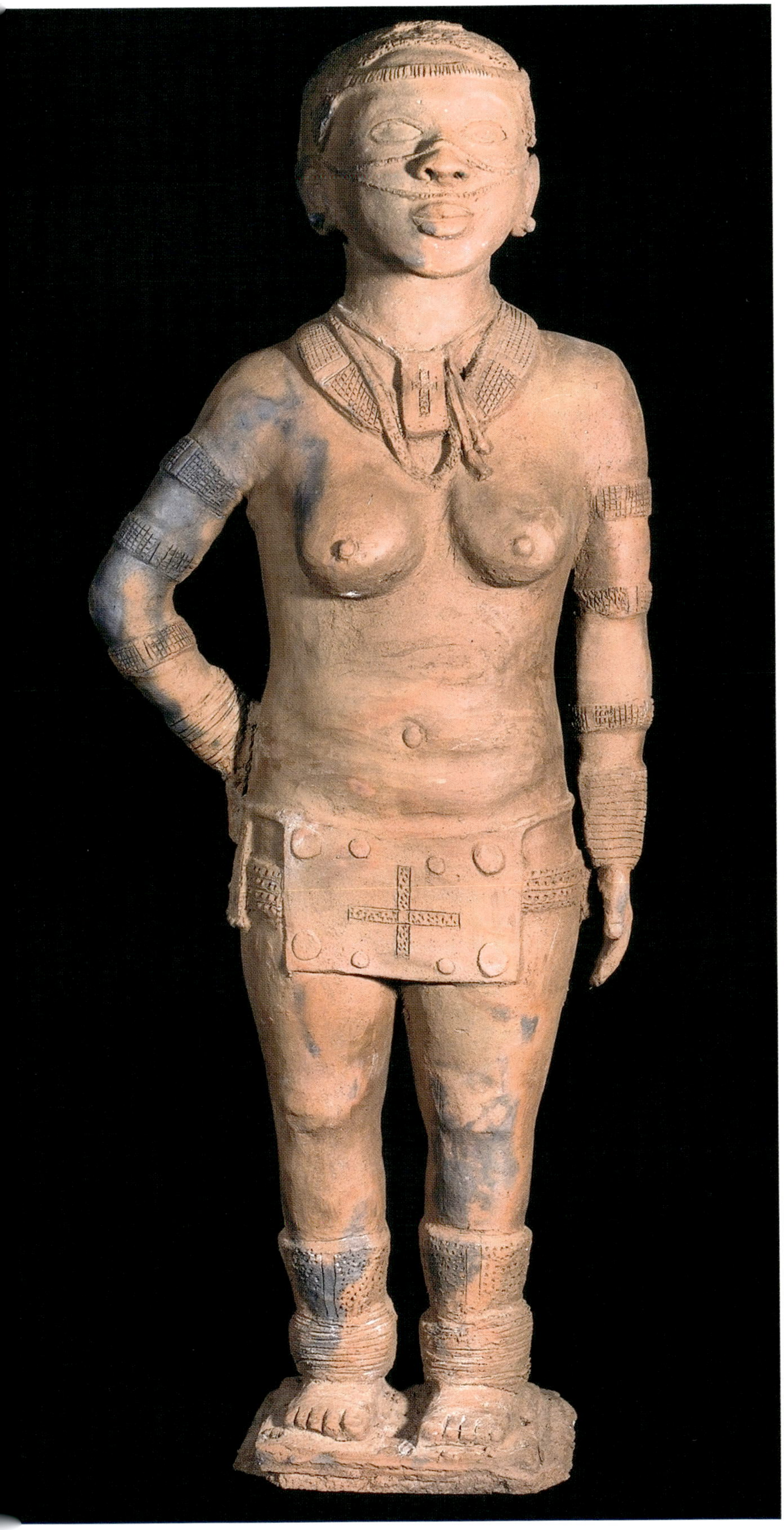

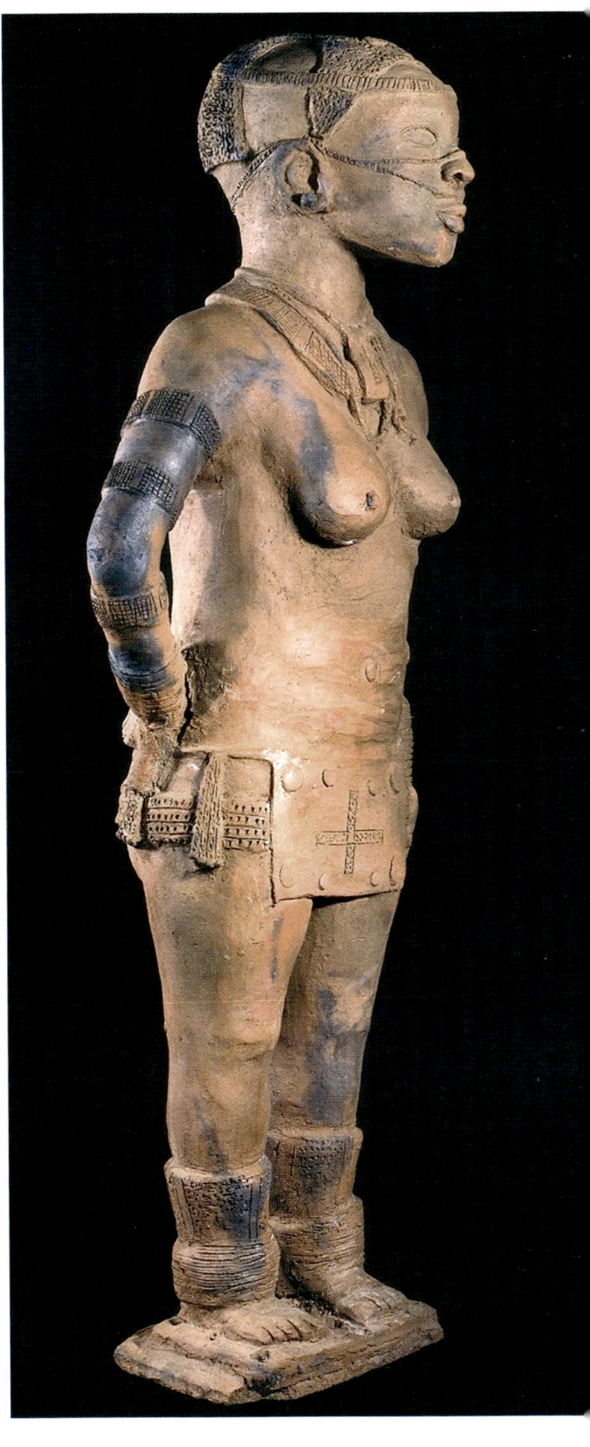

3. *Mukhali,* 1996, clay, 88.5 x 37.5 x 22.5 cm, Standard Bank Collection of African Art (Wits Art Galleries).

Photographs: Theresa Collins

she took it home. Having no tools to carve with, she ignored the wood and continued with the clay sculpture she had been working on. Yet the wood kept beckoning to her and she could not resist. An old man gave her an axe and with this single tool, she made her first carving – a figure of a woman, which she called *Sangwani*. She put the piece aside and did not work with wood again until 1981. Eventually she gave *Sangwani* away to her sister-in-law.

During these years Noria produced many clay works and had a number of exhibitions. She began to make more figures of traditional women – carrying pots, showing respect, breastfeeding. Then one day she was out collecting firewood and found herself searching for wood that she could carve. This time she managed to get a chisel and she started to carve again. Her carvings were left outside in the rain and she paid them no attention. When visitors came Noria would sell them for as little as ten rands each.

Avashoni Mainganye helped her to set more reasonable prices for the sculptures, He insisted that she should hold an exhibition. Three of her wood carvings were exhibited at the Venda Sun Hotel in 1984 and all sold very quickly. Noria became the first black woman in South Africa to carve wood, and with this new medium she was suddenly freed from the confines of making small pieces, as wood offered the possibility for producing much larger works than she had been able to achieve with clay. Her first big works in wood included *Bushman* and *Carnage (Natal Flood Disaster)*.

Noria's move from clay modelling to wood carving sparked controversy and threats. Some of the members of her community laughed at her and she was considered a rebel, since she defied the traditional social order in which carving was considered to be a man's job.

Noria loves to carve and is undaunted by her critics. 'There were some people who said my ancestors were going to punish me for going against tradition. I was not worried because I was told by my ancestors to carve.'

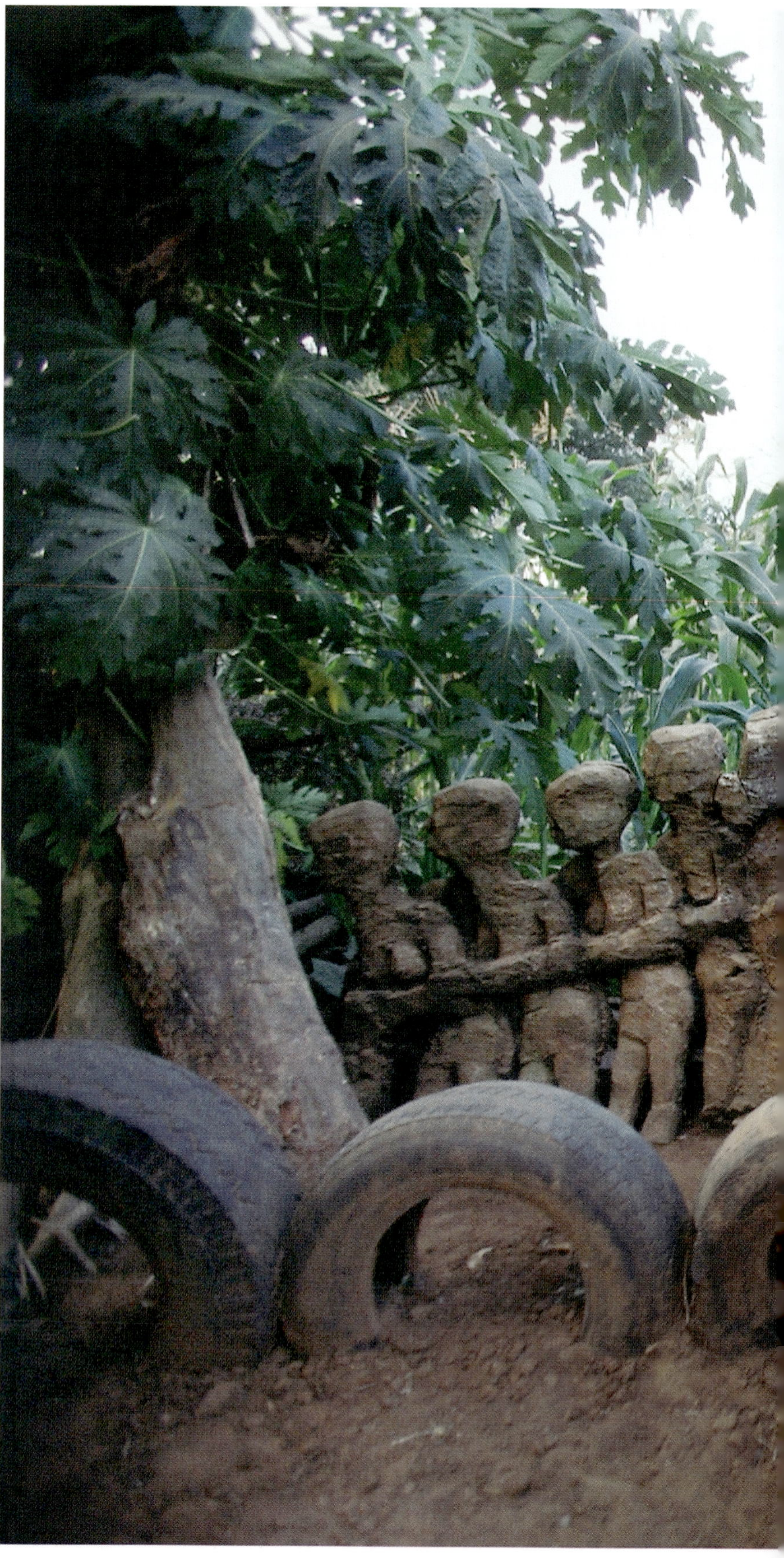

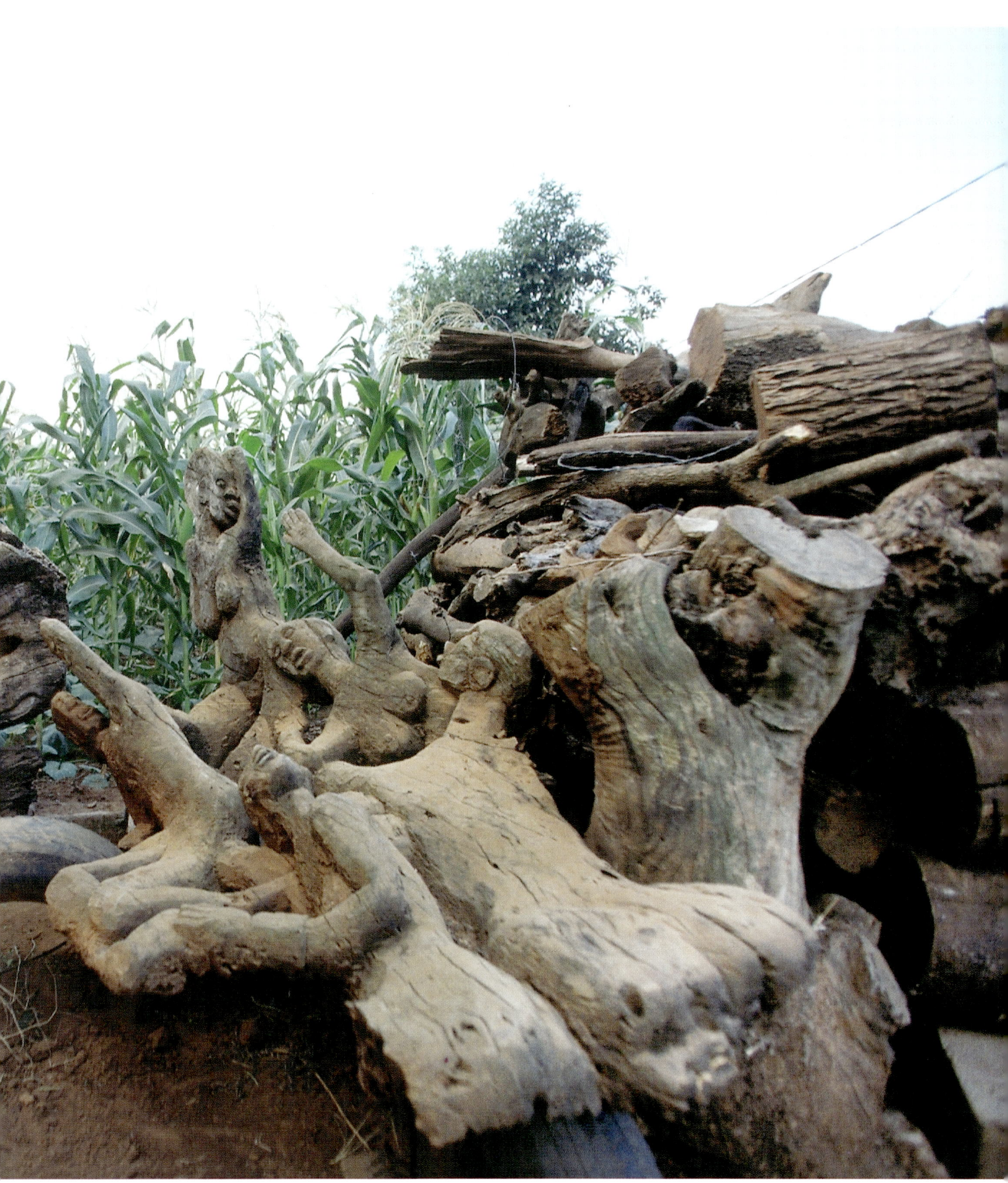

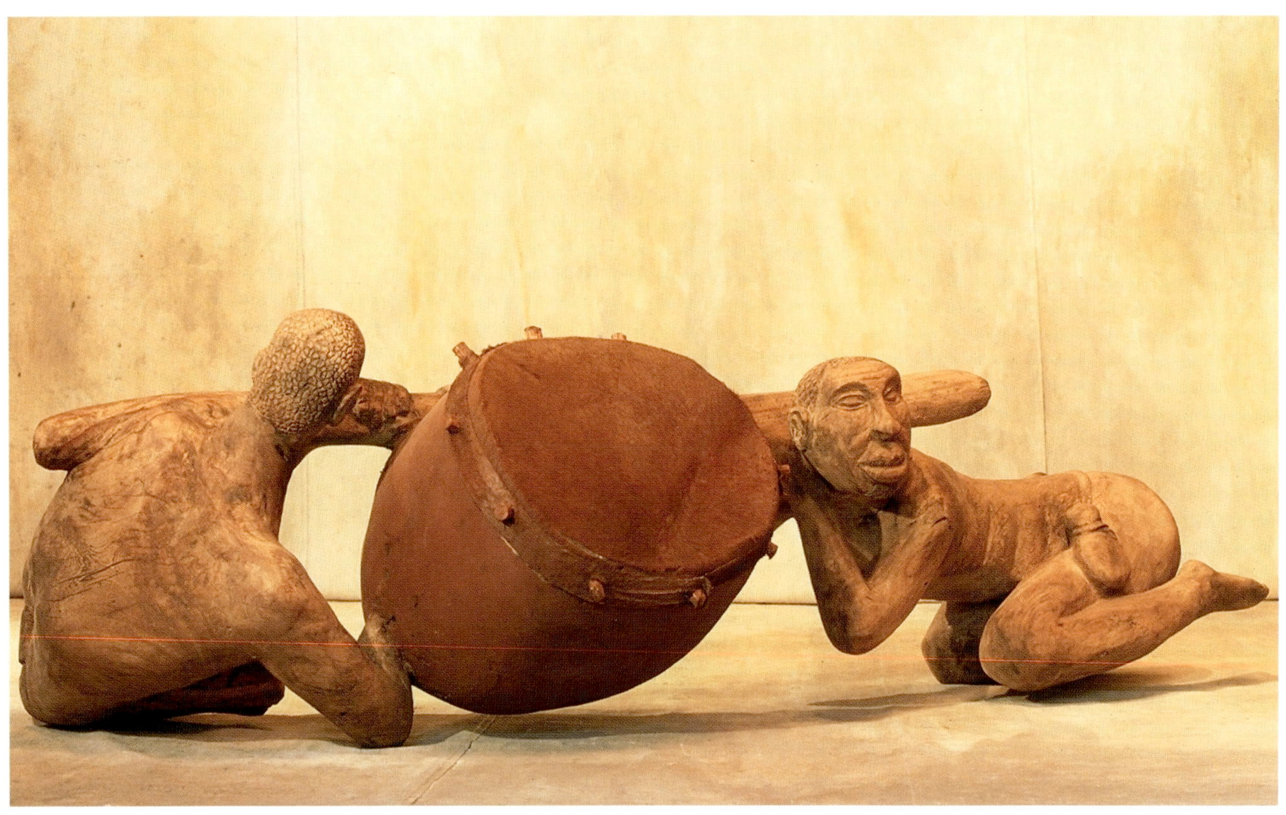

4

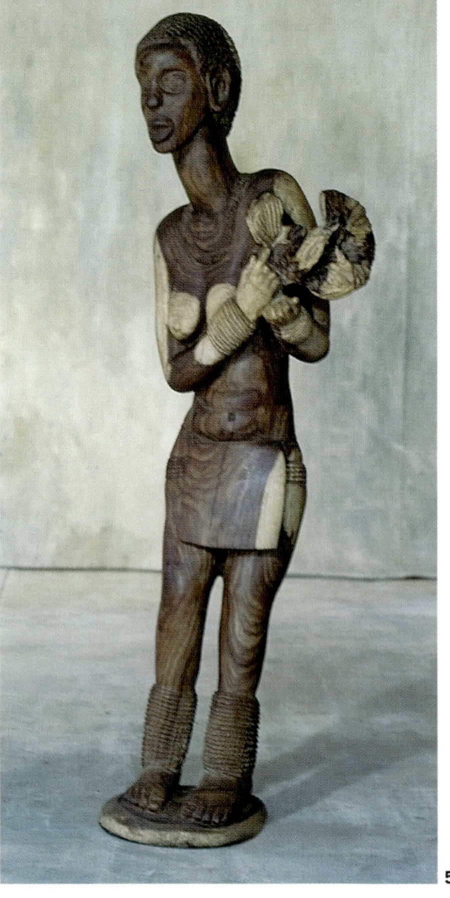

5

4. *Ngoma Lungundu I,*
1999, wild fig
wood, 80 x 60 x
220 cm,
Mukondeni Fine
Arts Gallery
Collection.

5. *Young Woman with
Flowers,* 1993,
kiaat wood, 120 x
30 x 30 cm,
Mukondeni Fine
Arts Gallery
Collection.

VENDA CULTURE AND TRADITION

Roots and culture are very important to Noria. She acknowledges the traditional roles played by men and women, and does not believe that men and women are equal or that they should be. However, this does not imply that one sex is better than the other, only that they have different roles in society. Asked whether she felt that it was important for men to be able to cook so that women did not have to cook every meal, she replied, 'Women must cook for their husbands. It is not right for a man to cook while a woman sits and anyway, women cook better!'

Her clay pieces and carvings reflect the rituals and traditions of the VhaVenda people, as well as the Shangaan and Zulu cultural traditions present in the communities of the region. Many of her works show women dressed in traditional clothing, and the details in the style of dress, beadwork and other adornments that she uses are significant. These fine points portray the status of the character she is depicting. In VhaVenda culture, certain items of clothing such as the *shedo* relate to the initiation schools. Noria explained how important initiation

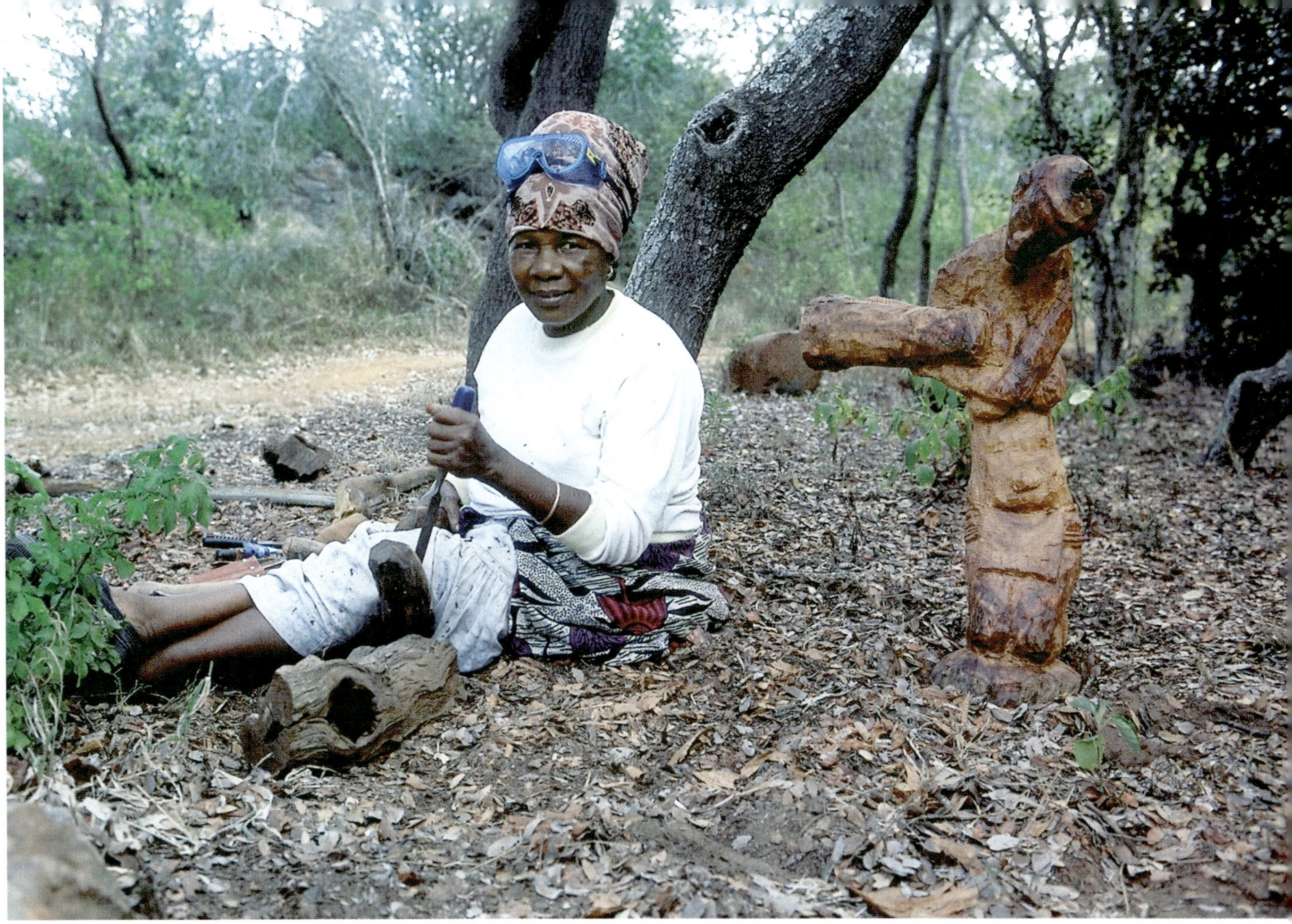

Mabasa at work, 1990.
Photograph: Lesheba Wilderness

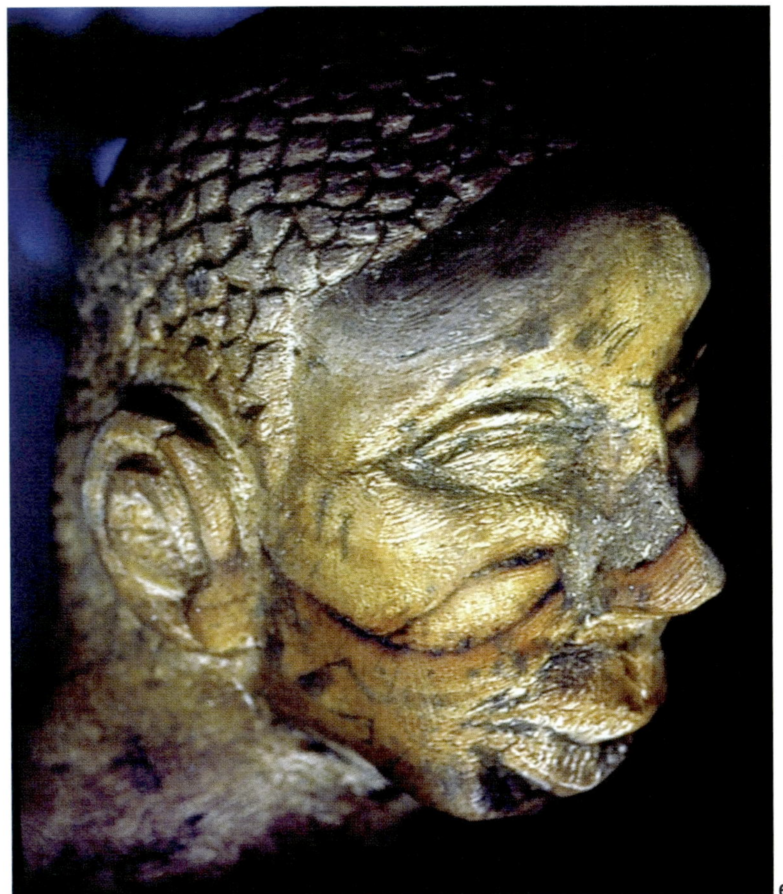

6

" There were some people
who said my ancestors
were going to punish me
for going against tradition.
I was not worried because
I was told by my ancestors
to carve."

6. Detail of *Ngoma Lungundu I.*

27

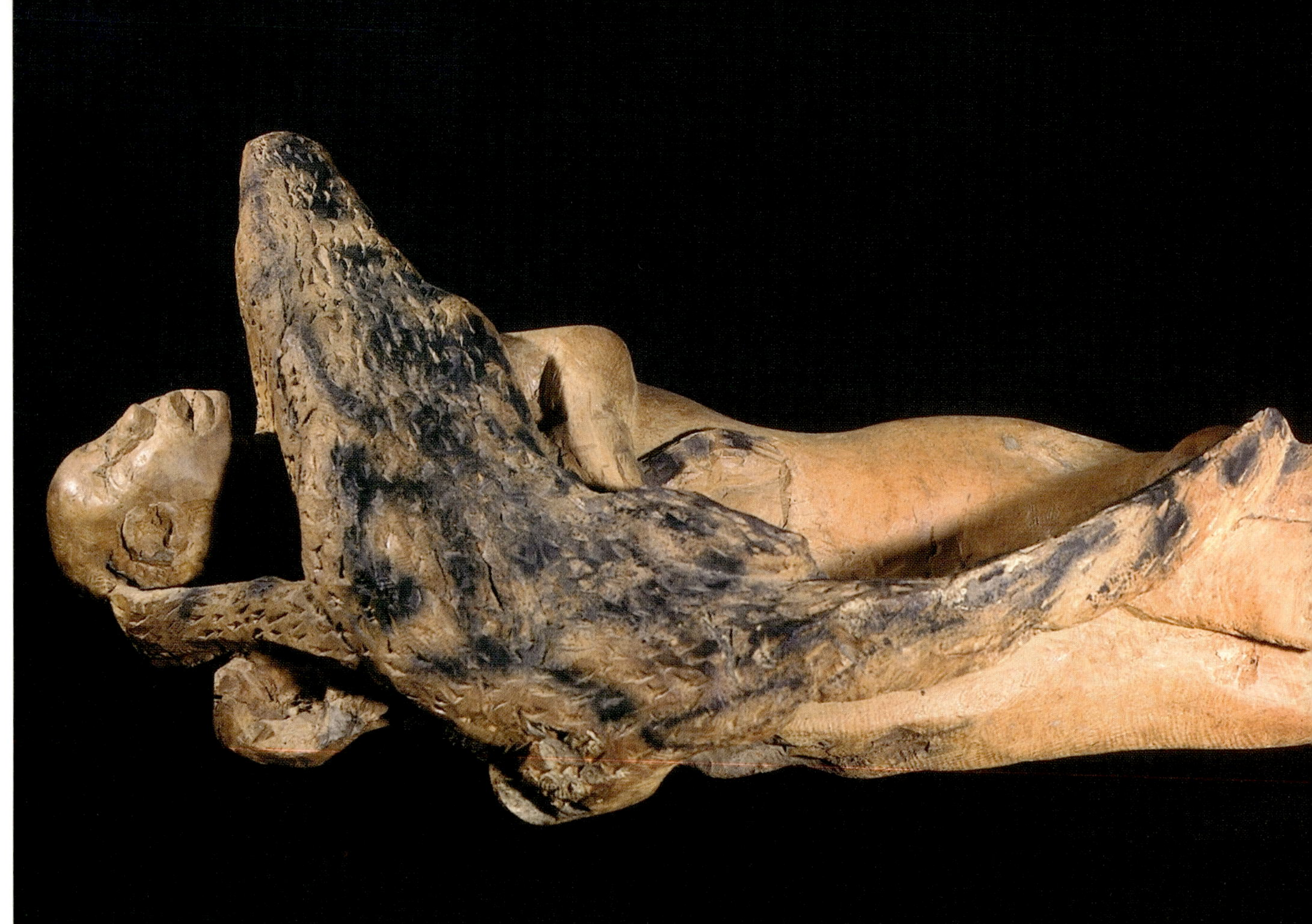

7

7. *Man and crocodile*, c.1987, wood, pokerwork, 21.5 x 135 x 52 cm, Wits Art Galleries.

8. Detail, *Man and crocodile.*

schools are for her. This was the only schooling she had received, and its influence is mirrored in her work. 1938, the year that Noria was born, was the last time that girls left home to attend initiation school for six months. Thereafter the schools were closer by and a girl went for shorter periods of time. In order to interpret her work and to have an understanding of Noria herself, knowledge of the initiation rites is of great importance.

In indigenous southern African cultural traditions, women are generally considered subservient to men. However, in Venda, women do not necessarily share this inferiority. Within her own courtyard (*muta*), a woman is in charge. Women are allowed to own property, which is usually given to them by their fathers or inherited when there is no male heir. Noria is the head of her household, owns her property and is respected by her family and community.

Nevertheless, there are still many areas of daily life in which a Venda woman's position is inferior to that of a man. Women are still expected to perform basic duties such as cooking, cleaning and drawing water.

Traditionally, a Venda girl is expected to attend three major initiation schools before marriage: the *vhusha*, which takes place at puberty; the *tshikanda*, an intermediary school designed to reinforce the lessons of the puberty school, and the *domba*, a pre-marital school for young women.

The development of the individual is seen as a series of distinctly separate stages: puberty marks an important stage and marriage another. Transition from one stage to the next is made possible by external forces (such as the ancestors, both good and evil spirits and witches[3], who can be both male and female), which can exert good or bad influences on people's lives. The role of the initiation schools is to instruct initiates about what to expect and how to behave in the next stage of their development: by performing ceremonies and dances, the initiates are enabled to break with the mistakes of the past and to embrace the challenges of the

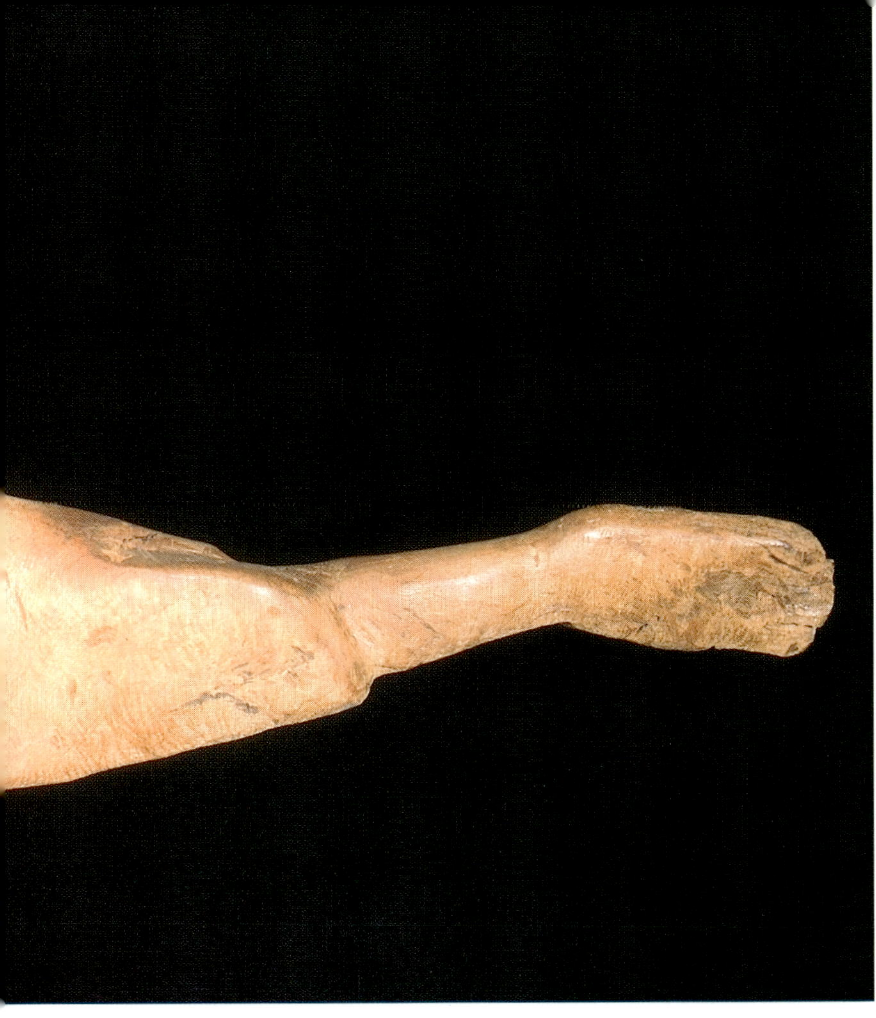

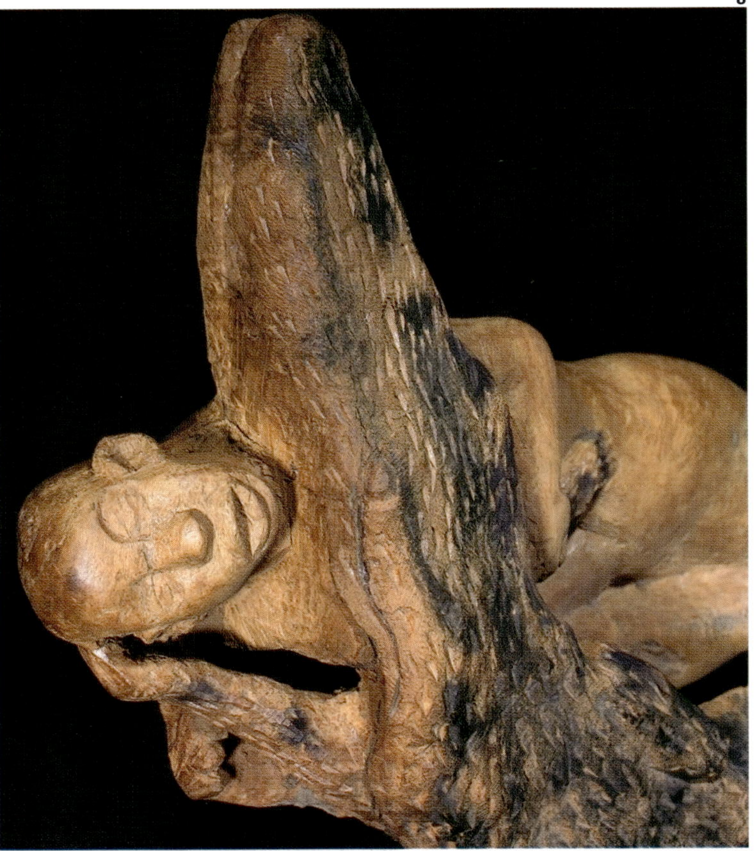

future. These ceremonies also invoke the support of the ancestors and strengthen the initiates through magic.[4]

Vhusha is an eight-day course held at an initiation lodge where girls are kept in seclusion and are taught that the essence of Venda womanhood is humility. Initiates are given extensive education in matters relating to sex, sexual behaviour, betrothal and marriage, with emphasis on avoiding pregnancy outside marriage.

They are taught to sing, dance and learn the *milayo*, a combination of everyday lessons and cultural symbolism. Noria explained that knowing the *milayo* endows her with special knowledge and entitles her to participate in women's special meetings and ceremonies.

The intermediary school, the *tshikanda*, takes place at intervals of three or four years, just prior to the holding of the final school, the *domba*.

The *domba* marks the culmination of the initiation process. This provides the final qualification for marriage and the school runs for approximately nine months. The *domba* commences with the blowing of the *phala phala*, a kudu horn. A sacred fire is lit at the king's village and is kept alight for the duration of the *domba*. Once the fire has been lit, the initiates are treated with medicines by a ritual specialist, and everything used in the *domba* is sprinkled with medicine to prevent interference from evil influences. The objective of the *domba* is to acquaint the young with all aspects of marriage, as well as with the mores and customs of Venda culture. The *domba* is viewed as a national event by the VhaVenda.

Noria described the *domba* dance, which is an important part of the ceremony. The dance is performed by the girls around a sacred fire at the king's *khoro*. The dancers form a single file, with each initiate holding the elbow of the girl in front so that they fit snugly into a long chain that weaves rhythmically around the *domba* fire to the beat of the *ngoma* and *mirumba* drums. Originally the girls danced naked, but today they wear the *shedo* cloth,

29

which is passed between the legs, forming an apron in the front with a panel hanging down at the back. They also wear metal bracelets and anklets that glint in the firelight and rattle as they dance. The dance symbolises a python, which is associated with fertility and is regarded as a sacred symbol.

Many of Noria's figures show the symbolic teachings of the *domba* and how important these traditions are to her.

ARTIST AND TEACHER

In April 2002, Noria participated in a project designed by the Lesheba Wilderness Arts Programme to enable young artists of the region to work alongside well-known artists such as Noria, Paul Thavhana, Owen Ndou, Albert Munyai, Jameson Ramvuvhelo, John Baloyi, Jackson Hlungwani, Hendrik Nekhofi, Azwi Magoro, and Meshak Rephelelani. Four young artists were selected to work together with the established artists. The first course proved to be a wonderful success for the artists themselves, as well for the students. This was the first time that they were able to apply their talents in an environment where they were under no pressure.

Of this teaching process Noria says, 'For twenty years I have worked on my own, now I am working with young people and other artists. The children are learning and it is fun to work with the other carvers. We can share our ideas and it will make Venda art grow. International artists can be brought in to teach us new ways and to give us ideas and we too can teach them. I like to work at home in Vuwani but I also like to work at Duluni Camp (Lesheba). The spirit is good at Duluni and the dreams come to me quickly there. Wood is easier to find and working is working, there are no interruptions. I am able to teach the other artists how to be more accurate and to share my knowledge. They (the other artists) call me mawe – mother. I also like to be shown new ways to fix problems I have with my work such as when I fire things and they crack. The artists have shown me how to make holes to stop this and how to improve the texture in my works.'

Noria Mabasa continues to explore her chosen media, and to expand her technical range as she undertakes new projects. Her fortitude and creative ability have set a standard that many of the local male wood-carvers find difficult to match. Motivated by her dreams, she is compelled to use her gift. Her belief in the ancestors is as strong as her pride in the customs and culture of VhaVenda society. She combines this belief in the power of the ancestors with a firm belief in a Christian God. She says that God has a big job and should not have to listen to the worries of each individual. This is why she doesn't speak to Him directly. She speaks first to the ancestors so that they can pass the message on to God.

She says: 'The Venda people have always made everything themselves. This is why they know art. Venda is the number one place for art and I like the style of the Venda. I am proud to be Venda. I am also proud of myself because I am "big", even if a man is carving, me, I am not a man, I am a woman and it makes me happy!'

Notes

1. Tshigalo is also sometimes spelled Xigalo. There are variant orthographies for many place names in the region, based on the different languages spoken by the inhabitants. This point is discussed further in Rayda Becker's essay in this volume. Geographical designations of regions within South Africa have changed several times during the past century, as apartheid policies defined and re-defined areas to which certain sections of the population would be confined, and designated these as 'tribal homelands' (bantustans). In the latter years of the apartheid regime, the bantustans of Gazankulu and Venda were created in the northern parts of the Transvaal, in the region where Noria Mabasa was born and now lives. This region now forms part of Limpopo Province.

2. Many South African churches combine Christian worship with indigenous rituals that acknowledge the role of the ancestors and other traditional belief systems in the lives of their members.

3. In Venda culture a woman may be regarded as a 'witch' if she appears to behave in a manner that is threatening, abnormal or unacceptable to the community.

4. Alan Kirkaldy, personal communication.

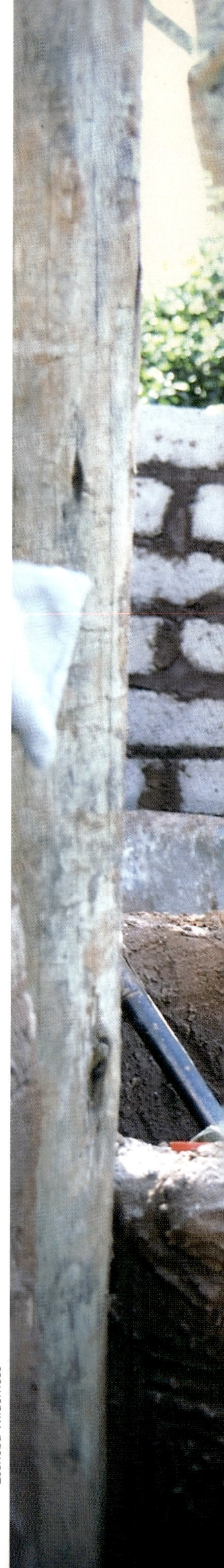

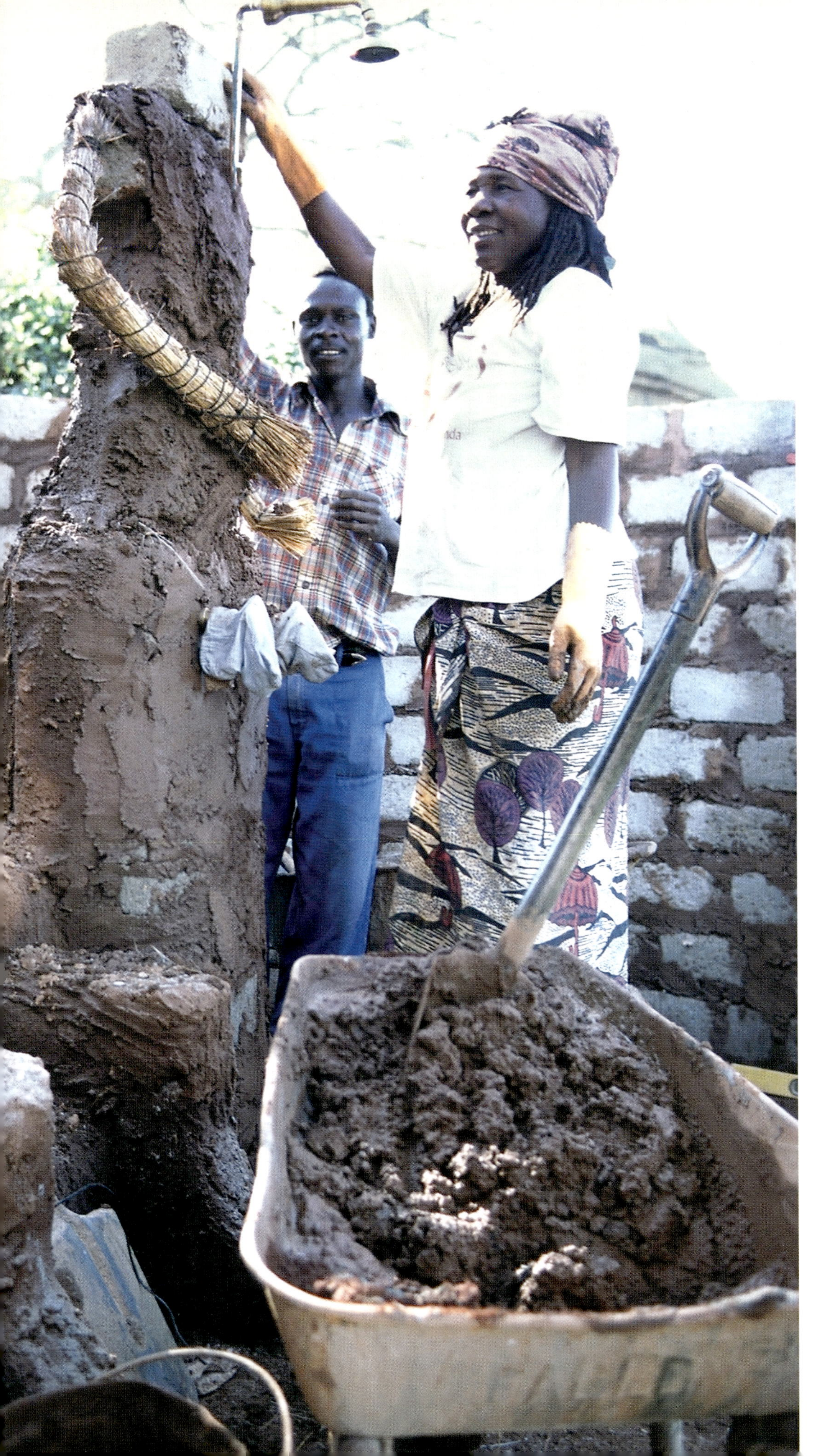

"For twenty
years I have
worked on my
own, now I
am working
with young
people and
other artists.
The children
are learning
and it is fun
to work with
the other
carvers. We
can share our
ideas and it
will make
Venda art
grow."

MAJOR WORK

VENDA VILLAGE

The Venda Village at Lesheba Wilderness Private Game Reserve, situated in the Soutpansberg in Limpopo Province, was an old Venda settlement built by the Ralidzivah family. It was restored to its original condition in 1995 with the help of two local Venda women who made the bricks out of a mixture of cow dung and mud and baked them in the sun. Noria Mabasa had seen the village and mentioned that she would love to create something there. In 2001 she was offered the opportunity to help recreate the camp, becoming a co-founder of the Lesheba Venda Arts and Culture Trust funded by De Beers.

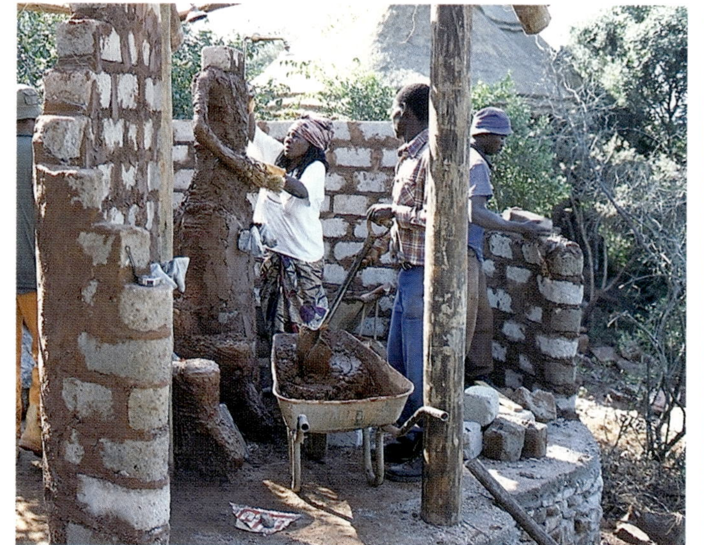

On arrival she knocked down all the interior courtyard walls and began to reconstruct the village. Over a period of five weeks this slight woman of 65, with the assistance of two young workers who helped her mix cement, completely transformed the structures into a magical masterpiece. All the sculptures and walls are made out of concrete, which is a very difficult medium to work with as it dries very quickly. The floors were thrown in the traditional manner using various coloured oxides and pigments – blues, reds, yellows and greens. Engine oil is then applied and left to soak into the floors, bringing out their rich colours, after which they are polished with a mixture of candle wax and paraffin.

On arrival, the visitor is welcomed by a figure of a tall man in a loincloth standing next to a small hut. Inside the hut, a young woman is kneeling and alongside her a sign proclaims: The Venda Village by Noria Mabasa.

As one enters the first courtyard, one finds oneself surrounded by sculptures that rise from the floors and materialize from the walls. There are figures of women and children, a crocodile and an aeroplane, drums, giraffe, lions and a massive bull that belongs to the village chief, 'Sam'. 'Sam' is a life-size figure who sits beside a large clay pot and overlooks the valley.

Venda Village is run as a eco-tourism destination and has attracted visitors from all over the world. Noria poured a tremendous amount of her energy and imagination into it. The camp is, as she puts it, '... the place where my heart is'.

Pages 32–35: Details from Venda Village.

Photographs: Lesheba Wilderness

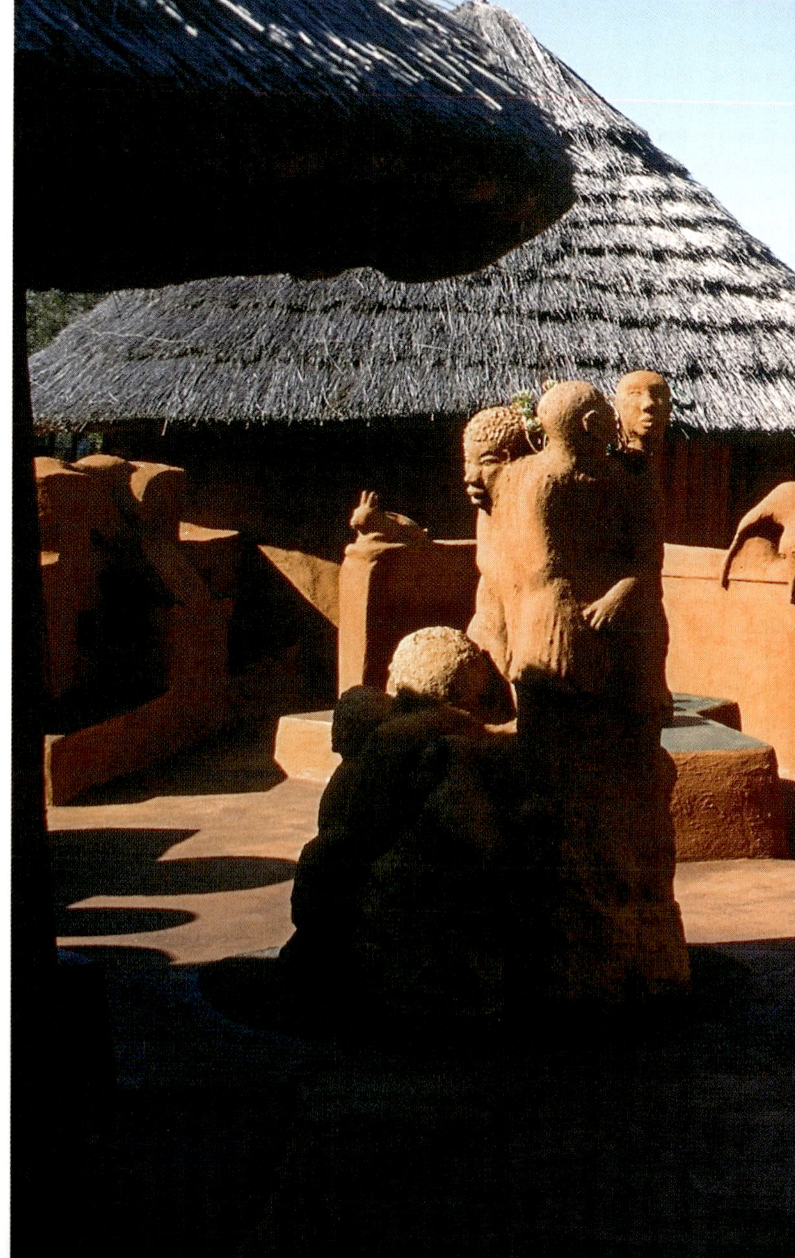

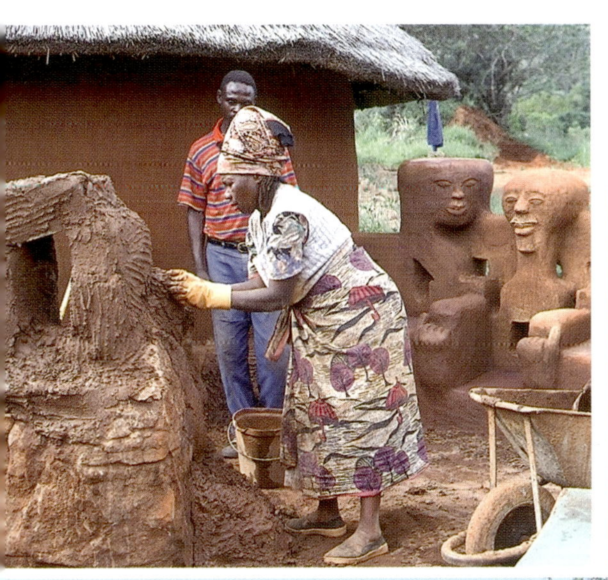

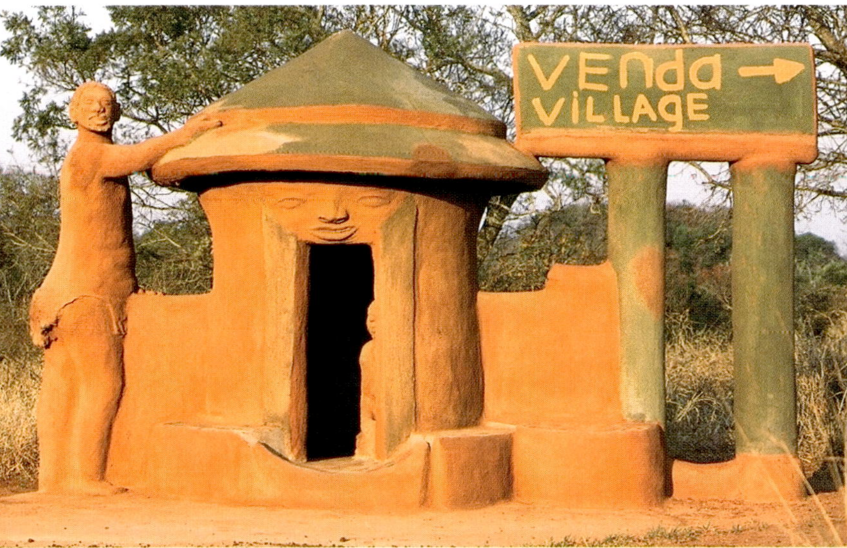
VENda →
VillAGE

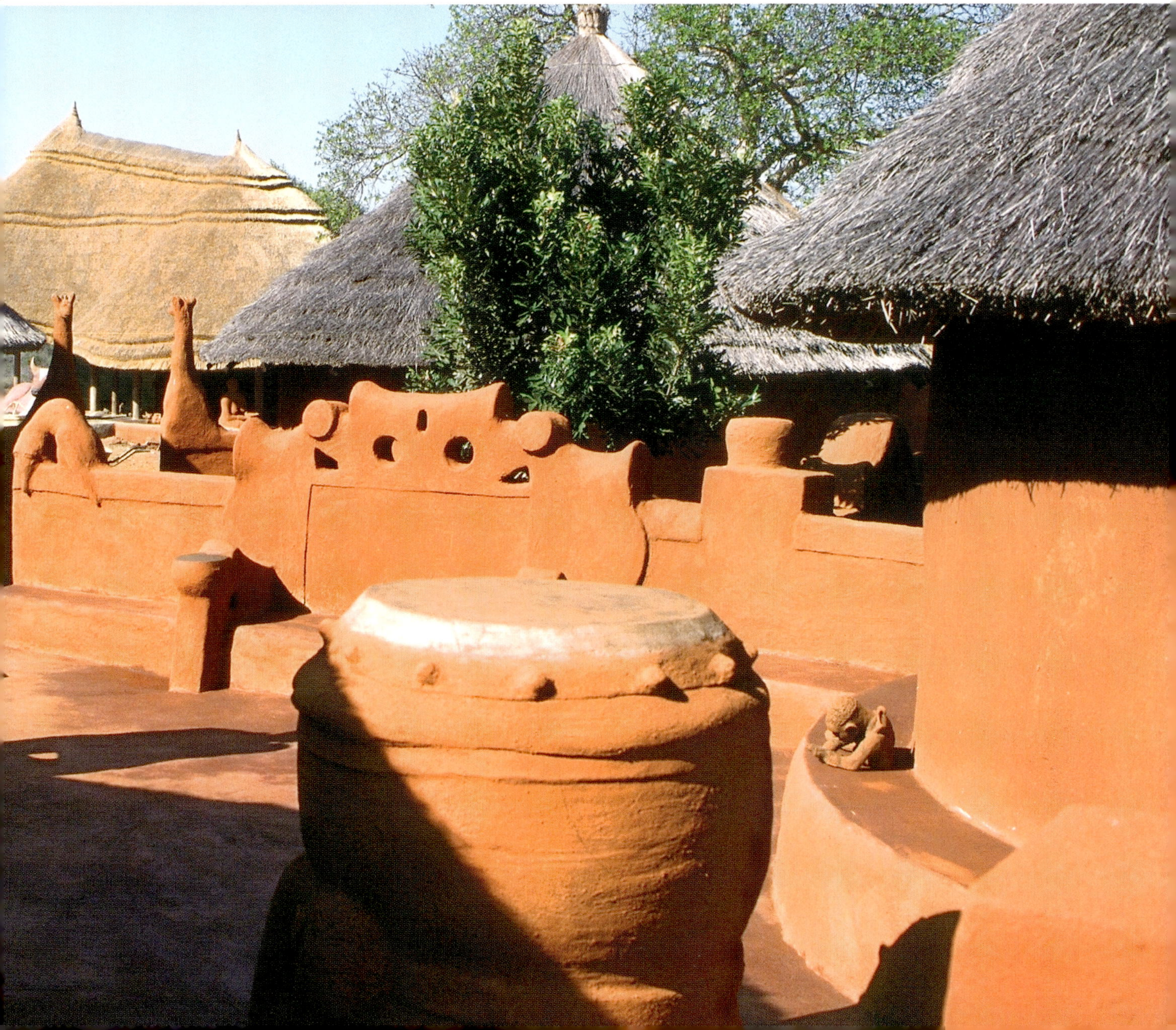

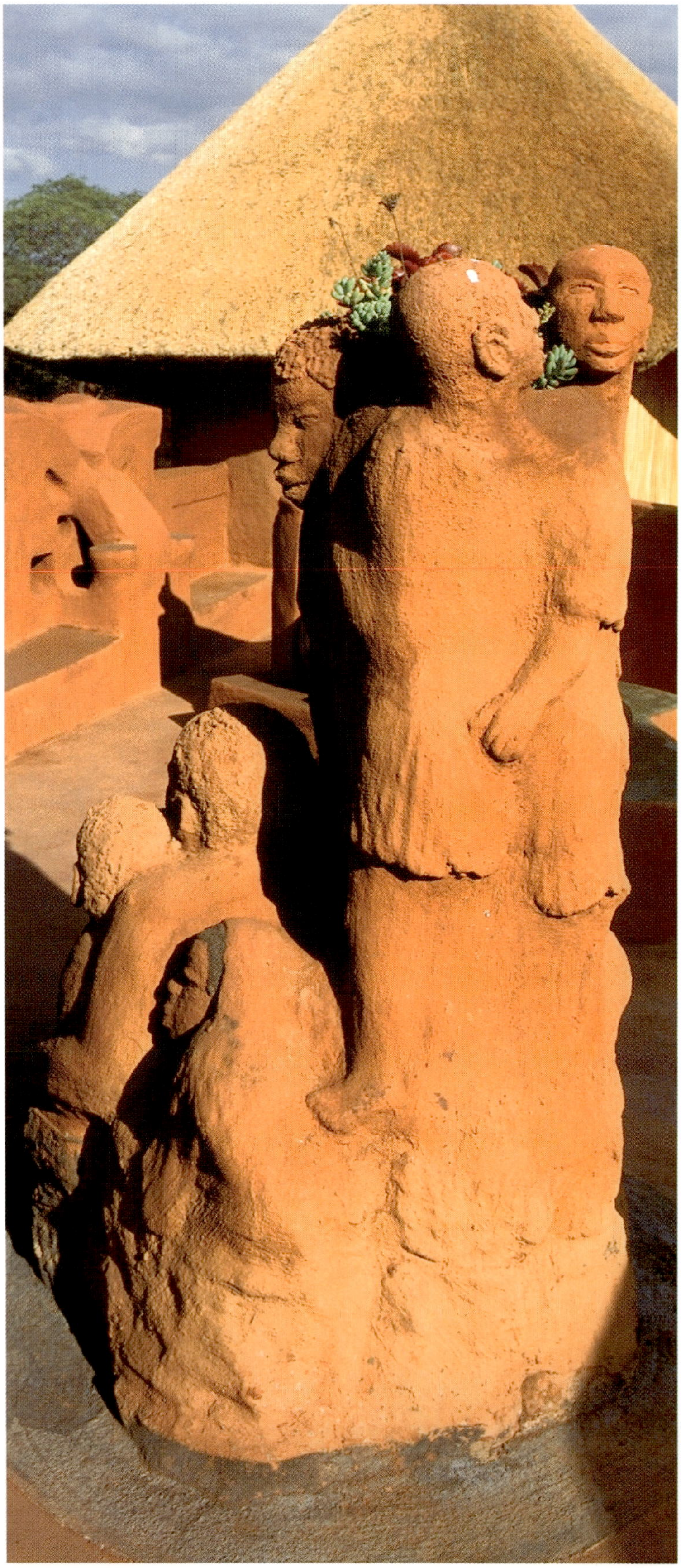

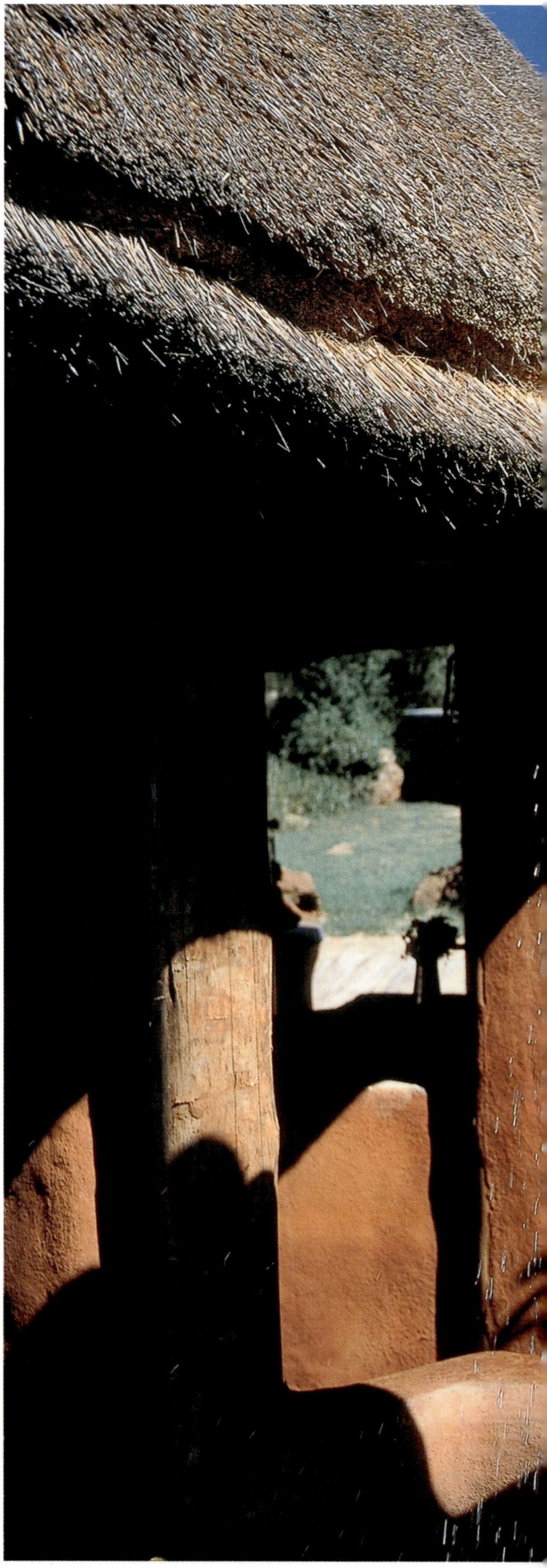

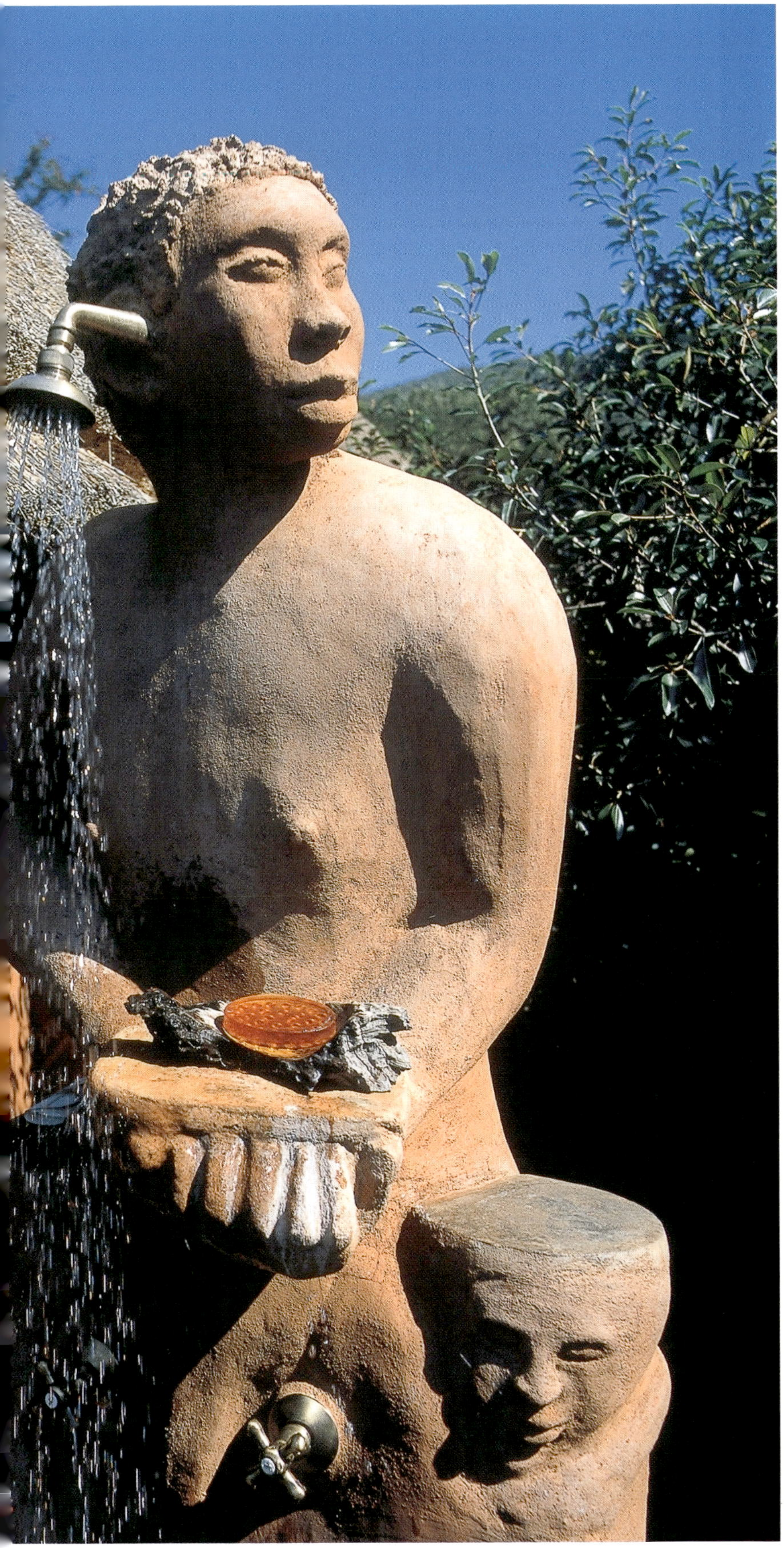

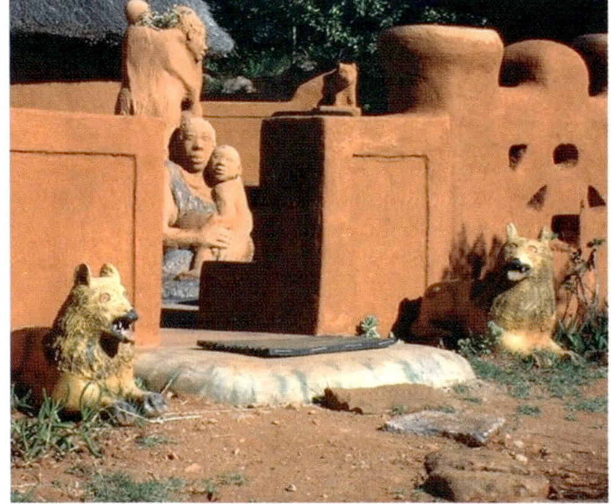

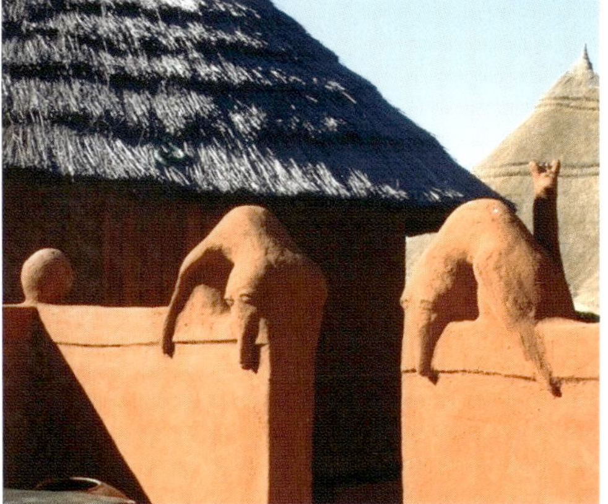

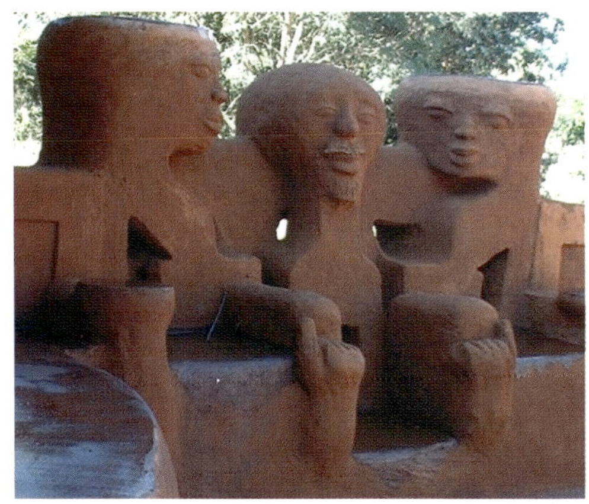

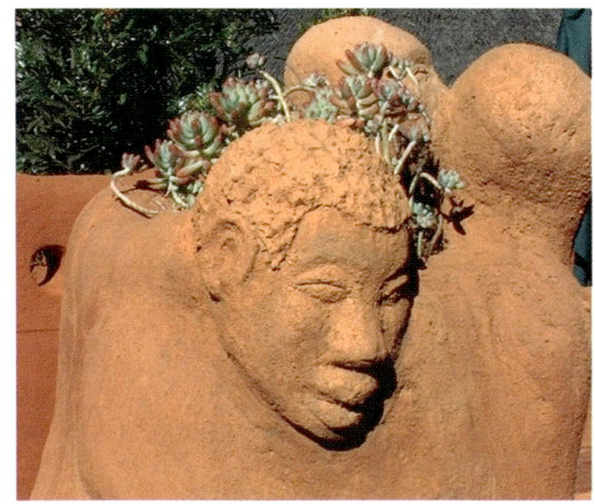

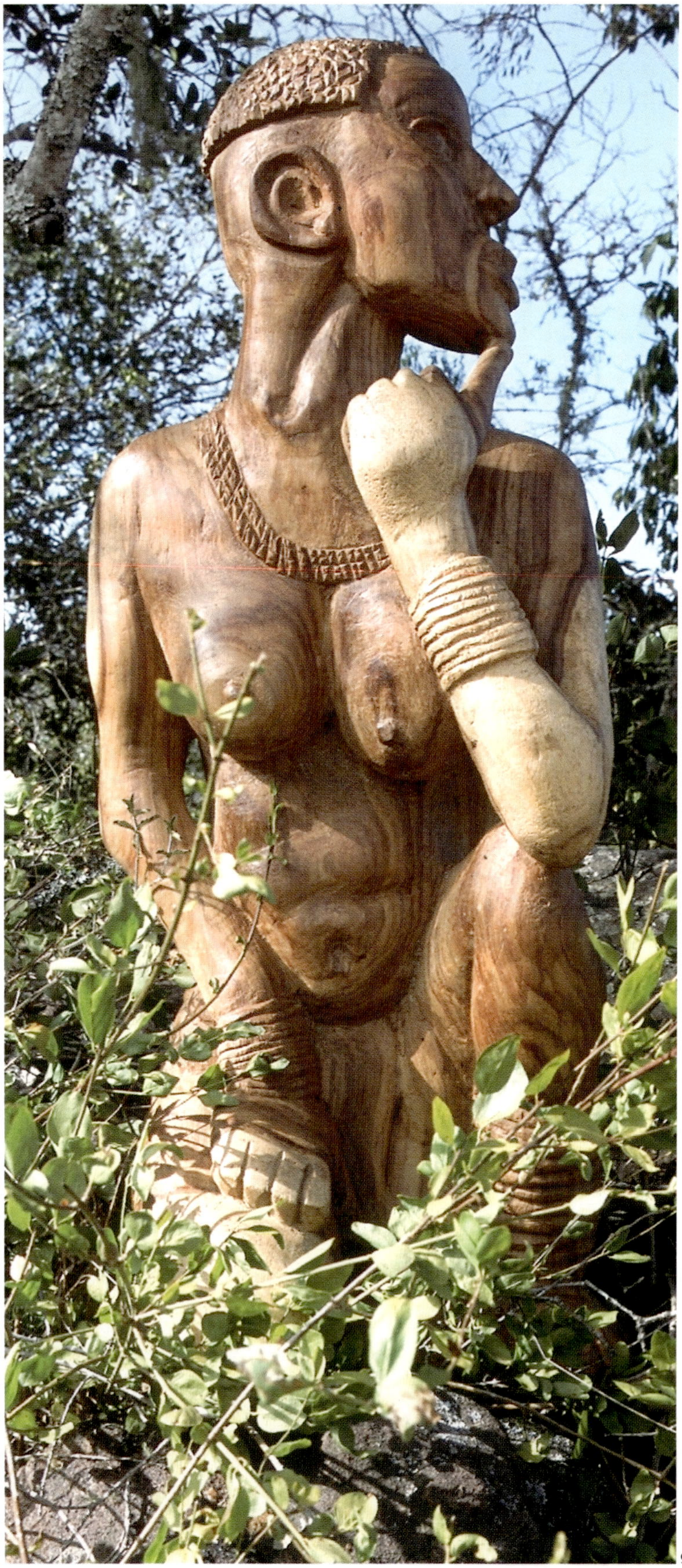

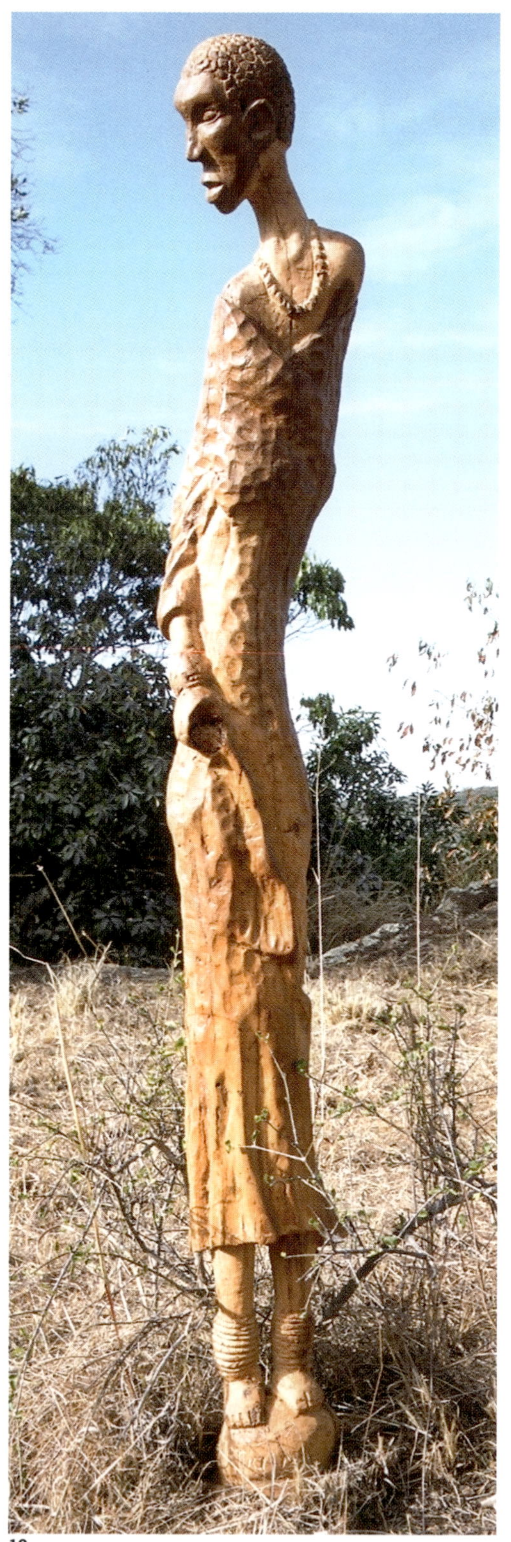

9. A polished wooden sculpture at Venda Village.

10. Recent wood carving at Venda Village.

THE NEW POTS

Noria worked at Lesheba to produce sculptures that would form part of an exhibition for the World Summit on Sustainable Development held in Johannesburg in September 2002. She became inspired and after completing a very large but simple pot that stood taller than she did, she decided to try something she had never attempted before. She made two pots and began work on a third, on which the independent figures she usually made were created as part of the pot itself (**11**). A woman breastfeeds her child beneath the leaves of a tree while a young man watches over her and the baby, offering protection. Noria describes the characters as hungry and seeking shelter. Another of the pots has a woman and a child, and a large bird of prey with a rat in its mouth sits above the woman (**12**). Above this an elephant's head dominates the front view. On the reverse, the pot is made like any other and one cannot see the figures depicted on the opposite side. Both these pots are approximately one and a half metres high and more than a metre in diameter.

Noria says of this new work: 'These are not pots. These are sculptures.'

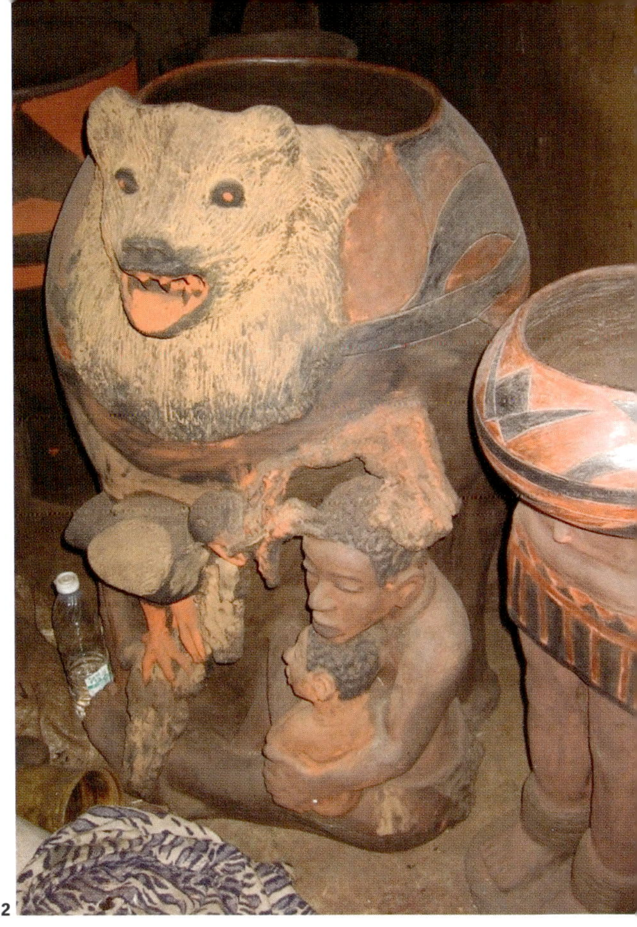

12

11

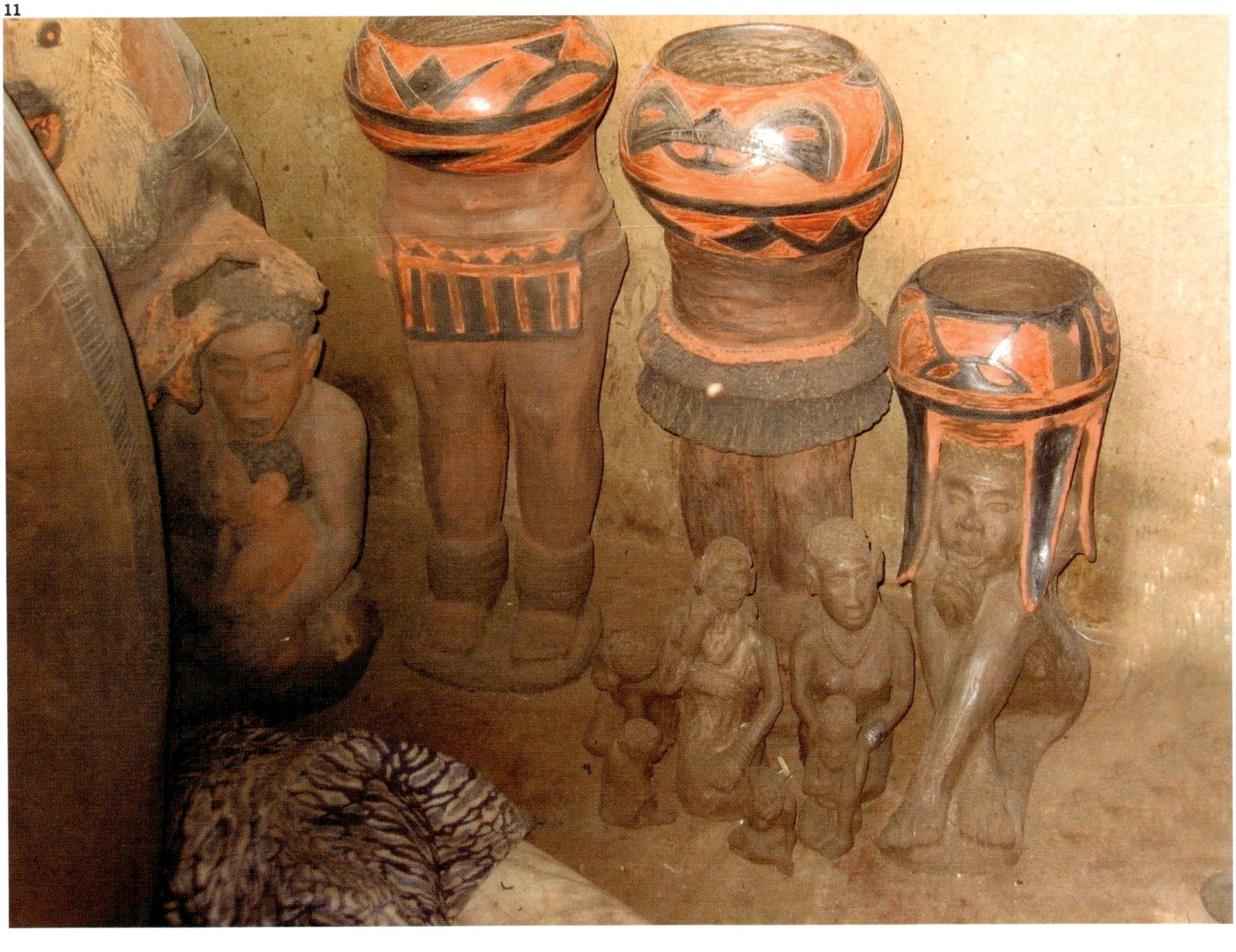

UNION BUILDINGS

In 1999, during the floods that devastated parts of
southern Africa, a massive fig tree (*Ficus
craterostoma*) washed down the Levuvhu River below
Noria Mabasa's house. The piece of wood was too
big to carry back with her and so she began carving
beside the river. The tree was cut into five pieces, the
biggest one being used for *Union Buildings* (**13**),
seen here at her homestead. The name refers to the
complex of buildings in Pretoria which houses the
executive arm of the South African government. In
1956 thousands of women travelled from all parts of
South Africa to the Union Buildings in Pretoria and
gathered on the lawns outside the buildings to hand
in petitions declaring their refusal to carry the
dompas, the identification document which all black
South Africans were expected to carry at all times,
and without which they could be arrested. It was the
largest protest action ever by women against
apartheid policies.

The sculpture took nine months to carve and another
five months to sand down. It consists of fourteen
women and one man. The man appears to be
fleeing while the women are dancing and rising up,
as if singing and shouting in jubilation. Noria
describes the man as an employee running away
from the crowd of women. He represents everything
the Union Buildings stood for in apartheid South
Africa: the power and brutality of the oppressive
state. A few of the women hold their *dompas*
documents, ready to throw them down in protest.
There are two drums held high at the top of the
sculpture; they represent the voices of women, their
power and strength and the assertion of their rights.
Union Buildings portrays women's liberation from
oppression. This piece appears also to represent
Noria's own emancipation from the poverty and
abuse she has experienced in her life. It is a
celebratory piece, which she regards as one of her
finest works.

The sculpture was purchased for the nation in 2002
and placed in front of the Union Buildings in
Pretoria.

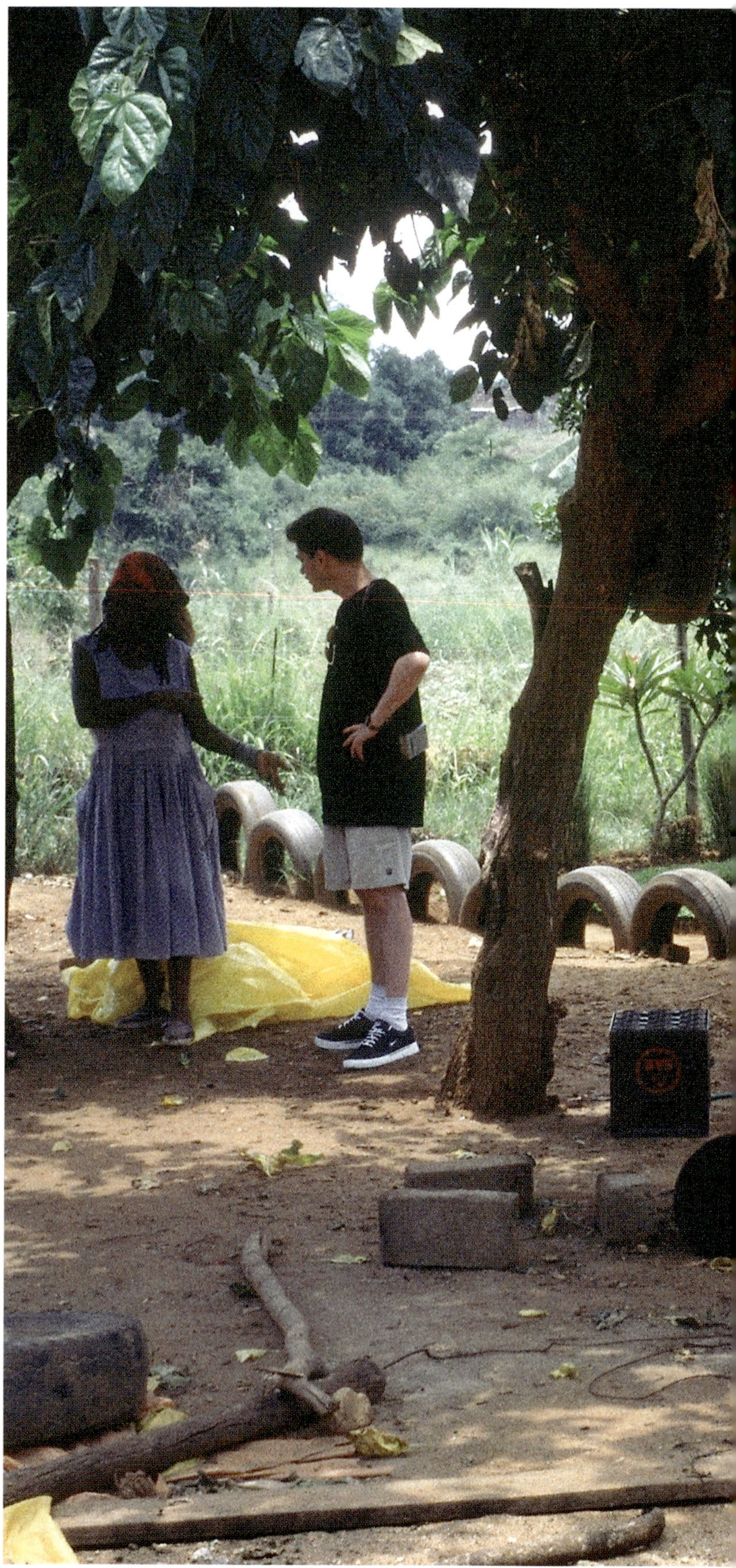

13

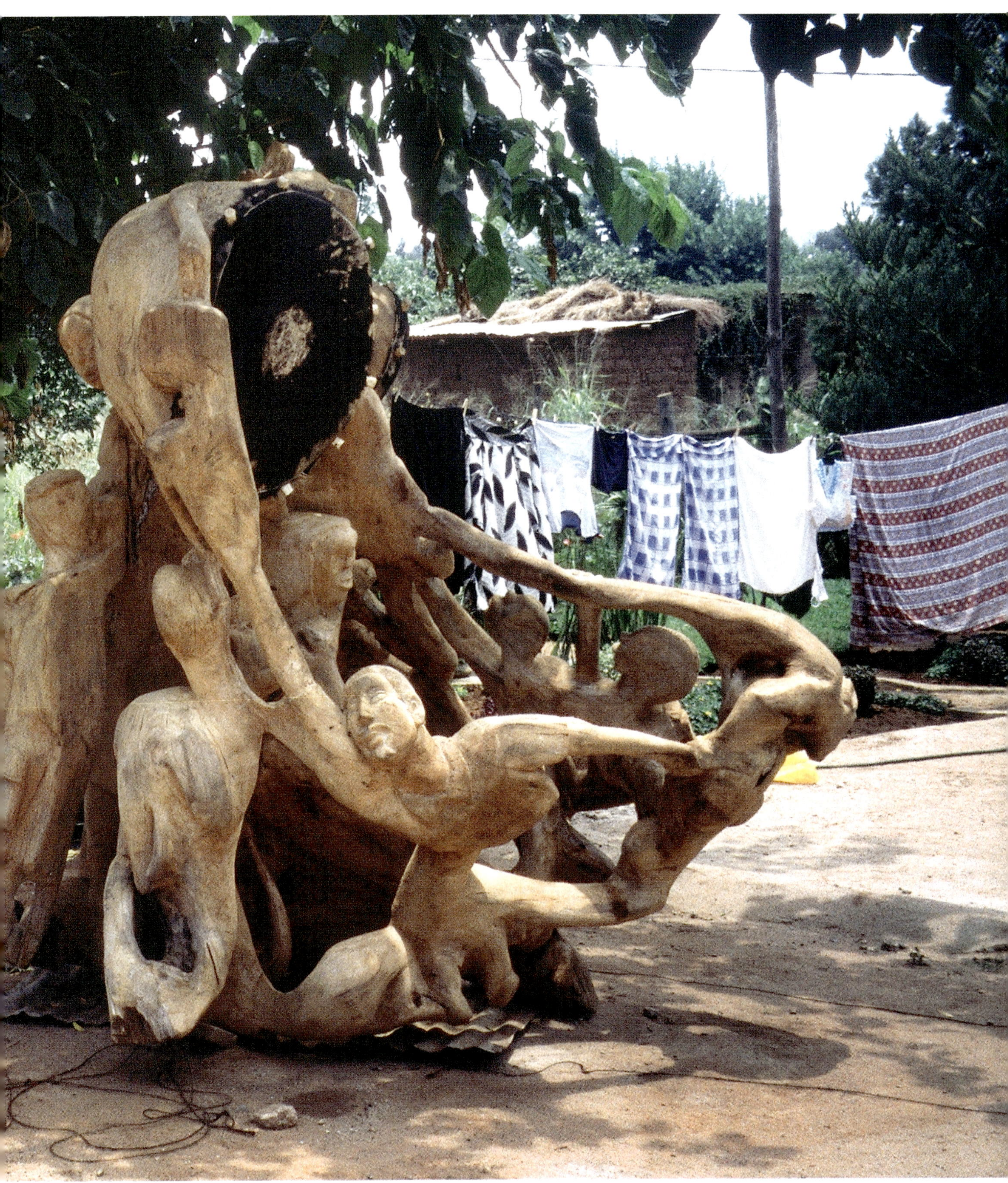

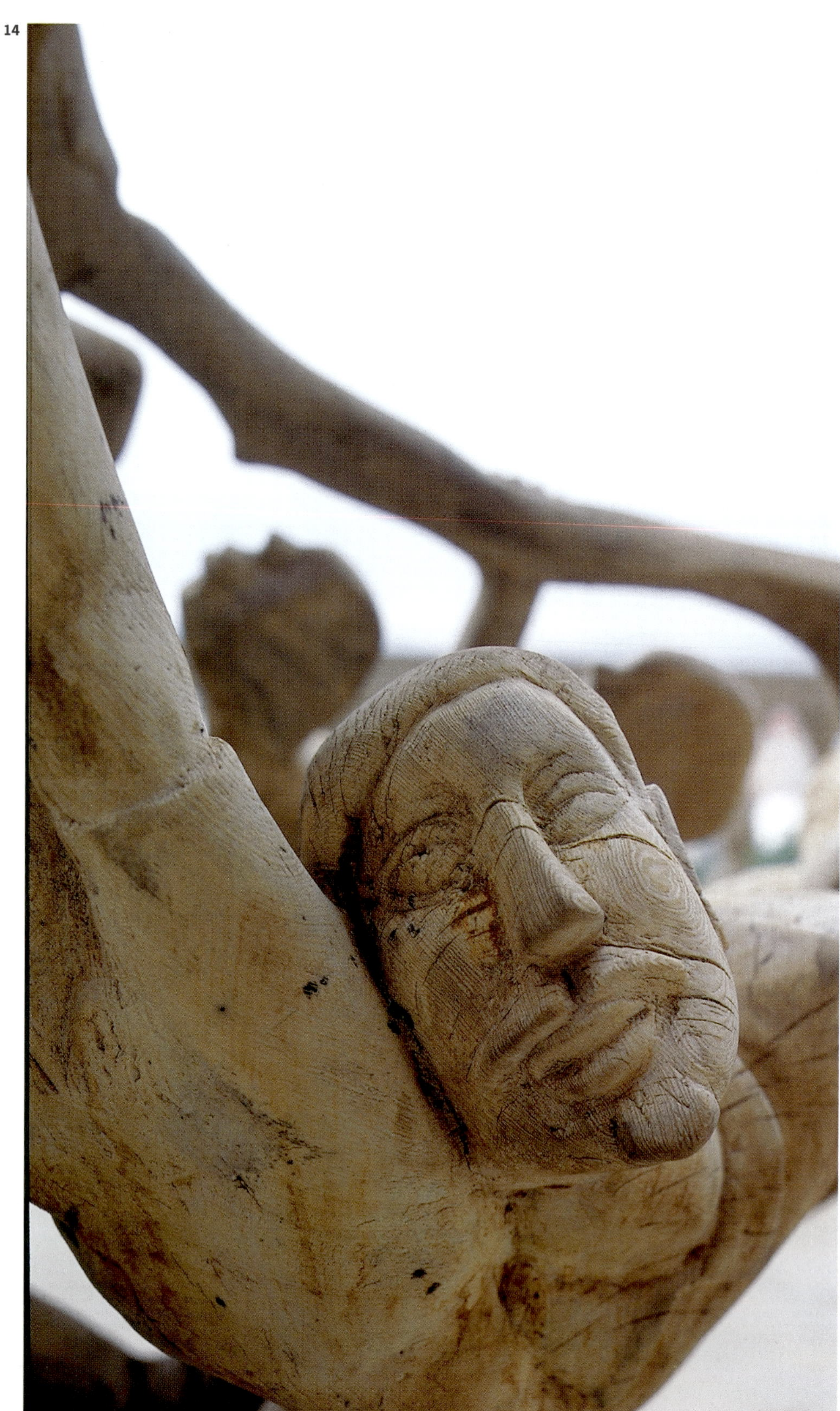

14

14. Detail. *Union Buildings.*

15. *Union Buildings*, 1999, wood and hide. Collection of the Department of Arts and Culture, seen here outside the President's Office at the Union Buildings in Pretoria.

Pages 42–45: *Union Buildings.*

Photographs: Theresa Collins

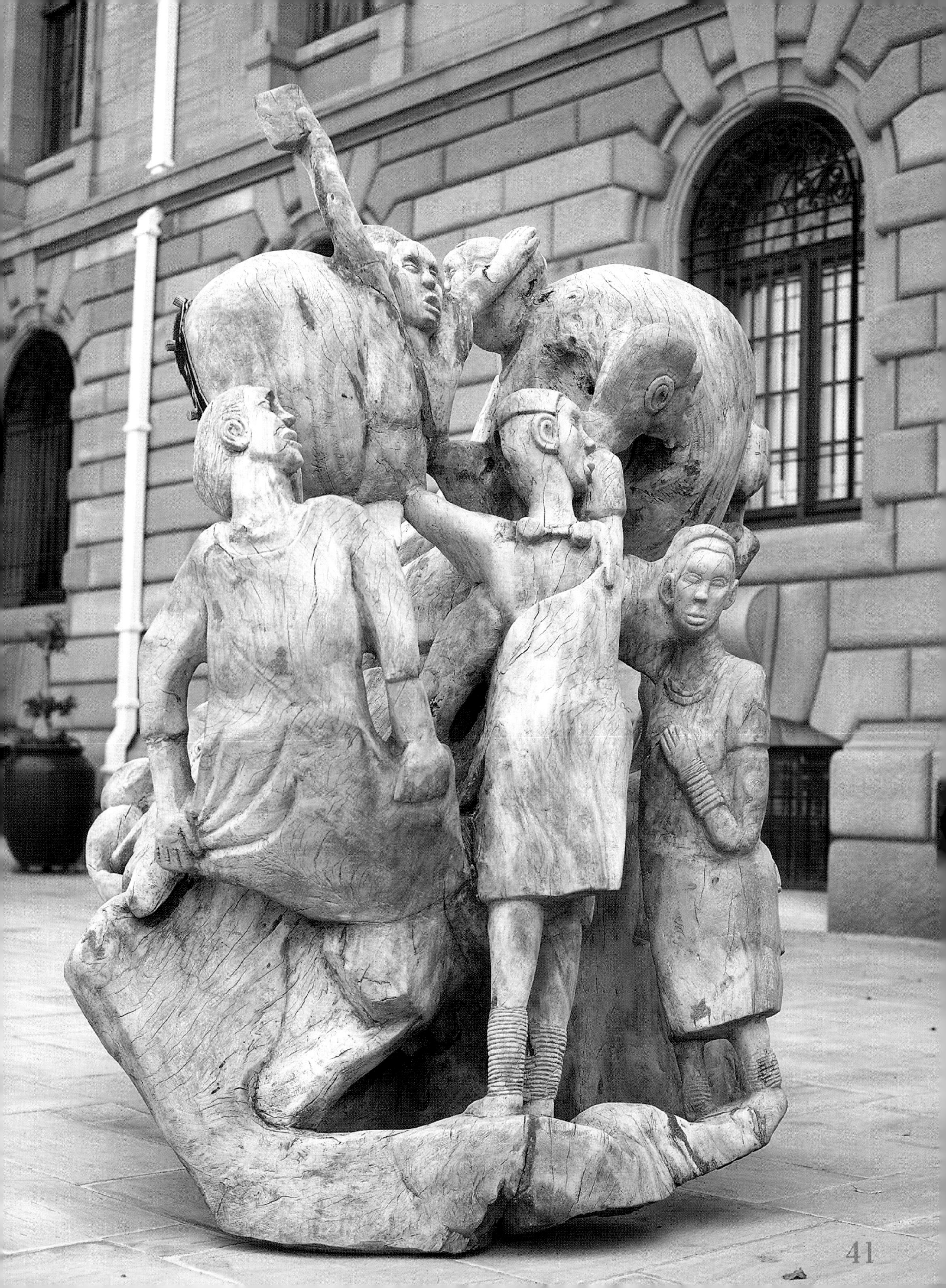

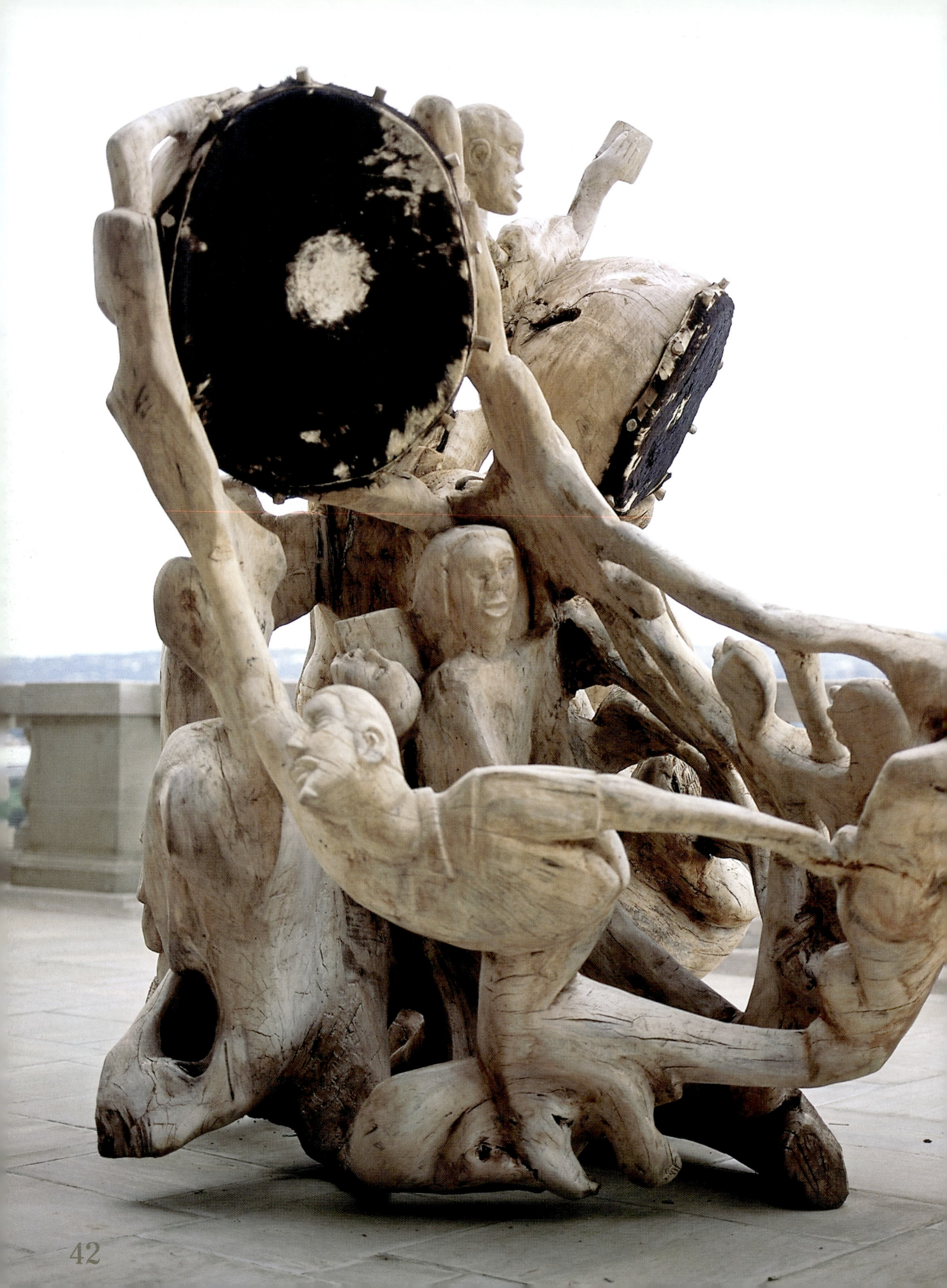

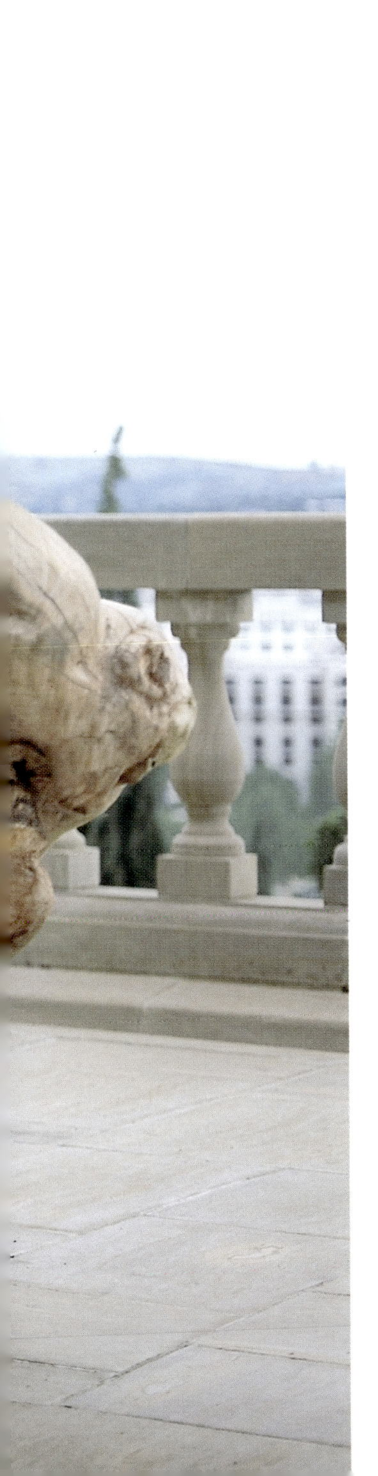

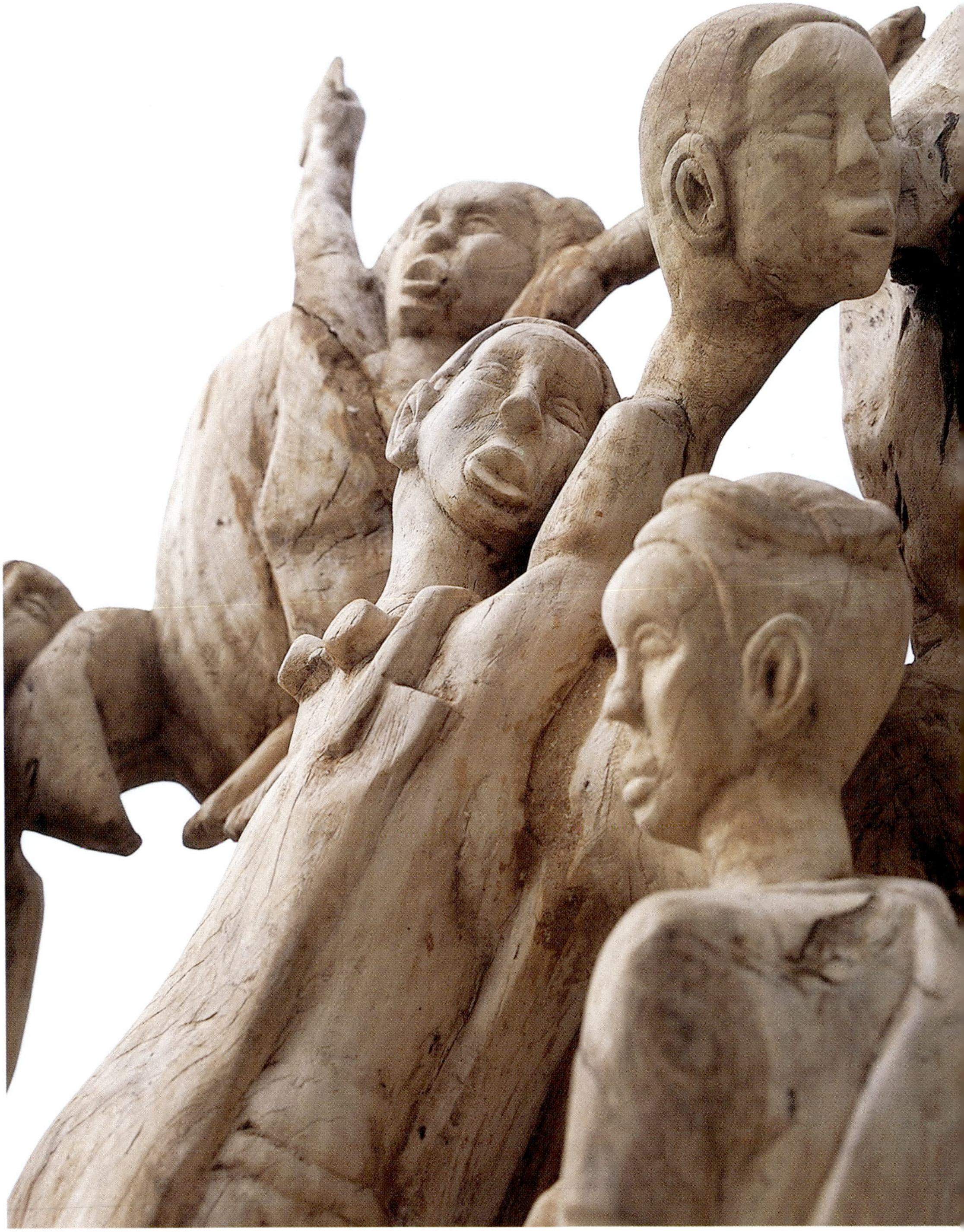

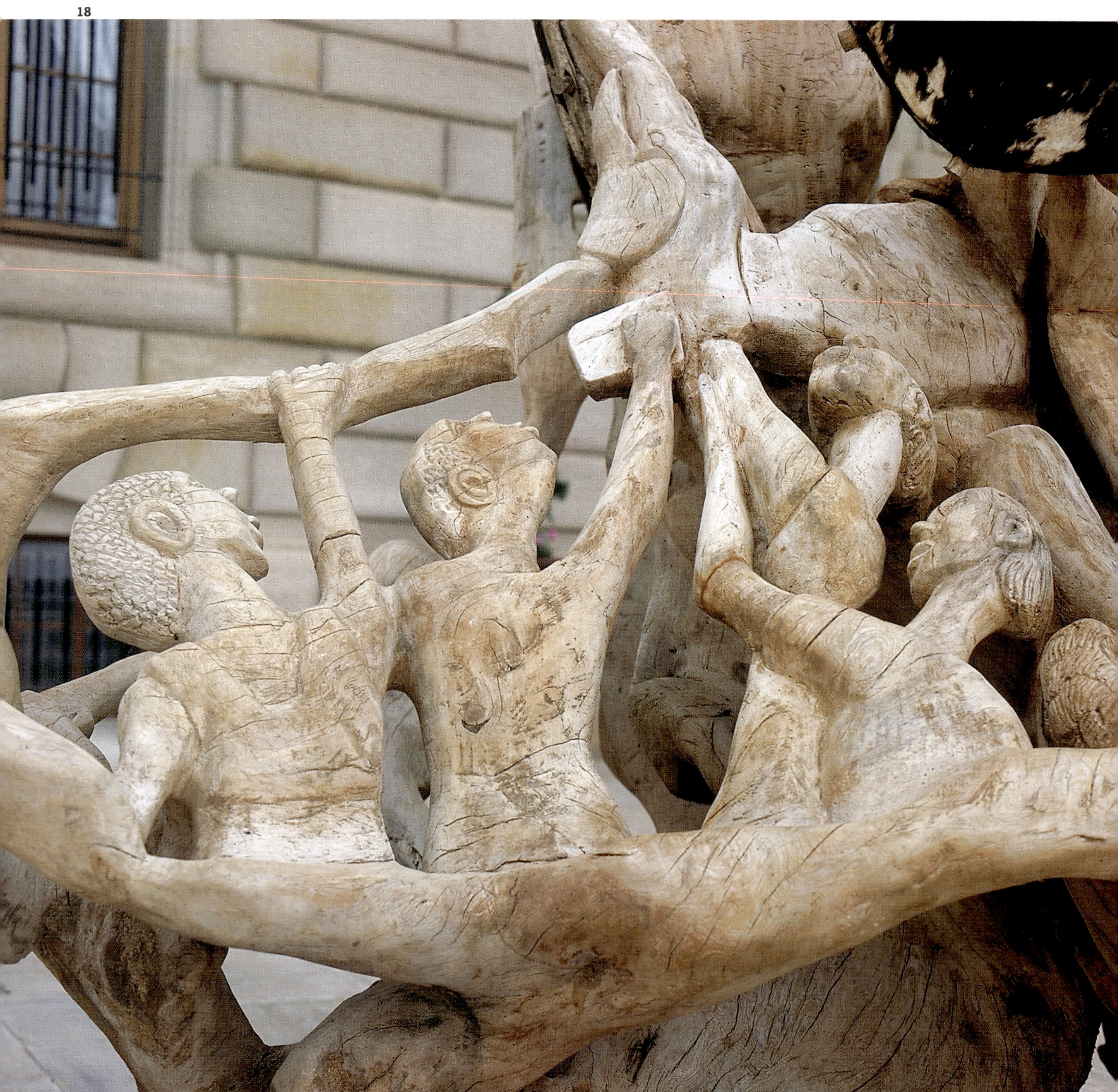

18

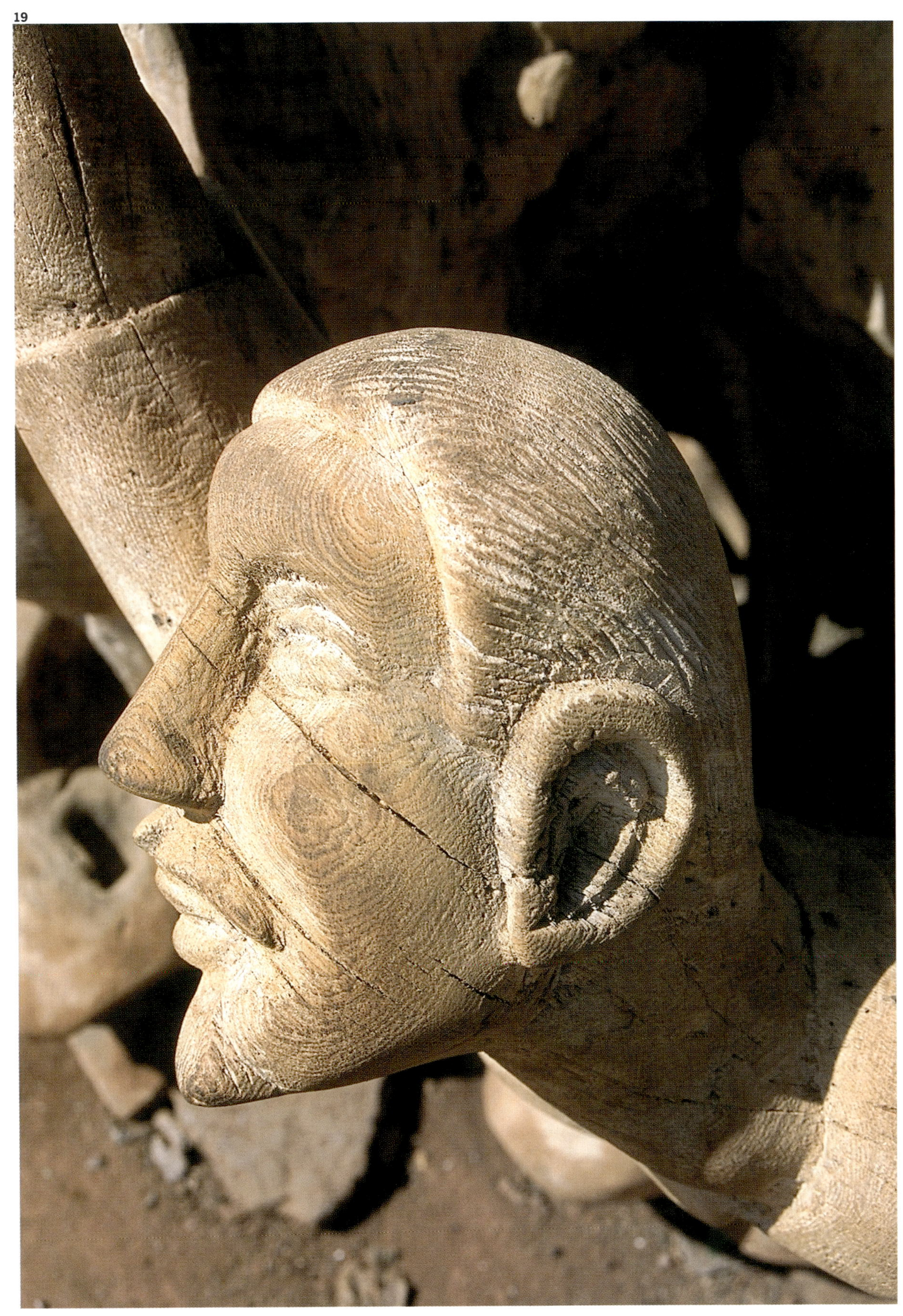

CARNAGE

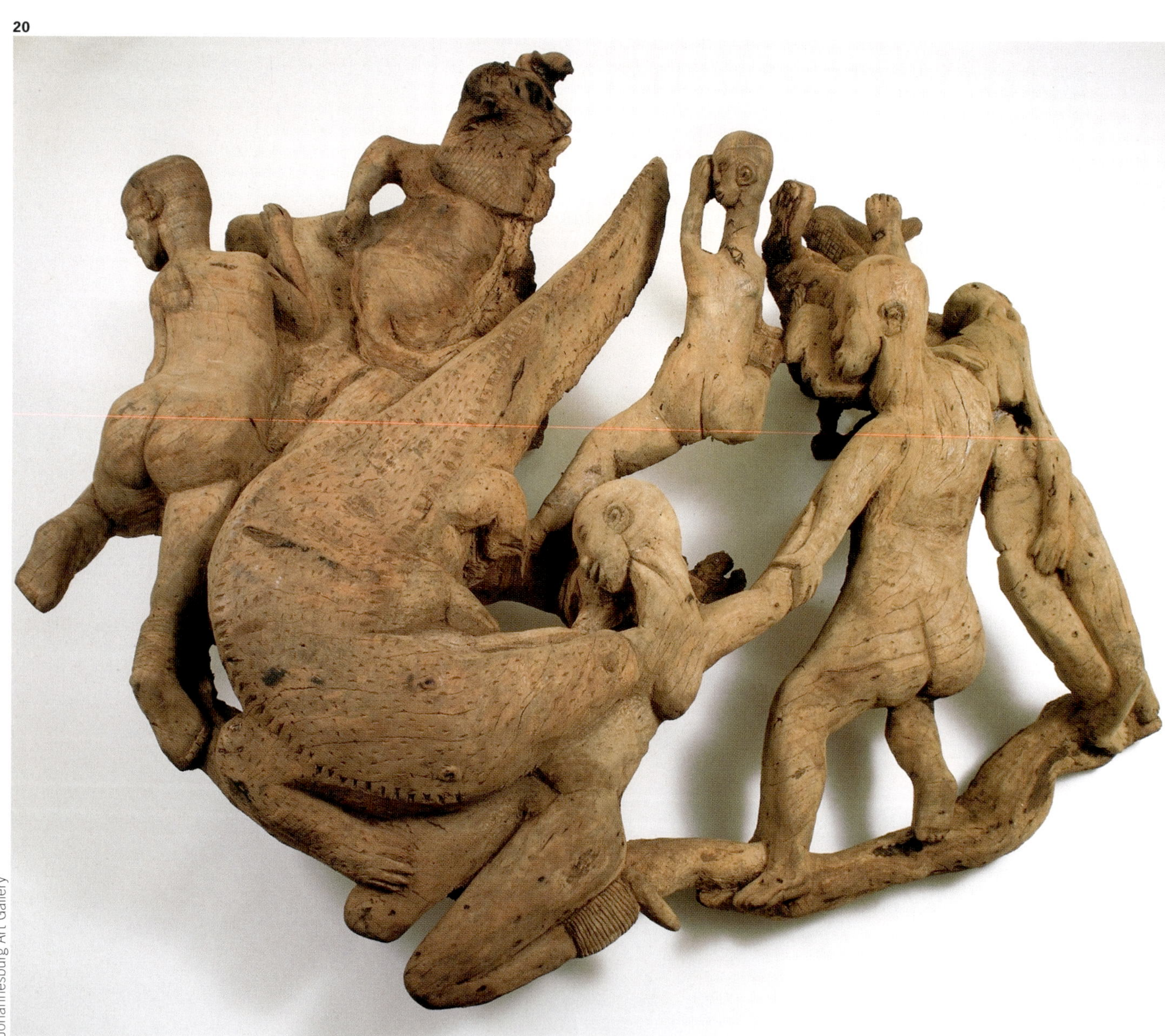

20–22:

Carnage II (Natal Flood Disaster), 1988, fig tree
wood
79 x 218.5 x 197 cm,
Johannesburg Art
Gallery Collection.

21

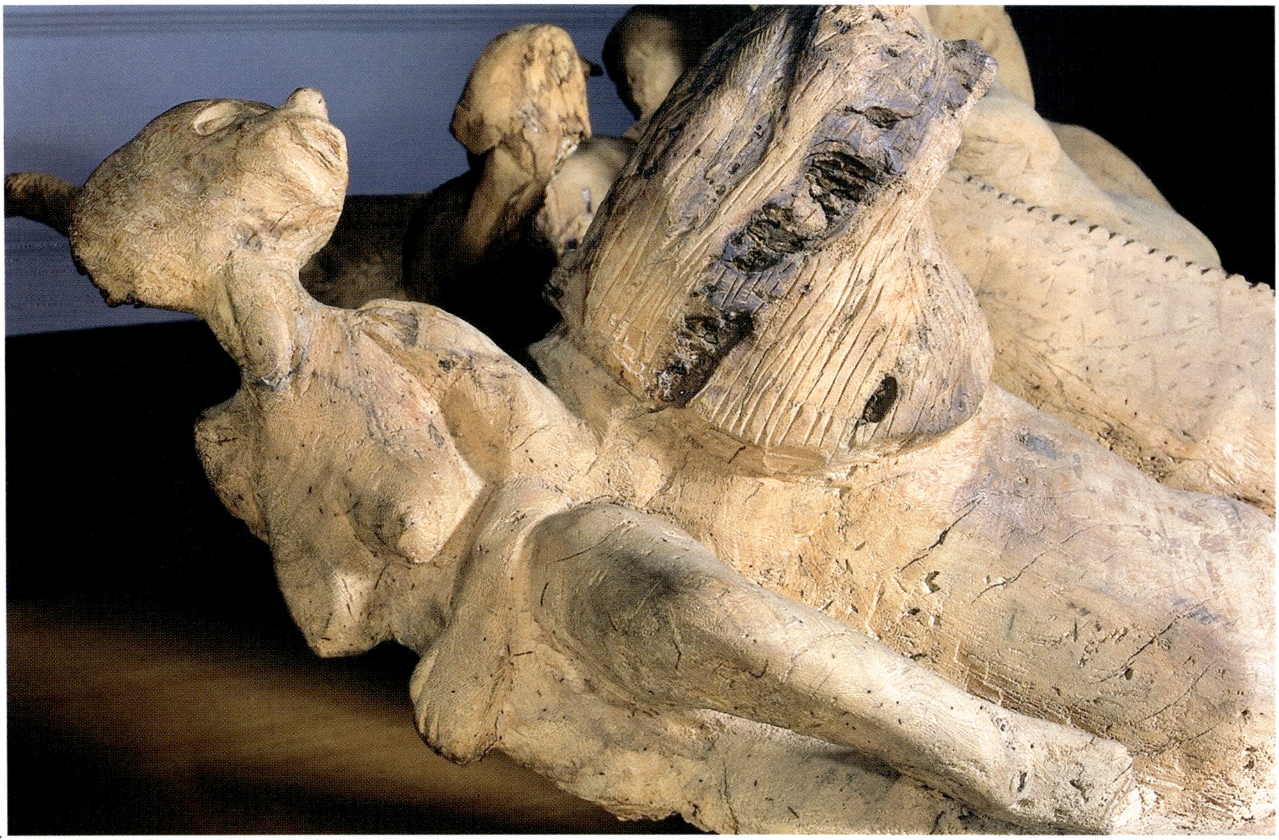

22

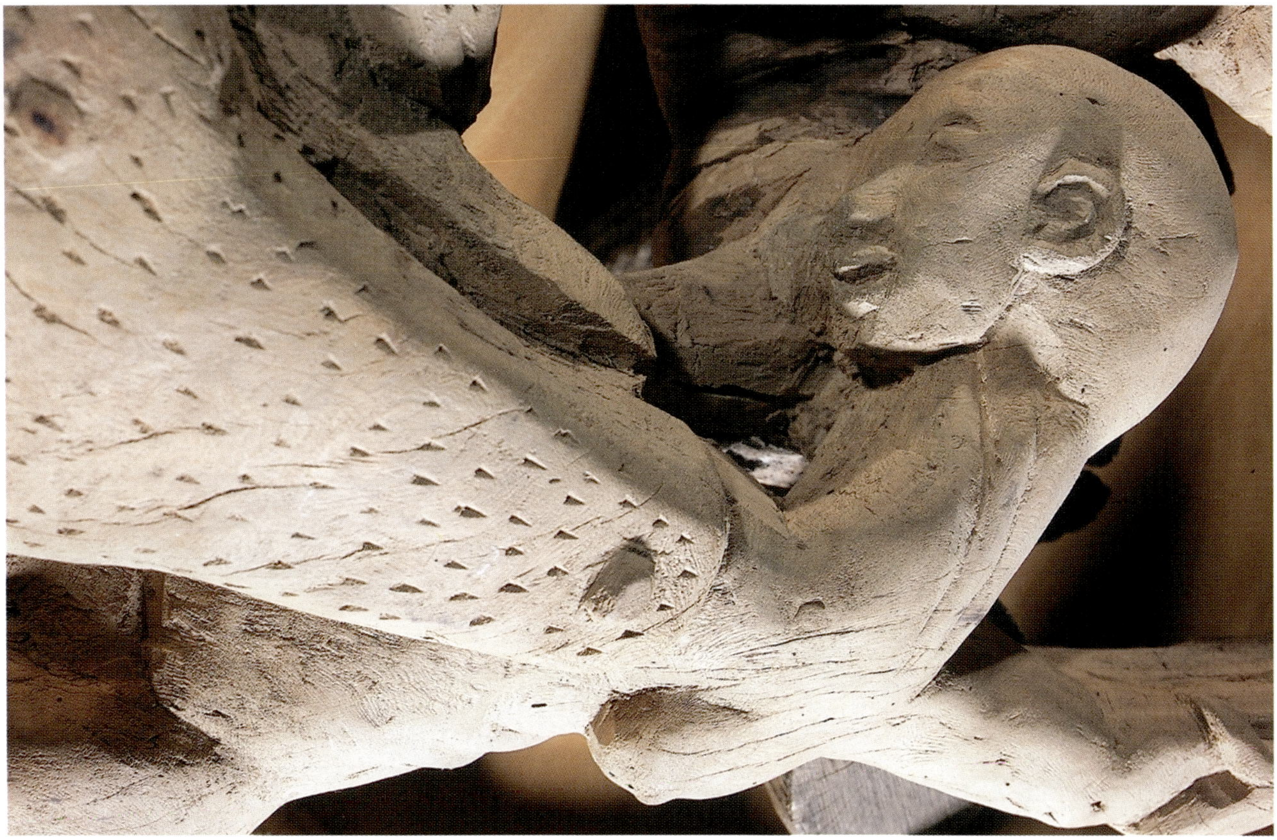

Photographs: Theresa Collins

NGOMA LUNGUNDU

Noria Mabasa has produced two pieces which she calls *Ngoma Lungundu*, which is the magical *Drum of Thunder, Drum of the Dead* or *Drum of Mwari*.

Noria explained the legend of the drum as follows:

"When the Singo people migrated south from Zimbabwe to what is now known as Venda, they carried this drum. The drum was enormous and had to be carried by many men. It was not allowed to touch the ground, as it was believed to be filled with medicine and magical powers which protected the people from their enemies. Human arms were used as drumsticks to beat on the human skin covering. According to tradition, as long as this drum was continually beaten during times of threat, it would help to defeat the enemy and protect the people. The drum struck such fear into the souls of the enemies that they fled in terror, fell to the ground in a swoon 'as in death' or actually died. If they stopped beating the drum, or allowed it to touch the ground, the Singo would be vanquished. It is said that it was the power of this drum that enabled the Singo to undertake their journey and occupy and hold land to the south of the Limpopo River. At times the power of the drum was so great that it would appear to play itself."

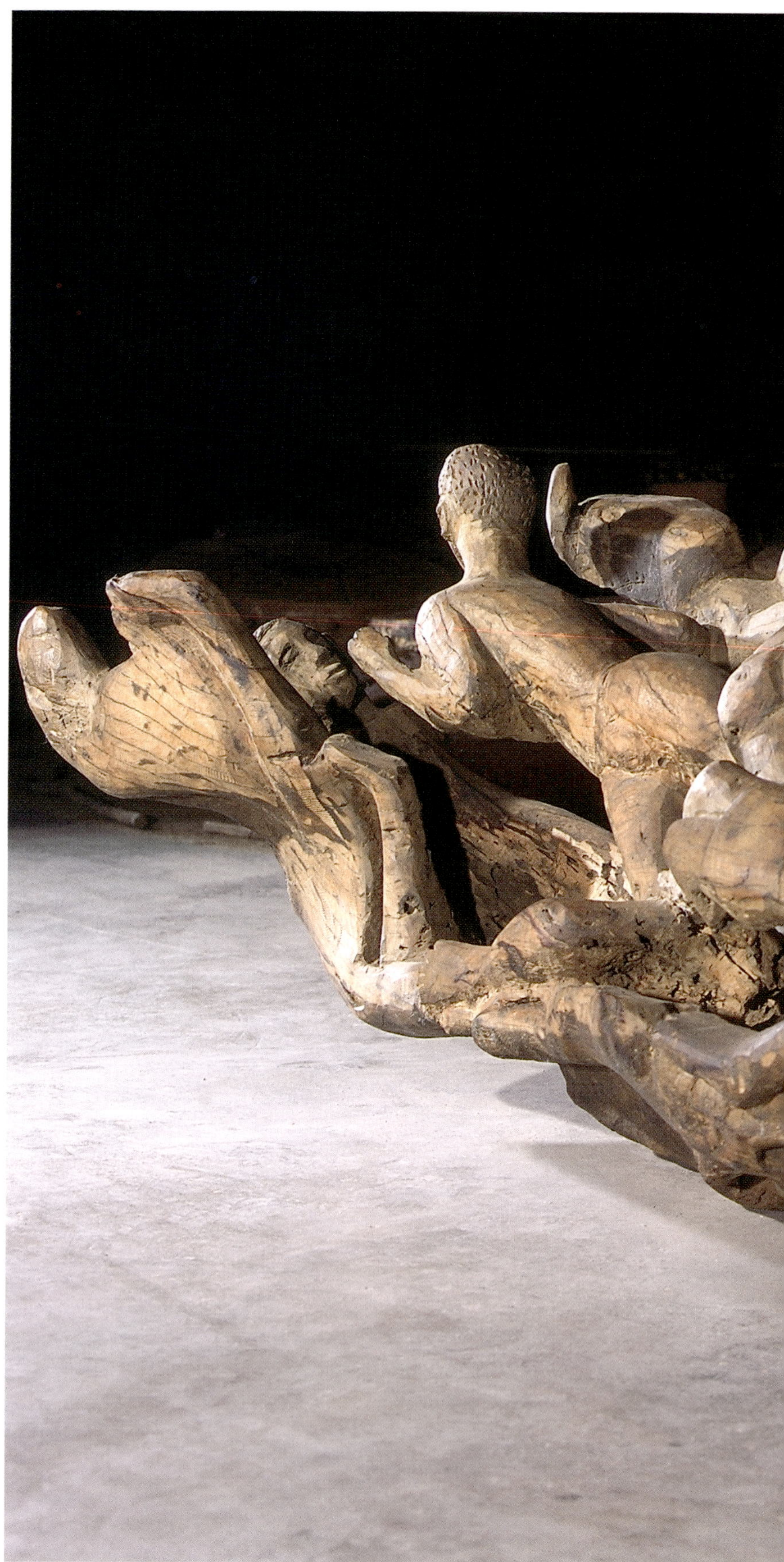

23. *Ngoma Lungundu II*, 1995, wood, 116 x 279.5 x 146 cm. Standard Bank Collection of African Art (Wits Art Galleries).

Pages 50–51:
Details of *Ngoma Lungundu II*.

Photographs: Theresa Collins

23

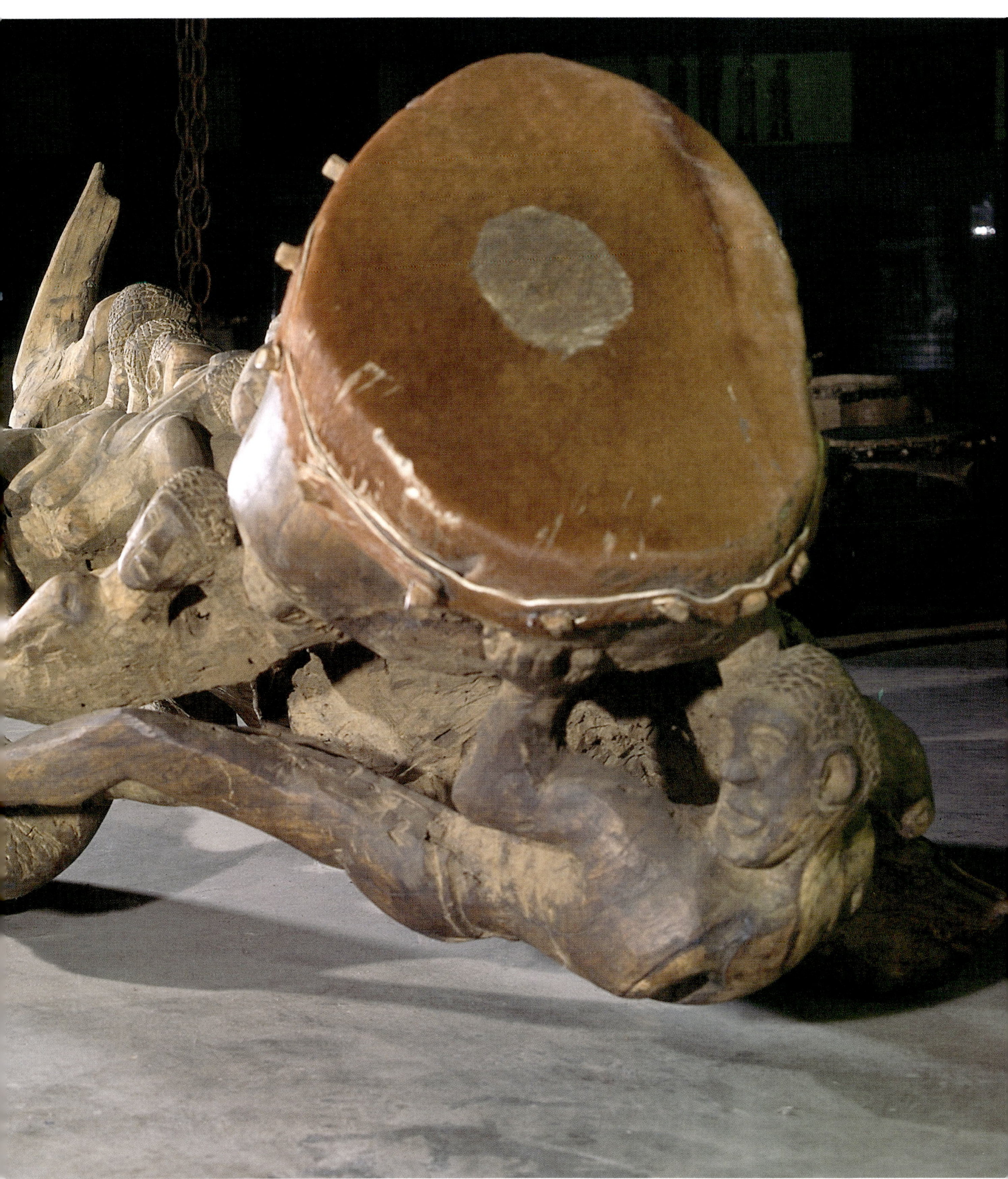

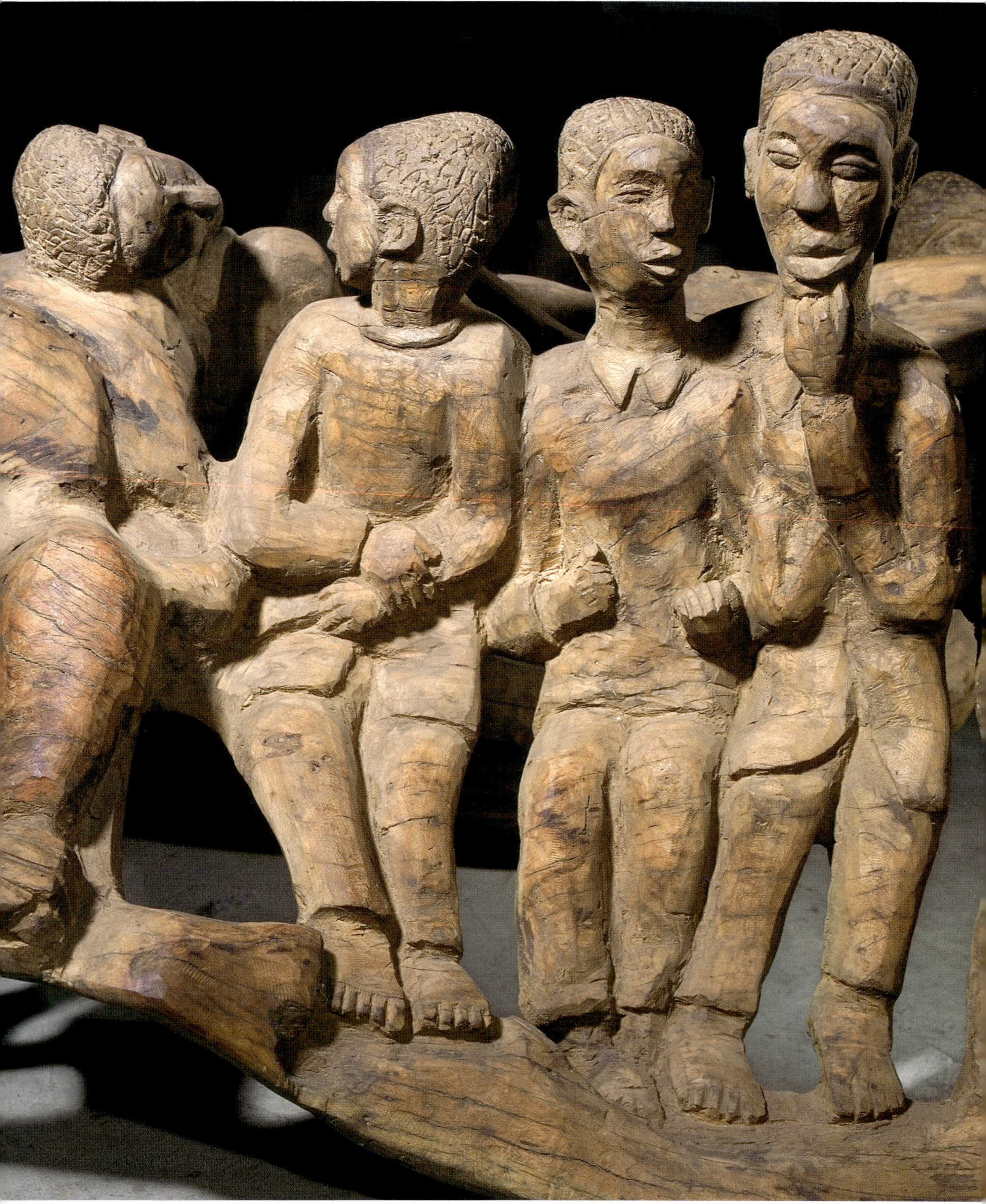

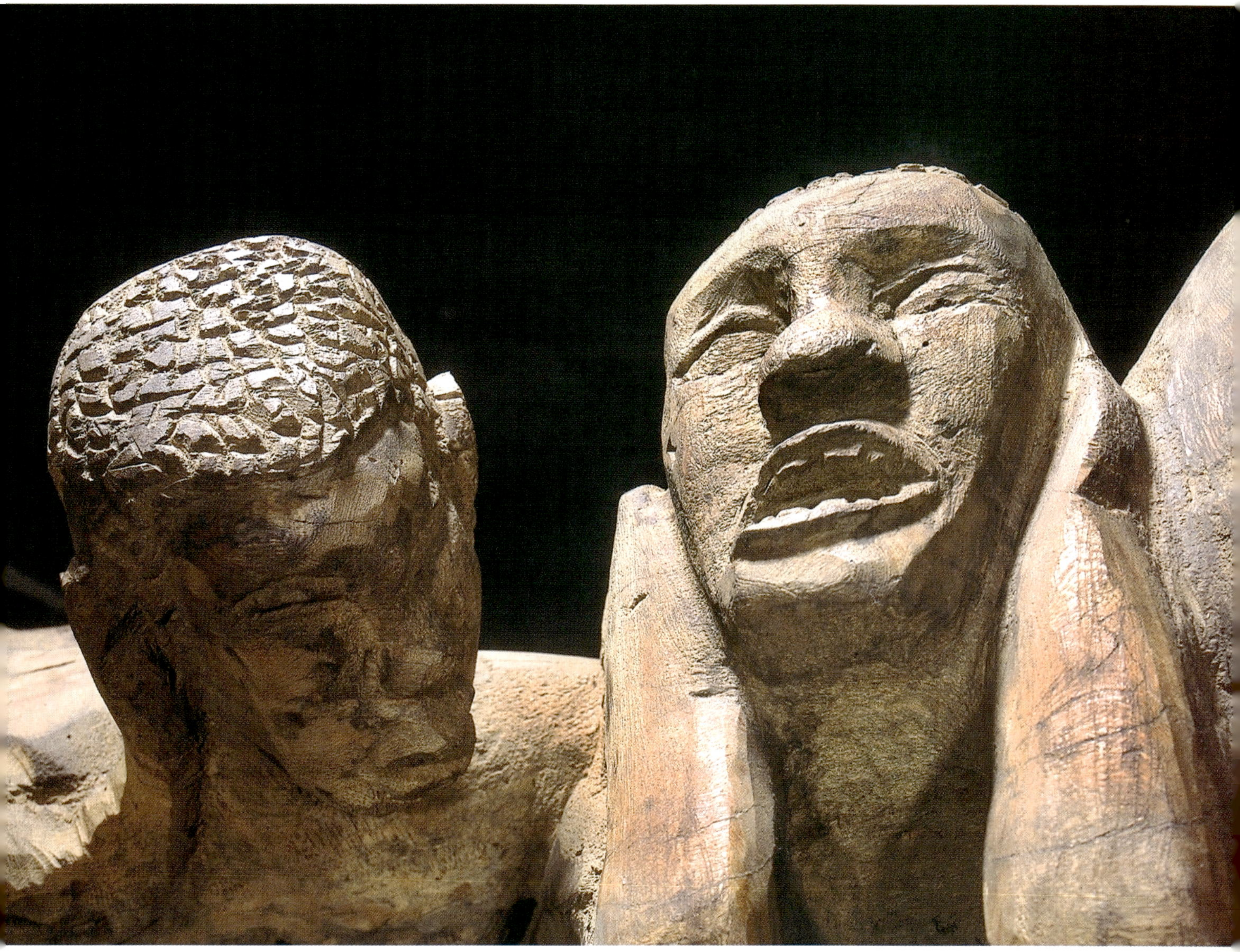

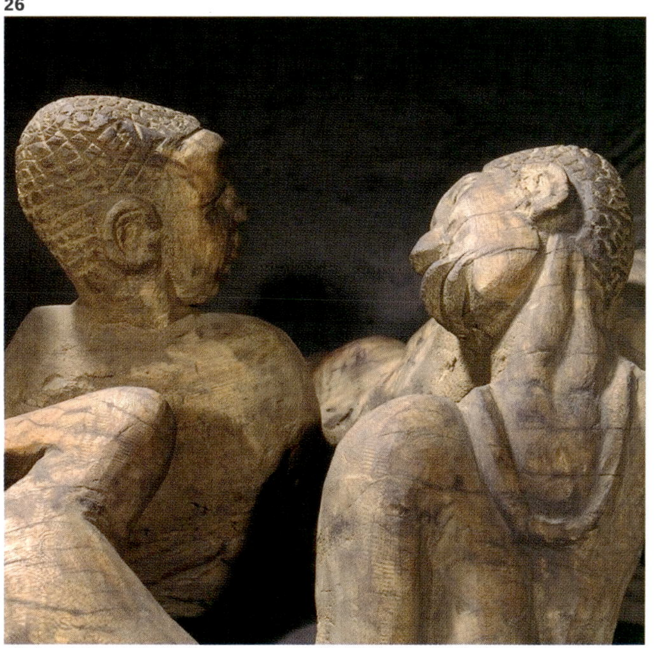

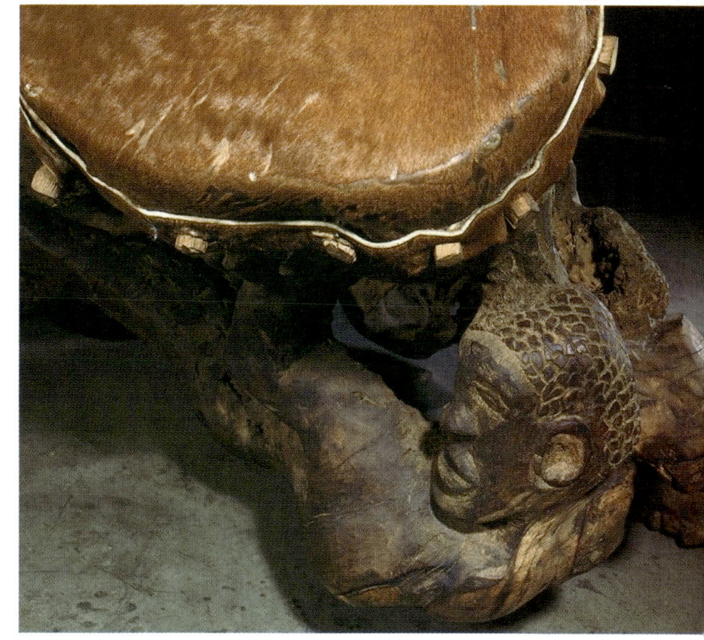

THE FLOOD

The Flood was created in the mid-1990s and took nine months to complete. The sculpture is carved out of a fig tree trunk with a circumference of approximately 2.5m and is almost 2m long. Noria found the tree trunk when visiting her son at his home in Hasane, Malamulele. *The Flood* is symbolic of all floods. It depicts figures of people and animals clamouring for safety and trying to escape raging waters. This work is permanently displayed in the foyer of the Sandton Convention Centre in Johannesburg.

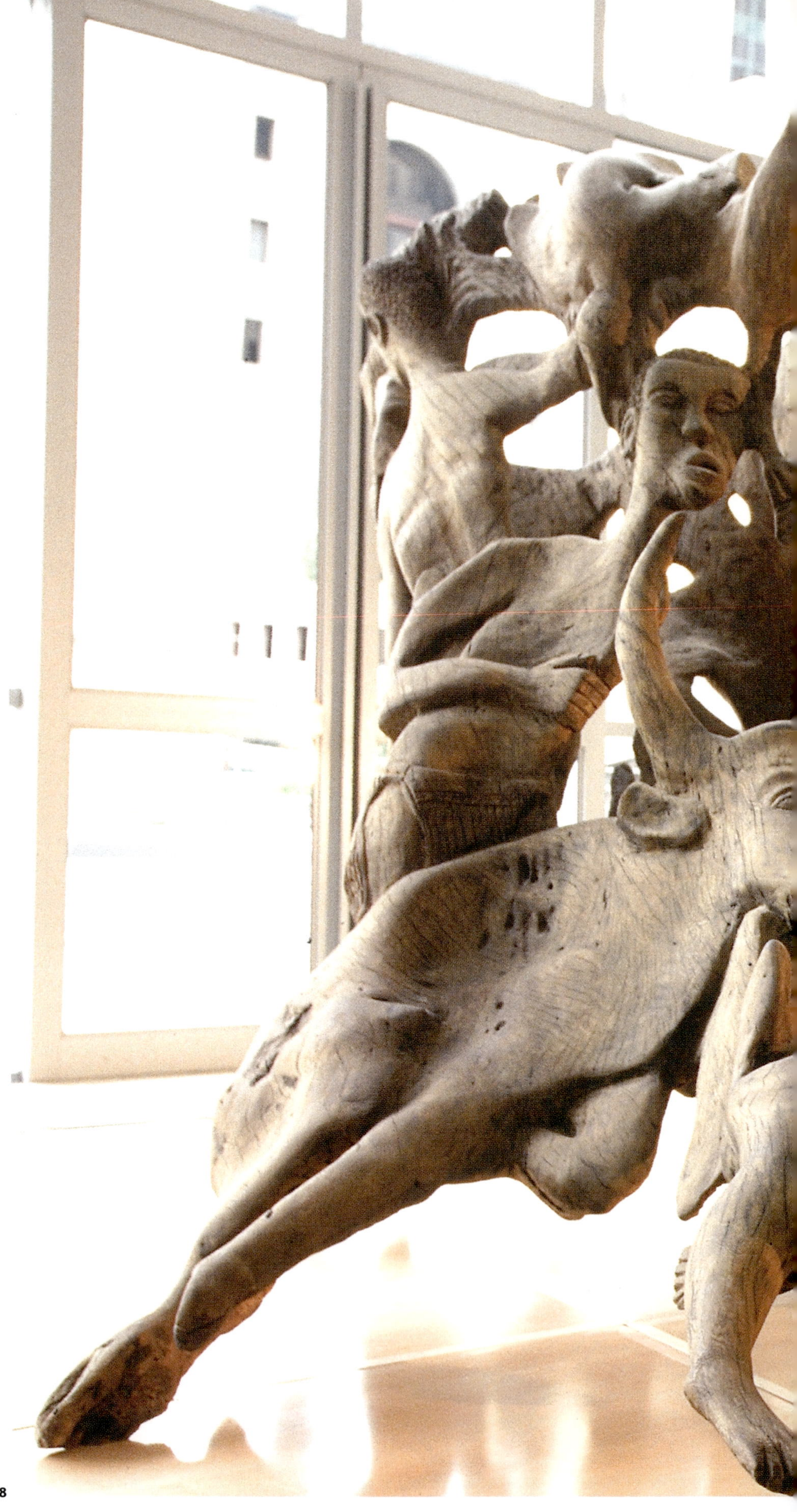

28. *The Flood*, 1994, marula, height: 2.8 m, circumference: 3 m. Sandton Convention Centre Collection.

Pages 54–57:
Details of *The Flood.*

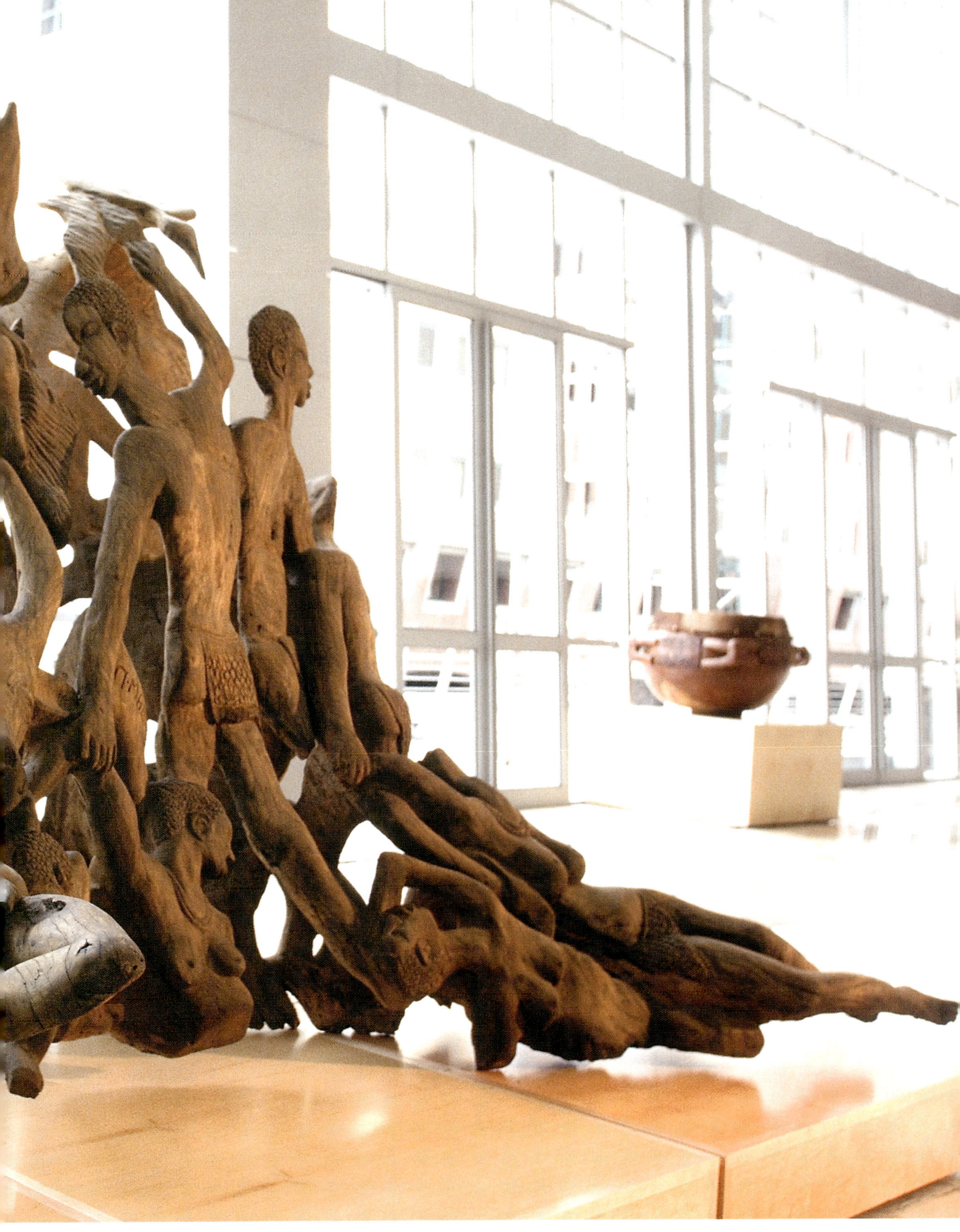

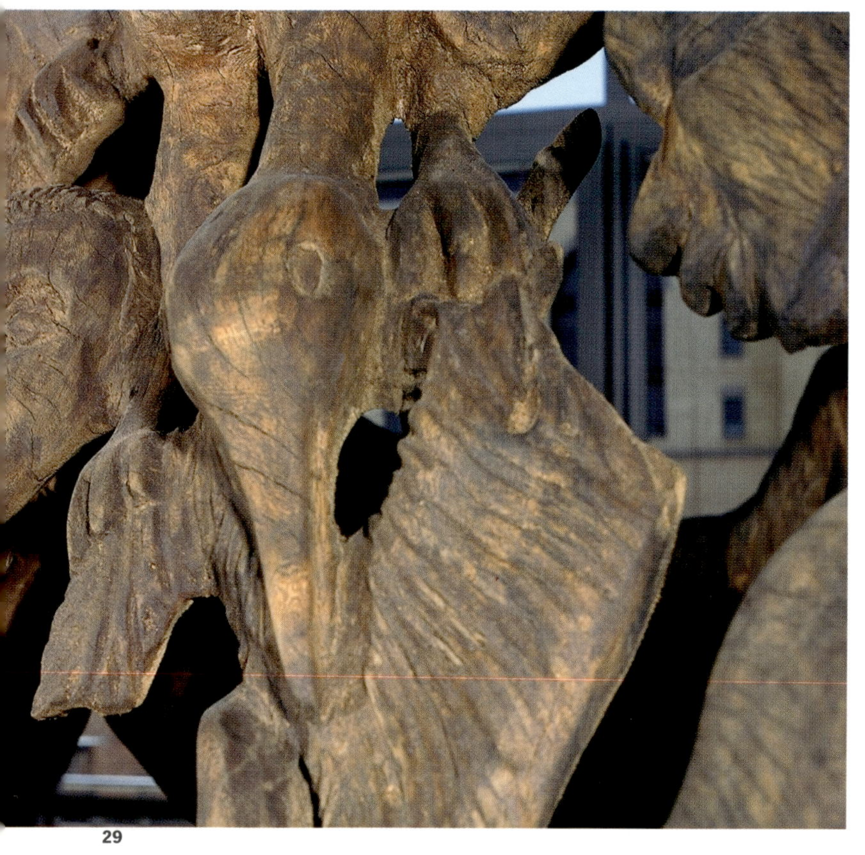

29

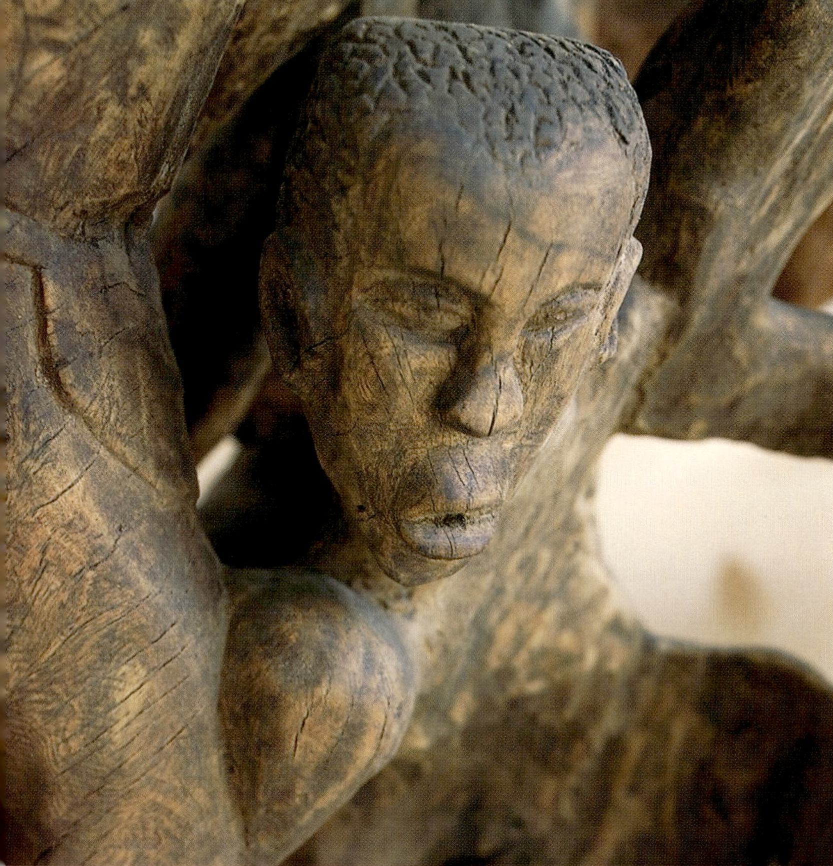

30

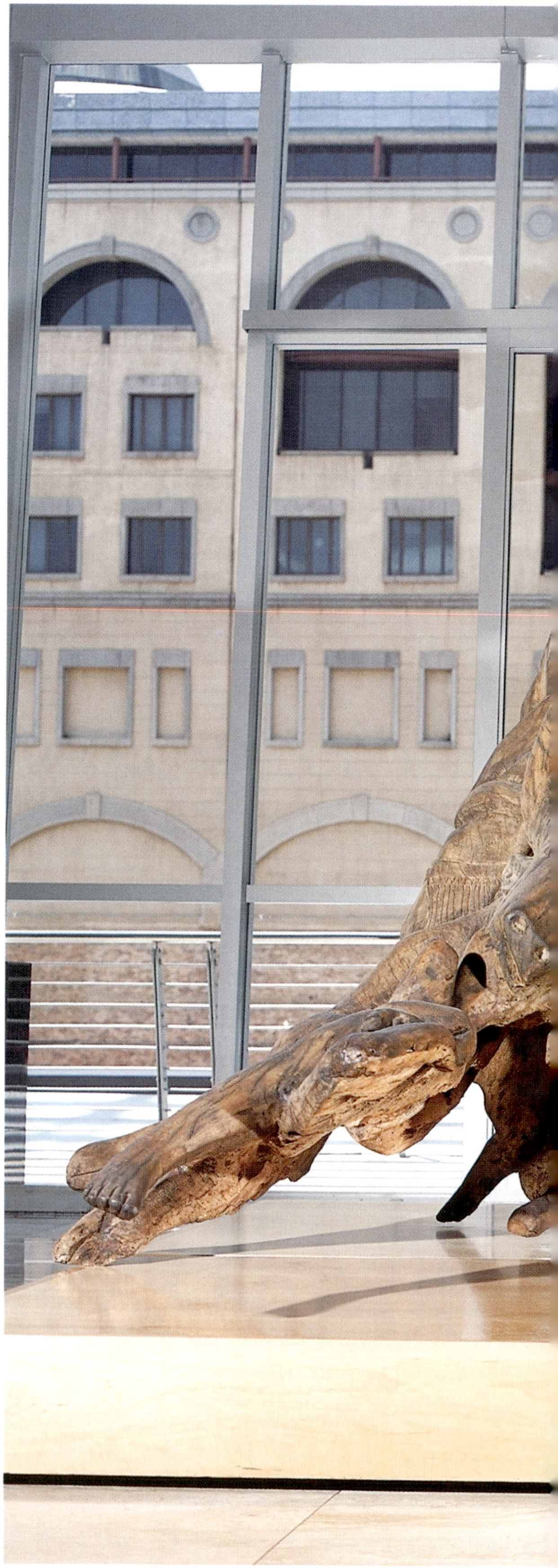

31

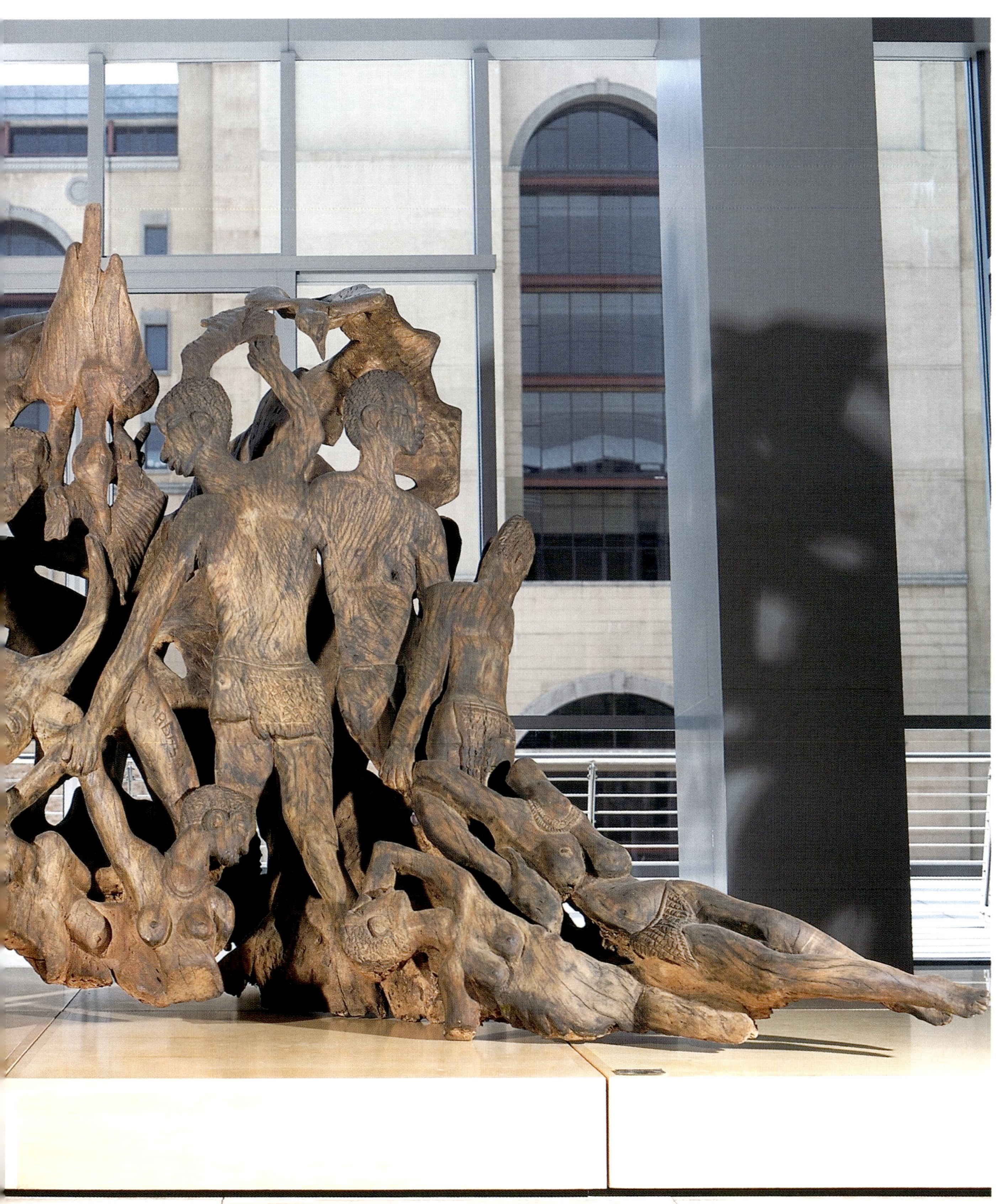

Photographs: Theresa Collins

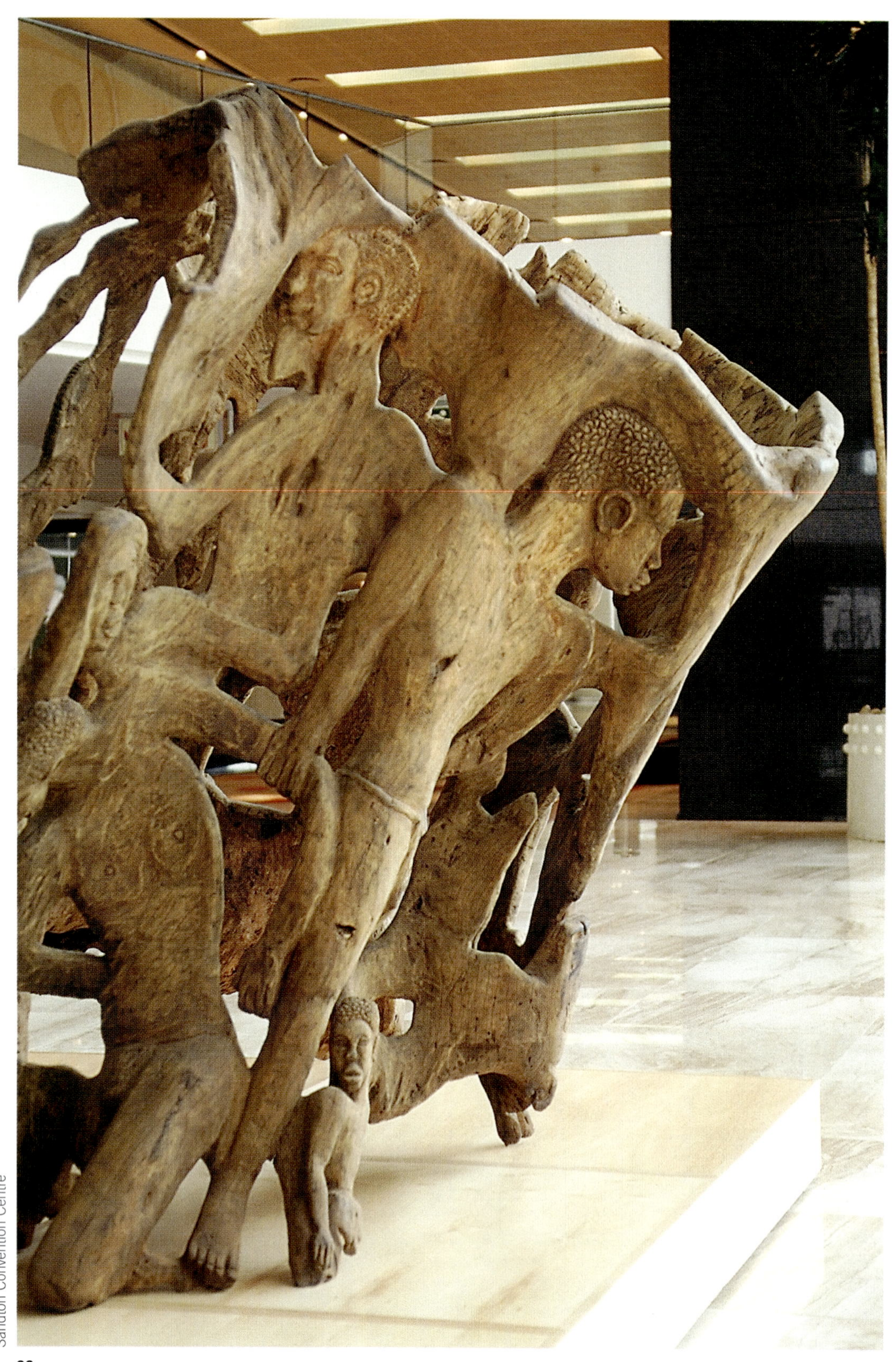

32

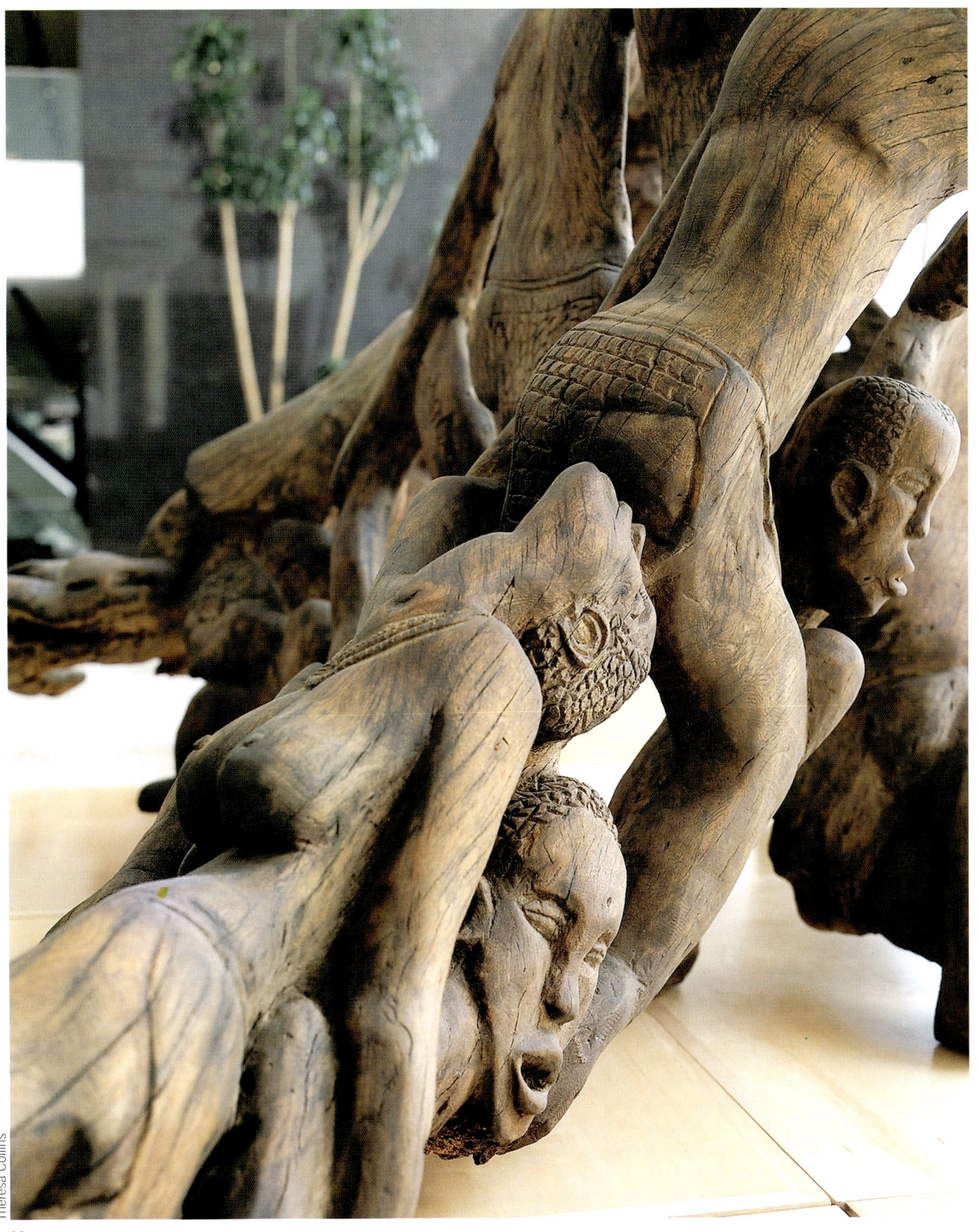

33

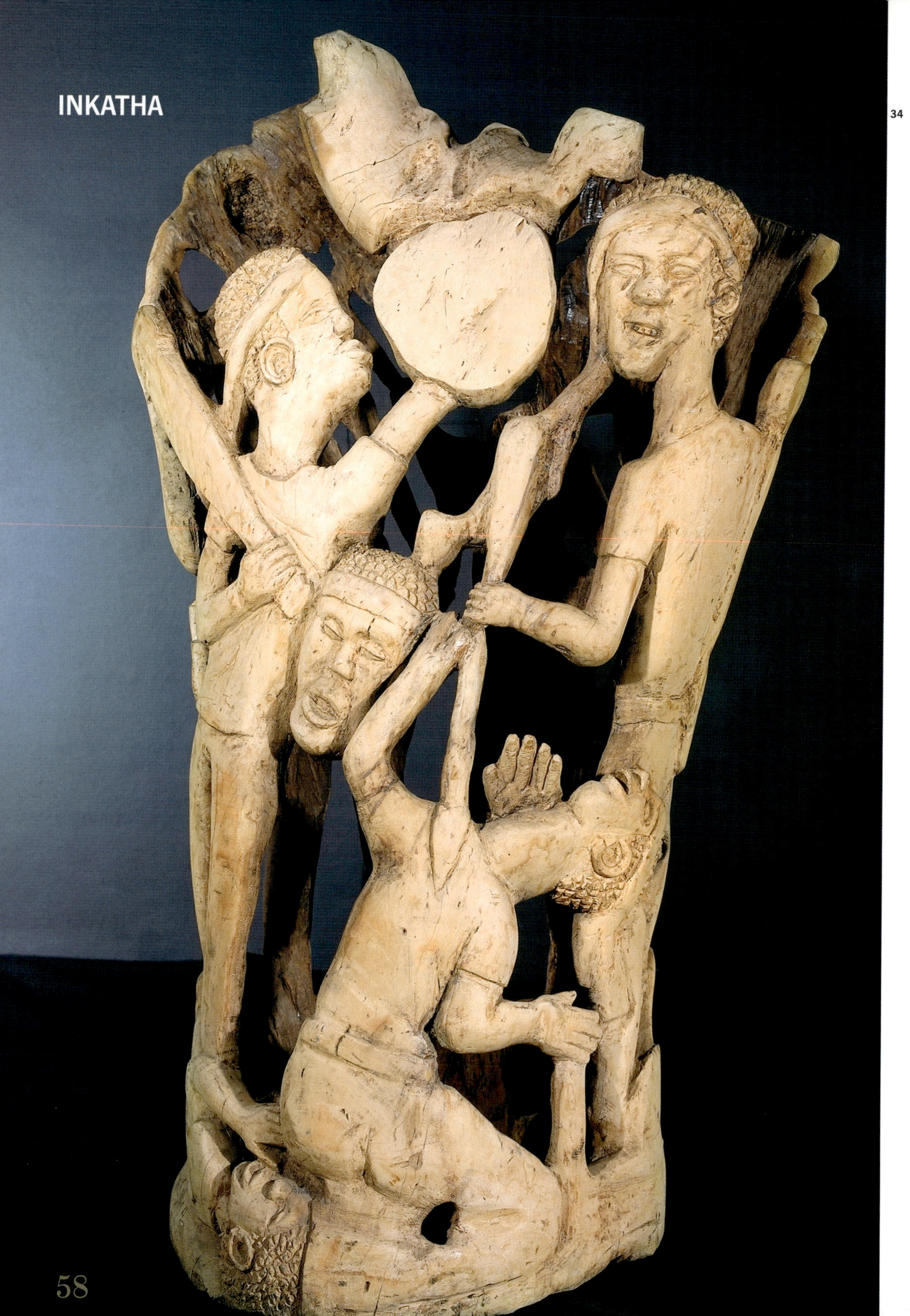

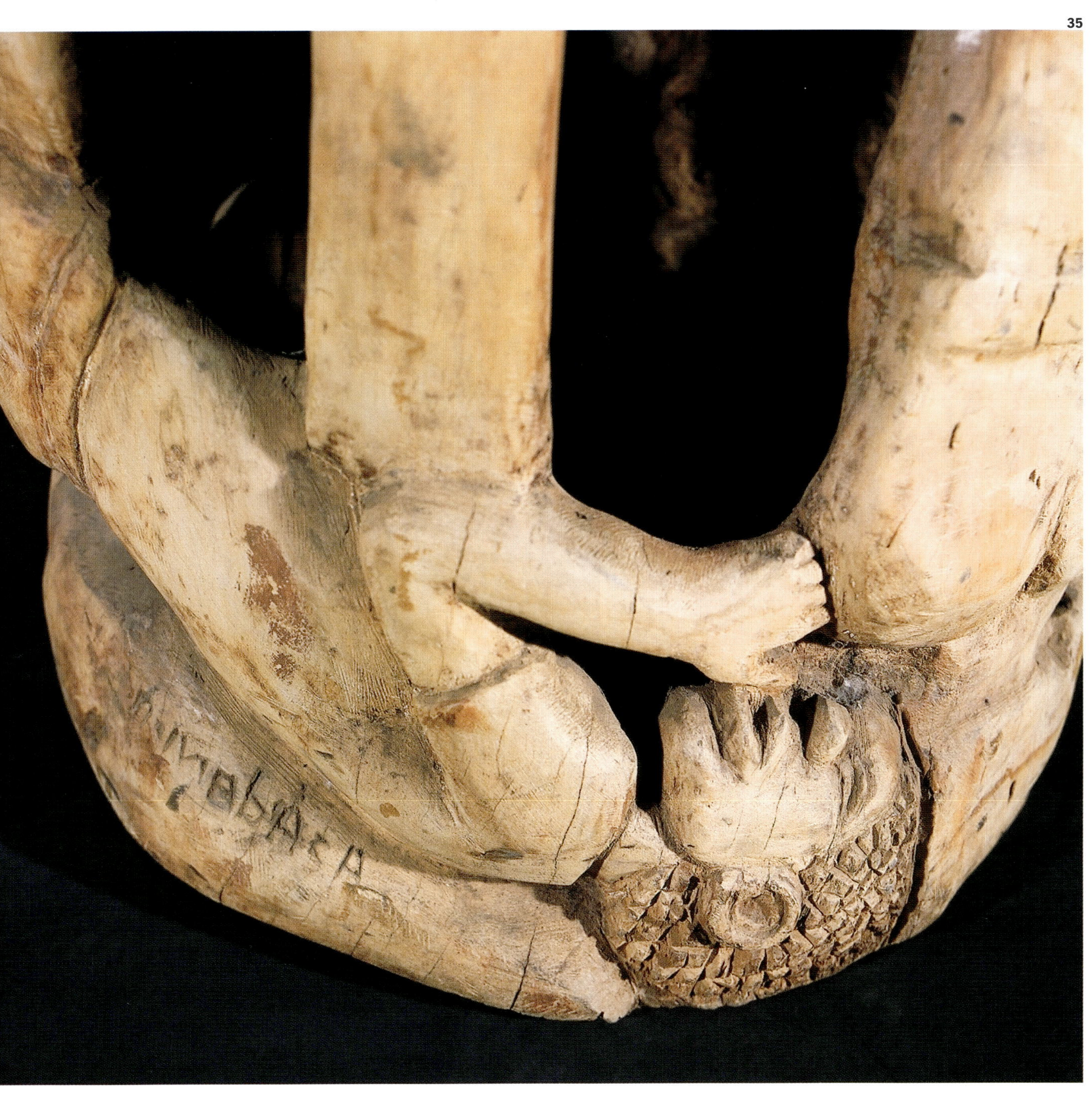

34: *Inkatha,* c.2001, wood,
163 x 106 x 53 cm,
South African
Broadcasting
Corporation (SABC) art
collection.

35: Detail of *Inkatha.*

Photographs: Theresa Collins

MIXED MESSAGES

Noria Mabasa and the art market

Rayda Becker

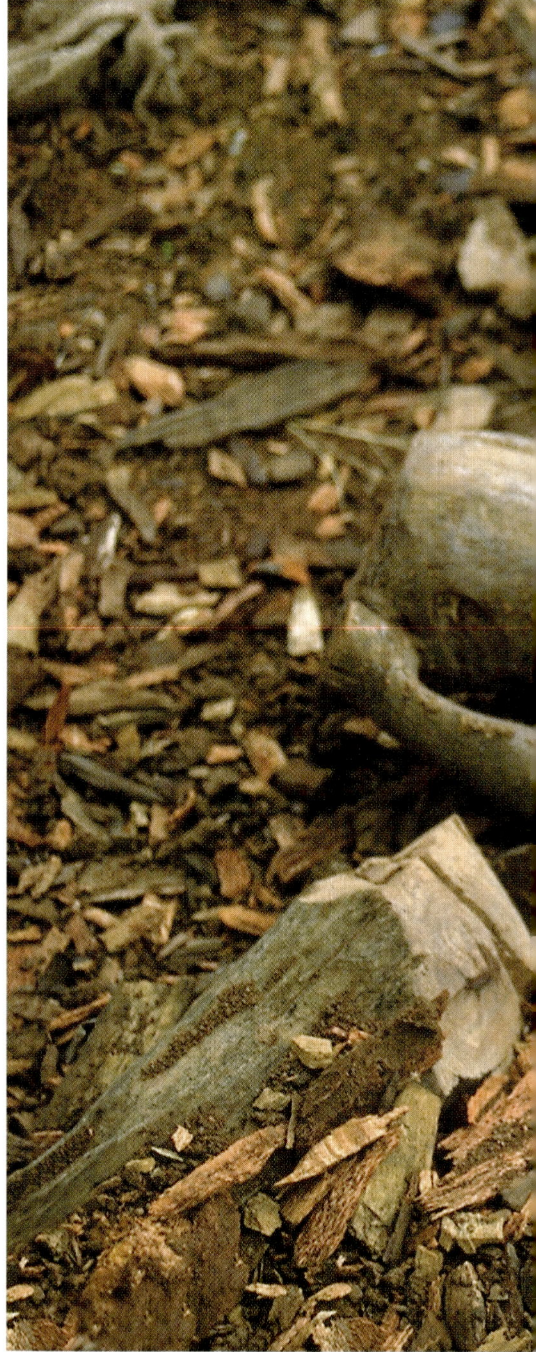

Noria Mabasa and her art are generally situated almost exclusively within the context of what has come to be seen as a unique group of artists working and living in the rural northern regions of South Africa and who, it is asserted, derive their inspiration and points of reference from cultural traditions deeply informed by spiritual influences. In her interview with Kathryn Straughan, Mabasa tends to reinforce this approach to an understanding of her work. The present essay takes a different bearing on the work and the artist by considering another context in which she has operated at times during her career – the city, with its network of galleries and exhibitions; and by foregrounding the reception that Mabasa has received in this arena of contested aesthetics and evolving cultural agendas. The fact that Mabasa's rise to prominence as an artist has coincided with fundamental changes in South African society, and with the cultural debates and challenges to settled aesthetic traditions that accompany these changes, has resulted in her work – like that of many other artists – being placed within diverse narratives by critics with different social and aesthetic preoccupations. This essay will highlight some of the interrogative strategies that can be brought to bear on this apparently 'traditional' artist, to locate her work within contemporary South African artistic production and consumption.

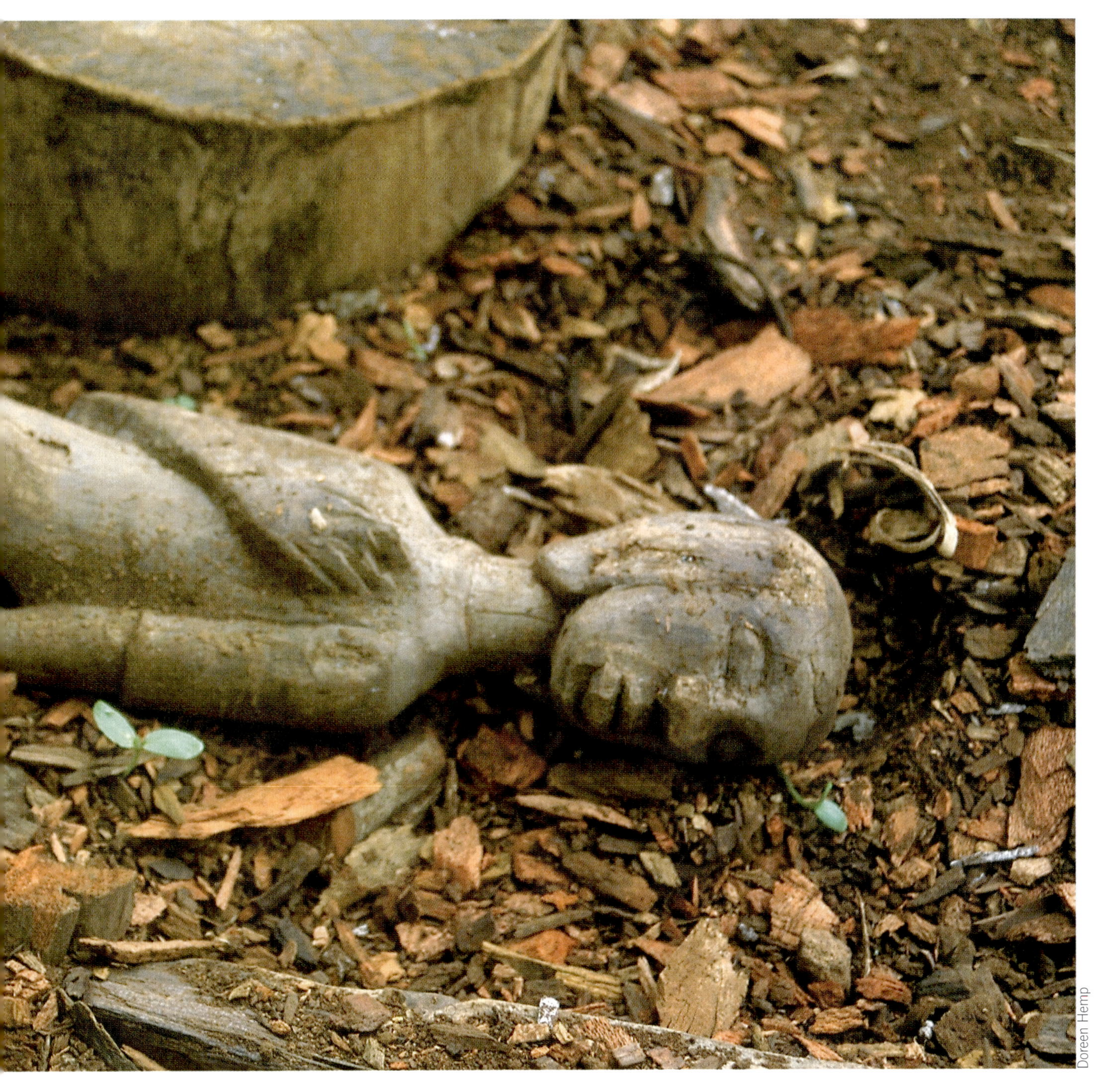

At Mabasa's homestead, 1990.

TRIBUTARIES

Mabasa first came to public attention in Johannesburg during the run of the *Tributaries* exhibition which opened there in February 1985, at the Africana Museum (now MuseuMAfricA). The exhibition was sponsored by BMW South Africa, and after it closed in Johannesburg it travelled to Germany.

Tributaries was an extraordinary event in the art history of this country. Ricky Burnett, the curator, chose to show art from all regions of the country and all sections of South African society. He wanted to cut across the constructed definitions of difference by showing the work of rural black and rural white, urban black and urban white artists. In the exhibition itself hierarchies of display were abandoned in favour of equality; all works were treated in the same way whether they were conventionally understood to fall into the categories craft, traditional or modern. The exhibition space itself was significant. It was a museum, that is, a space for serious contemplation, and not a curio shop or commercial gallery. All these factors invited destabilisation of the viewers' preconceptions, and yet the real surprise of *Tributaries* was not the juxtaposition of so many different kinds of work, or the revelation of the breadth of creativity in the country; it was the extent and complexity of the works of rural black artists, especially those from Limpopo Province (then known as the Transvaal) of whom Mabasa was one.

What was not indicated in the textual material linked to the exhibition, or in the critical responses that it generated, was how the thinking behind Burnett's curatorial selection connected to international discourses of the time. Neither the catalogue nor any of the reviews examined *Tributaries* in the light of current theories of aesthetic definitions and shifting meanings. Objects in official collections were in flux, as they literally and theoretically migrated between different institutions and mind-sets. Anthropology museums, for example, had opened their doors to artistic scrutiny. (Burnett had not only travelled the length and breadth of the country in his search for a South African art, but had raided the storerooms of anthropology departments as well as art collections.) This absence in the reviews may well have arisen from wilful ignorance, as South Africans at the time were experiencing increasing isolation from the international artistic community as a result of the anti-apartheid movement's strategy of cultural boycott. They were looking inward for affirmation in a way which expressed a degree of cultural resistance to further outside (read colonial) imposition or approval. A useful way to understand this shift, first articulated by Ivor Powell, is to recognise the growing appeal of 'the local' for South Africans at the time: 'Much more important, though, was the realisation that there is an indigenous independent and vital art in South Africa and that it has been flourishing for years, unheeded by and regardless of the machinations of the art world' (Powell 1986).

Ironically the exhibition, despite its good intentions, reinforced the divergent positions held by those within the art community, and a debate ensued about the language that should be used to define this 'indigenous, independent' work which was so different and unfamiliar. Initially it was categorised as 'transitional', a word that was meant to capture the ways in which the individual works operated between accepted notions of traditional and modern (old and new) art. In the end 'transitional' was dropped in academic circles, since it was seen as a thinly disguised cover-up for that more familiar and problematic concept, 'primitive' art. No work by a white artist was being described as transitional, and no other words were being sought to classify, or reclassify, their works.

In 1988 Steven Sack curated another groundbreaking exhibition, *The Neglected Tradition*, which included works in clay and wood by Mabasa. He evaluated the work from the rural areas as 'refreshingly different' and wrote that these works would have been classified as 'naïve or folk-art in other any other society' (Sack 1988: 27). But he too, in an oblique reference to the debate, acknowledged that even these words set up 'hierarchies'. The artists from the rural areas ignored the debate; only later were issues of disadvantage and lack of education submitted as explanations for their apparent indifference.

The art world received the work of these rural artists enthusiastically, and Mabasa experienced the effects of this positive reception. Hence it was in the city of Johannesburg that Mabasa first found real recognition and fame, and earned real money. Fame came not only from interested spectators but also from the urban art market and its support groups of commercial dealers, journalists, academics, students and, of course, collectors. For Mabasa and others like her, this success was as much about acknowledgement in the urban art world as it was about enabling their survival at a far more basic, economic level.

36

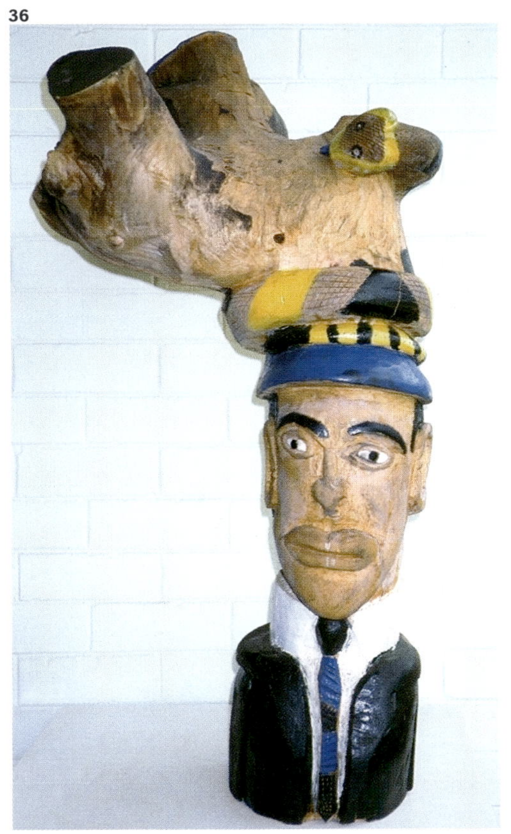

37

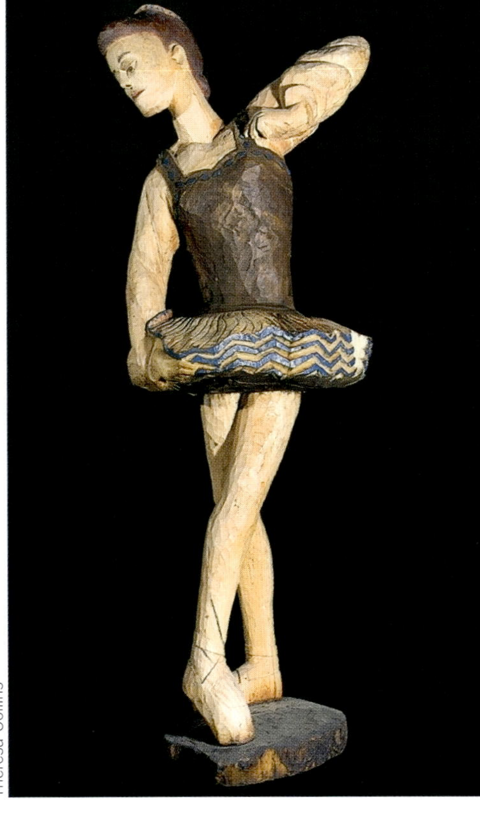

36. Phuthuma Seoka, *Head with snake*, 1983/4, wood, enamel paint, 111 x 57 x 55 cm. Private collection.

37. Nelson Mukhuba, *Ballet Dancer*, 1974, patinated wood, pigment, 118.5 x 50 x 38 cm. Wits Art Galleries Collection.

Pages 64–65: An installation view of Mabasa's solo exhibition at the Goodman Gallery, Johannesburg, in 1986.

THE ART MARKET: THEN AND NOW

In the 1980s, South Africa was a country caught up in the nightmare of regulated and institutionalised apartheid. The divide between rural and urban, black and white, poor and rich was more palpable then, impacting in every conceivable way on the lives of people. The movements of black people were severely restricted; they could not travel freely or be in the urban centres legitimately without the right documents. Yet they came, risking imprisonment and forced removal, seeking the jobs, money and opportunities that the city might offer them and that the barren rural areas to which they were confined clearly could not. The rural areas were slowly atrophying through a relentless programme of separate development that siphoned all resources into the creation of dummy 'governments' and 'homeland' bureaucracies. This process of impoverishment and enforced cultural balkanisation was the context for *Tributaries*.

The far-flung towns of Limpopo Province could not then, and still cannot now, provide sufficient financial support for the artists who lived and worked there. Their economic survival necessitated the establishment of relation-ships with the city. The biographies of all rural-based black artists, not only those who participated in *Tributaries*, include periods spent in the city — usually Johannesburg, the financial and commercial capital of the country. Many returned home; Anitra Nettleton suggests that this had as much to do with money as with a need to 'retain links with their own communities' (Nettleton 2000: 26). Mabasa, too, went to the city in the early 1950s, many years before she started making art, for family reasons. (She describes the experience of these city years in her interview with Kathryn Straughan in this volume.) By the mid-1960s, however, she was back home, poor, alone and making clay objects in response to directives from a female ancestor who appeared in her dreams.[1] The clay objects achieved their purpose in that they appeased the spirit; but they offered more than this, providing Mabasa with a way out of her desperate situation through an engagement with the art market.

A great deal of criticism has been levelled at the art market, especially at the dealers and their exploitation of artists. While one cannot deny that this has been a factor in dealers' relationships with artists, the situation is complex and cannot be seen in isolation from the current economic system and marketing practices for works of art. These have not changed over the years, despite a change in government. There has been little development of the mechanisms of the art market, and the artists remain dependent on the trade routes set up after *Tributaries*. Some, such as Johannes Maswan-ganyi, have managed to find ways to help themselves. He now acts as his own distributor. Some crafters and craft projects have received assistance from the Department of Arts and Culture and the National Arts Council, but the artists themselves have not received direct assistance.

The situation now is exacerbated by the loss of interest in rural art among collectors, and as a result there are fewer visitors seeking out the artists in

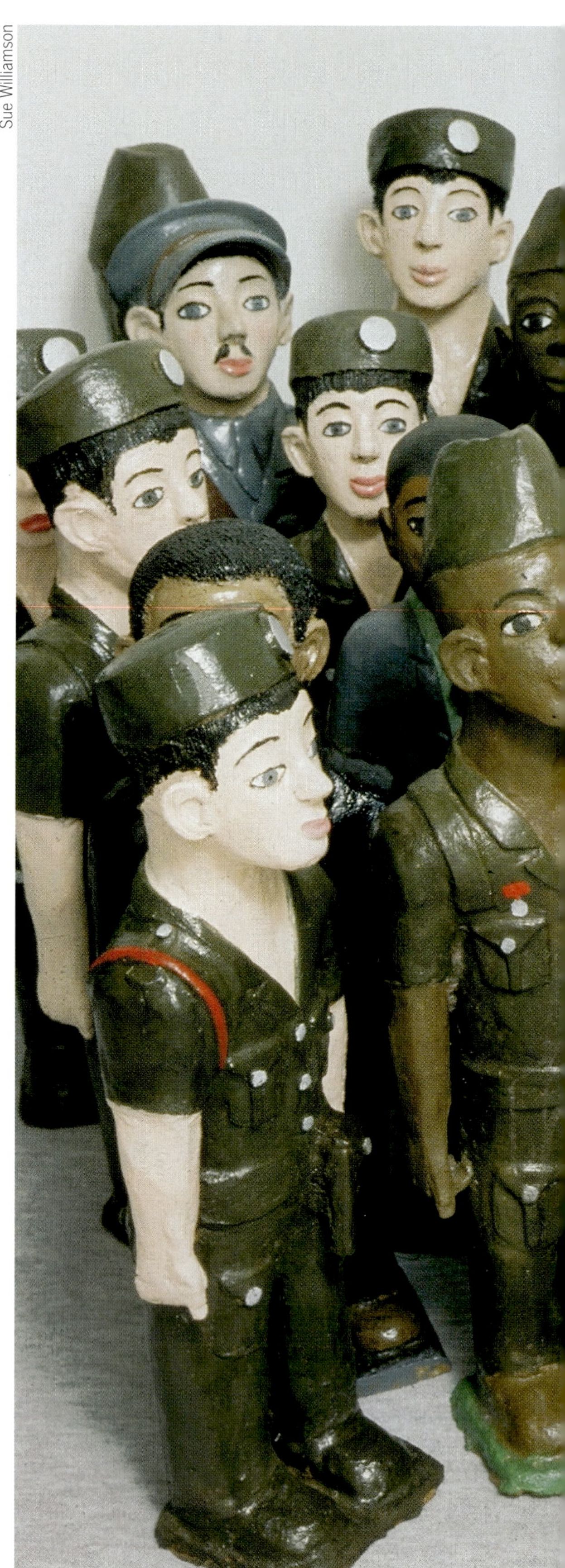

38

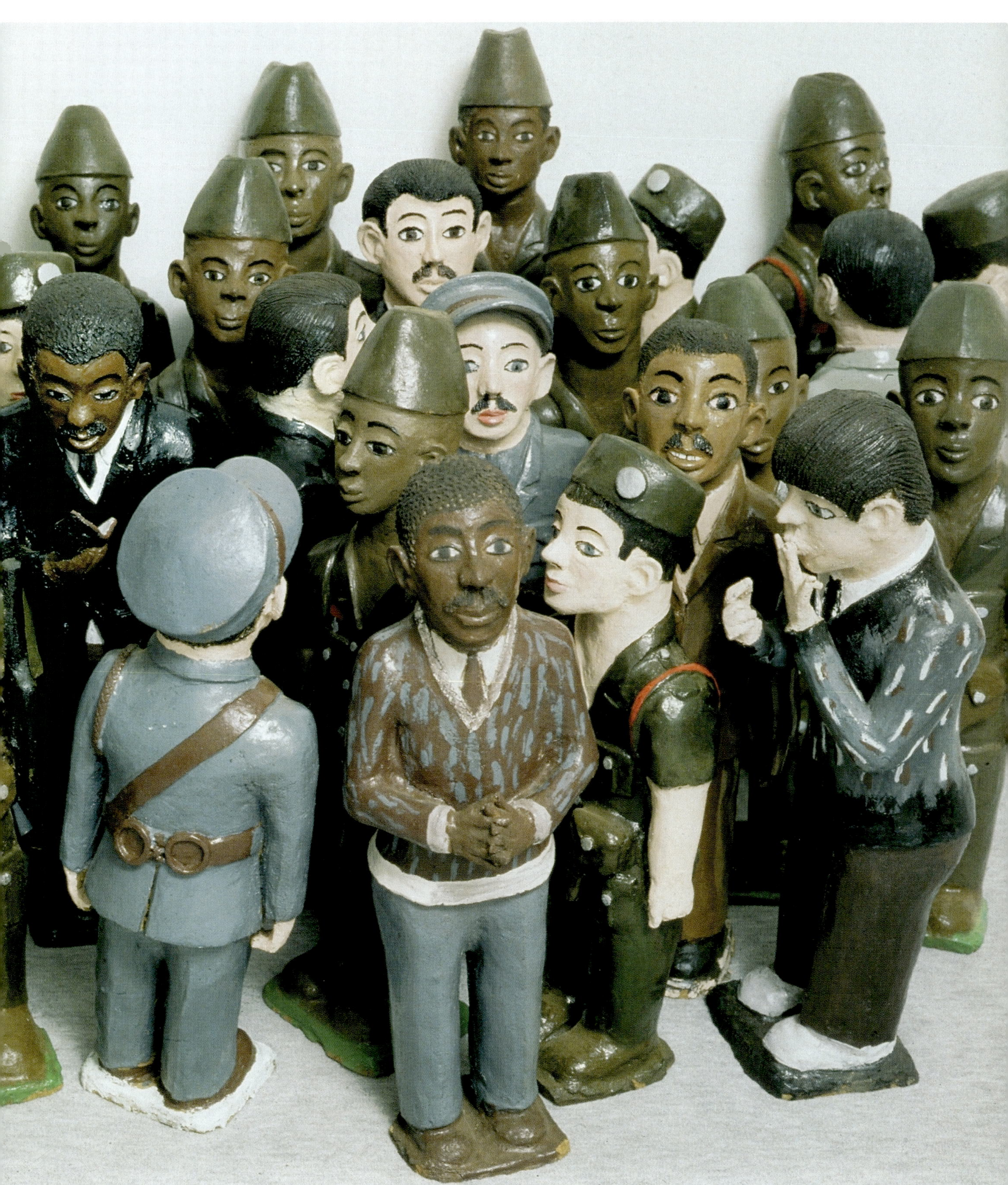

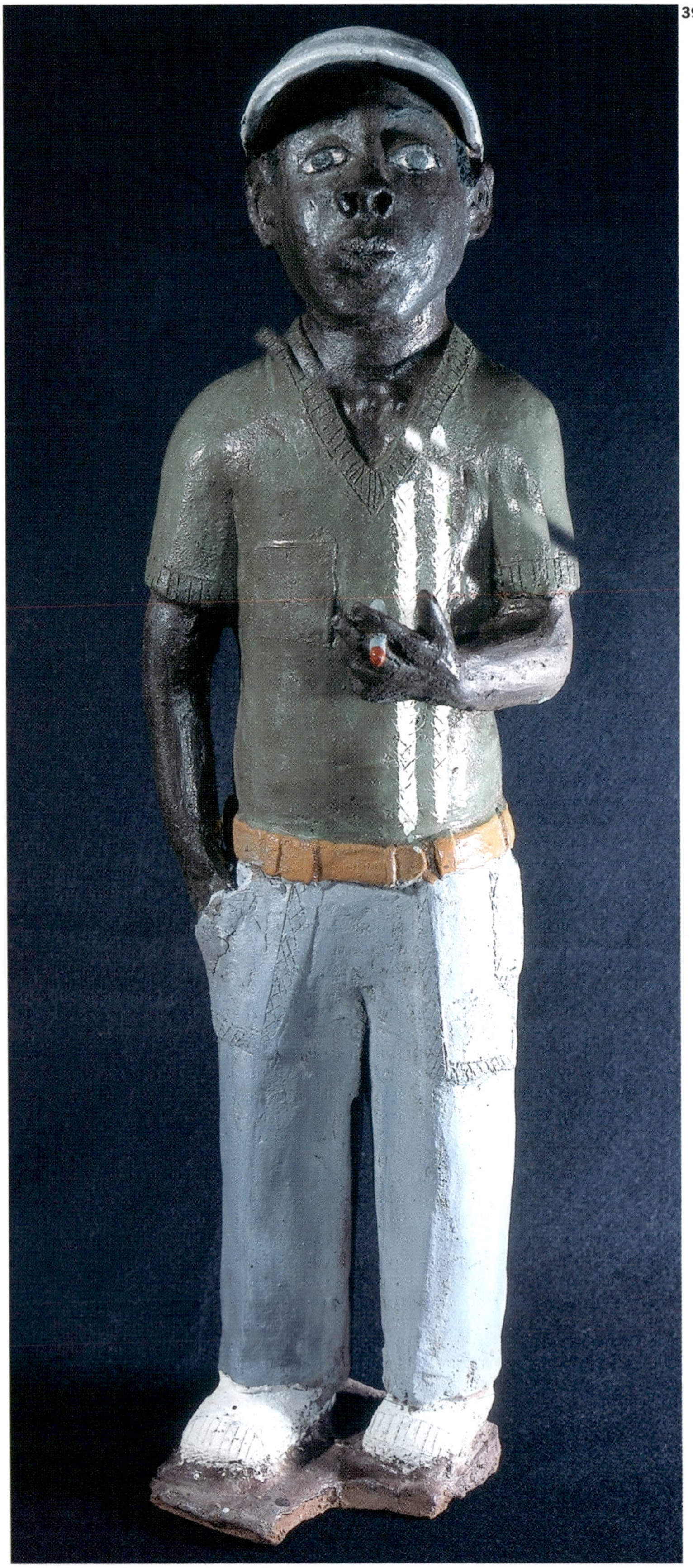

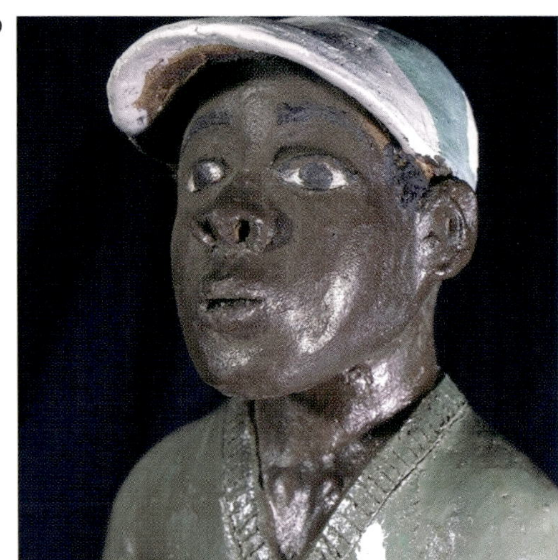

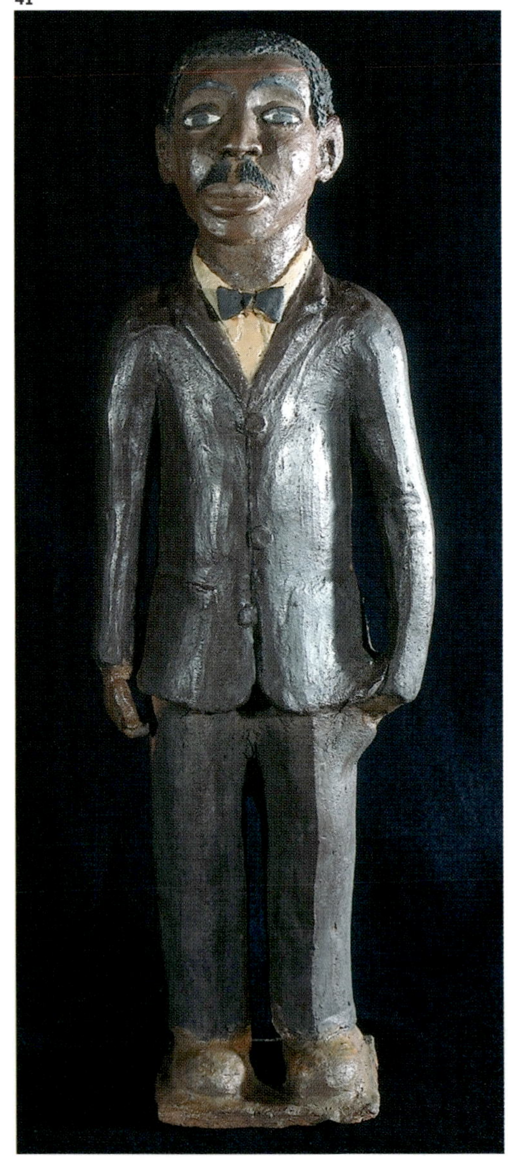

39

40

41

Photographs: Theresa Collins

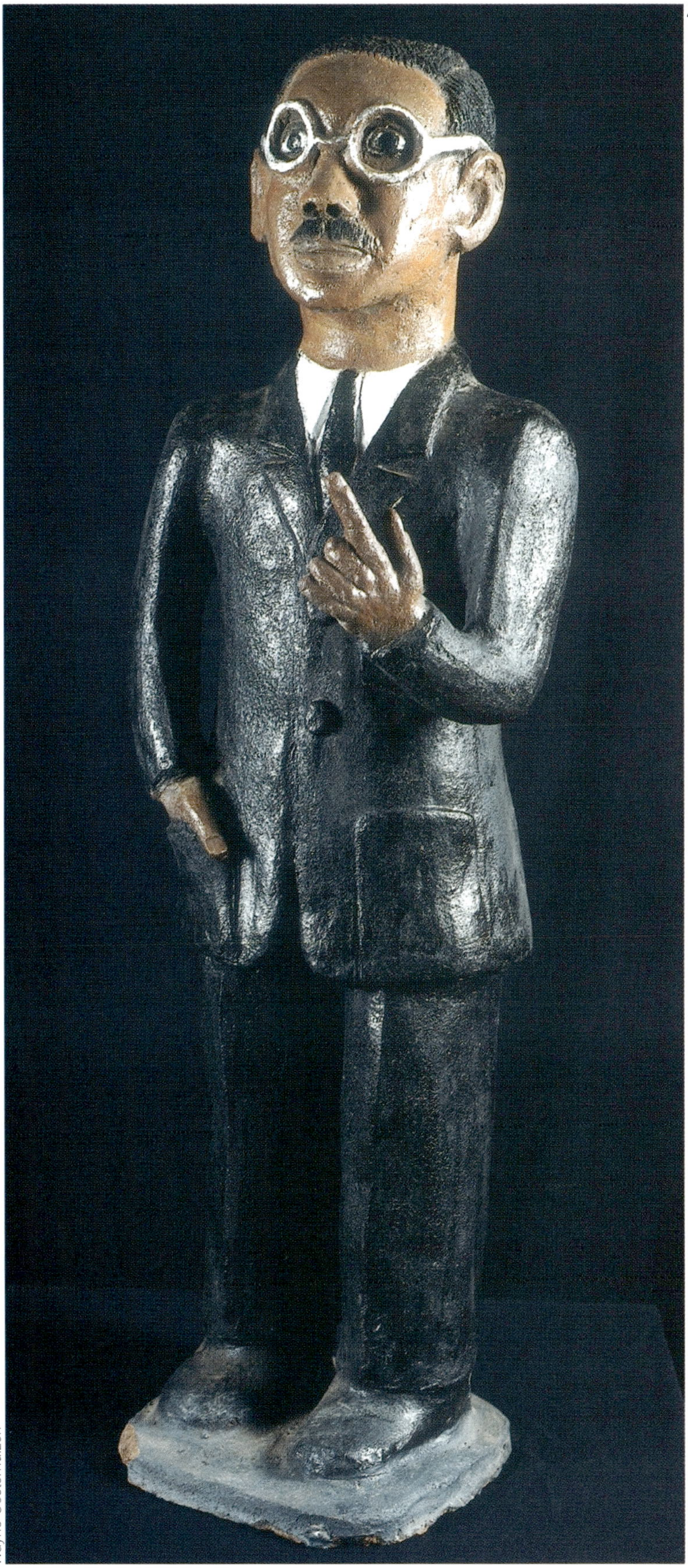

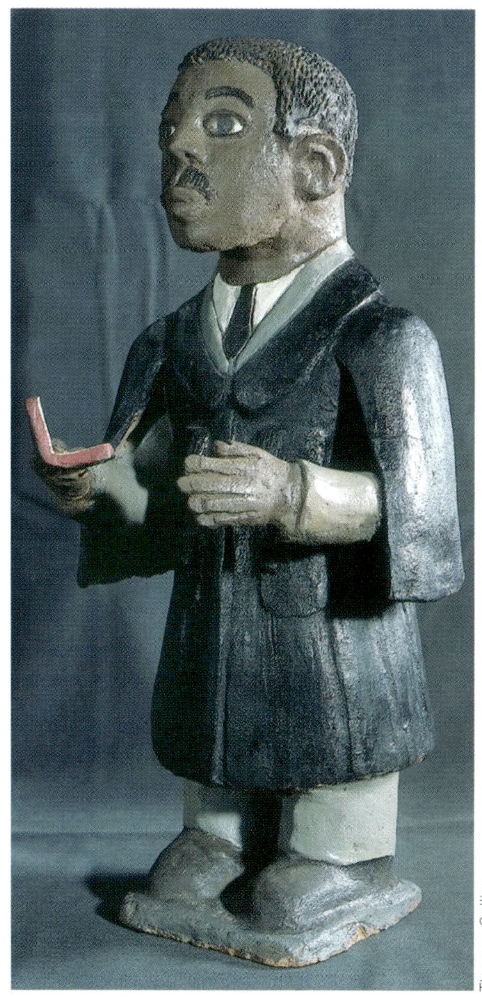

39. *Standing Man Smoking*, clay and enamel paint,
   69 x 20.5 x 20 cm, c.1980s. Standard Bank
   Collection of African Art (Wits Art Galleries).

40. Detail of *Standing Man Smoking*.

41. *Brown Suited Man*, clay and paint, 72.5 x 22.5 x
   15 cm, c.1980s. Wits Art Galleries Collection.

42. *Patrick Romano Mphephu*, clay and enamel
   paint, 1992. Johannesburg Art Gallery
   Collection.

43. *Clergyman*, c. 1987, clay and paint, 60.5 x 30.5
   x 26.5 cm, Wits Art Galleries Collection.

67

their rural studios. This, in turn, has led to an even greater reliance by artists on dealers and their intermediaries. While the relationship has always been fraught, the dealers nevertheless have literally provided a cash lifeline. Intermediaries and dealers have been willing to travel the long distances to find the works and bring them to the metropoles. They have understood that taking works on a consignment (sale-or-return) basis makes no sense for rural artists, and that cash in hand is the only way these artists can get access to the funds they need to continue working from day to day. It is too easy to criticise the dealers alone, instead of recognising that the whole network, from buyers to researchers, is implicated in the problematic situation that confronts artists wanting to find a market for their work. It is not without irony that Mabasa, after her first and only solo exhibition in Johannesburg in 1986, when she could finally afford to build a brick house and buy a television, remarked that 'Goodman [Gallery] bought this!'[2]

Lack of communication and an inadequate understanding of the art market affected two other artists who achieved fame through *Tributaries*, Dr Phuthuma Seoka and Nelson Mukhuba. Seoka, whom no one talks or thinks about anymore, set up a collective workshop with his sons, initially to meet the demand for his work. No one told Seoka the rules of the game. These collective works were not what the art market wanted: they were not 'authentic', they were repetitive, and they were not as valuable as his earlier works simply because they were not made by the 'master' (Rankin 1991: 23). Such attitudes ignore some of the accepted ways of working in African societies, where workshops are a common means of spreading knowledge; and they make no allowance for the fact that the maker can be part of a collective.

Mabasa has managed to establish a relationship with the art market, with all its vagaries and all its partners, and she has maintained that relationship despite the fact that she is no longer part of the Goodman stable. It is a remarkable achievement. Now she is more aware of how the market operates, though she continues to sell from her house and through a dealer in Johannesburg.

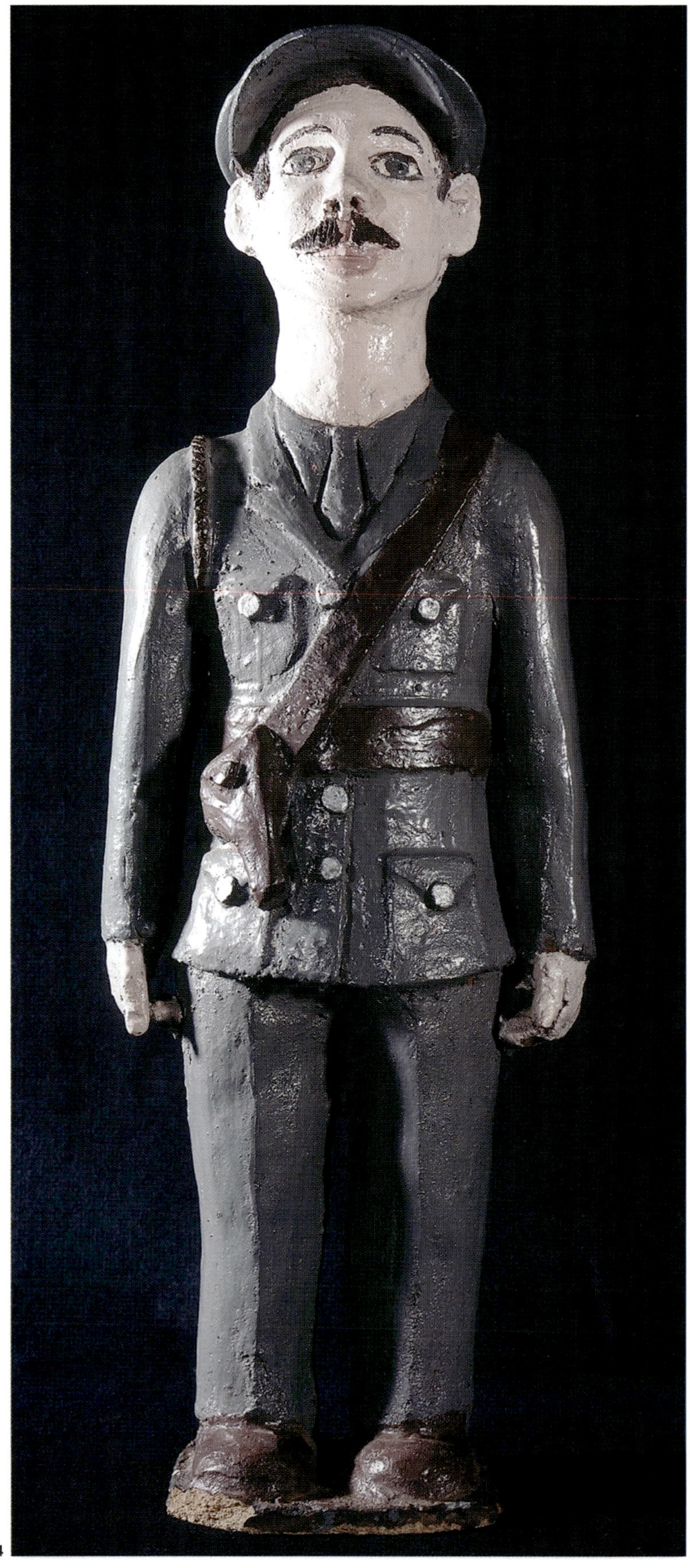

44

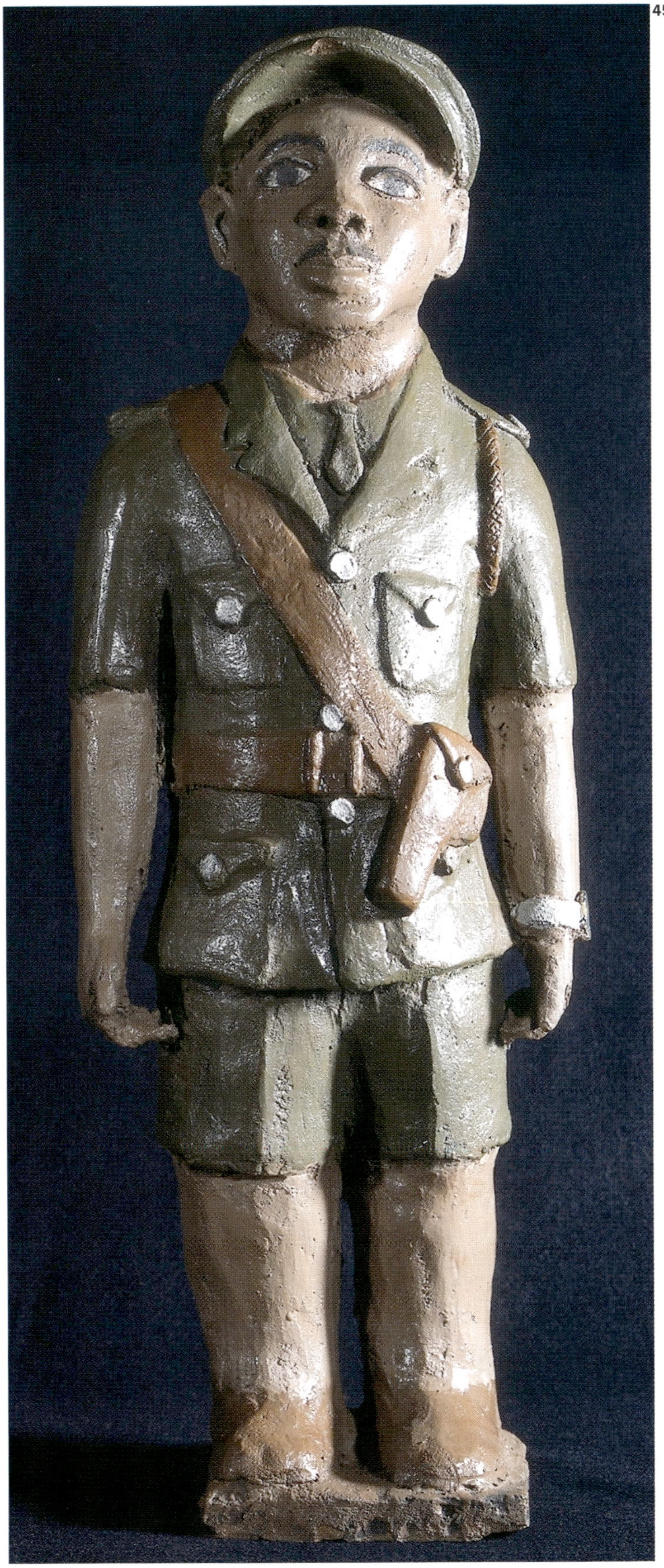

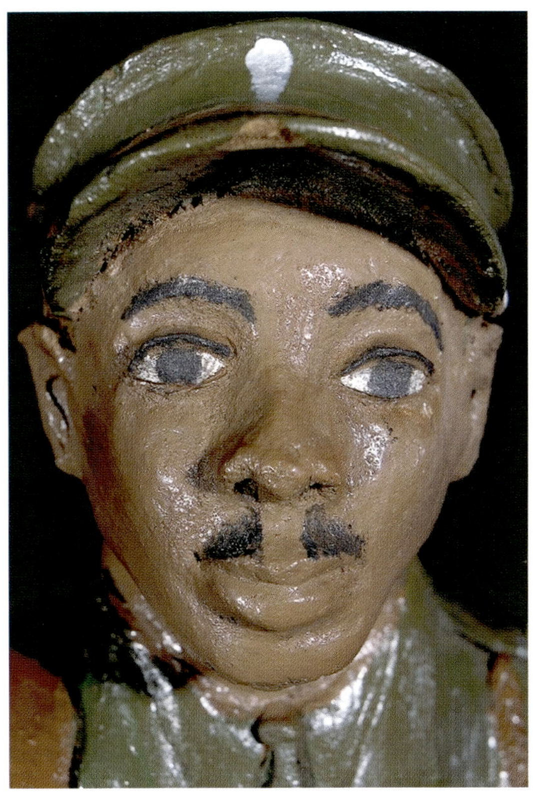

44. *SAP 1986*, clay and enamel paint, 68 x 22.4 x 20 cm, 1986. Wits Art Galleries Collection.

45. *SAP 1986*, clay and enamel paint, 74.2 x 26 x 17.8 cm, 1986. Wits Art Galleries Collection.

46. Detail of *SAP 1986*.

Photographs: Theresa Collins

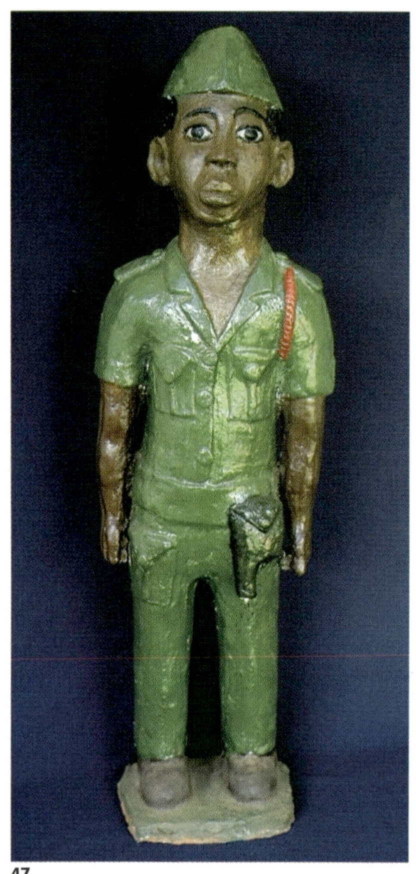
47

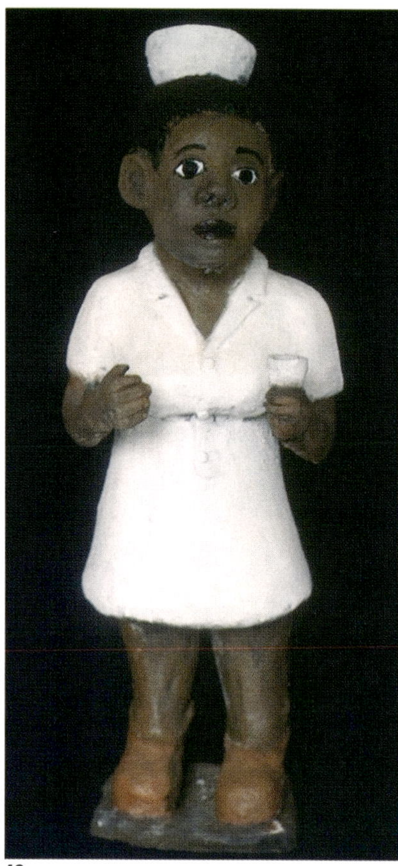
48

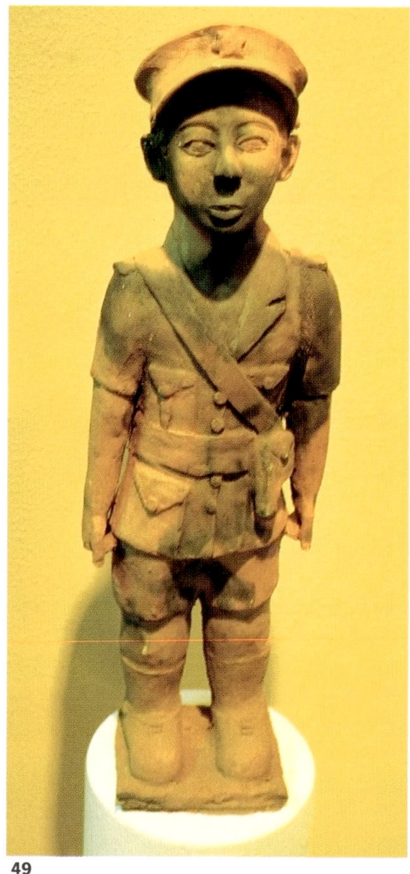
49

TRADITION AND IDENTITY: BEING BLACK AND A WOMAN

47. *SAP*, clay and enamel paint, height: 42 cm, photographed by Doreen Hemp in 1990 at Mabasa's homestead.

48. *Nurse*, clay and enamel paint, height: 40 cm, photographed by Doreen Hemp in 1990 at Mabasa's homestead.

49. *SAP*, clay and enamel paint, photographed in 1998 by Sue Williamson at Mabasa's homestead.

Two facts invariably accompany any introduction to Mabasa's work: that she is Venda and that she is female. They do more than describe her. On the one hand they identify and contain her; on the other, they provide outsiders with a point of entry into her work.

Born in 1938, Mabasa reached maturity as apartheid, with its ideology of ethnic difference, became entrenched and it began to matter to which ethnic group a black person belonged. Mabasa is Venda, but with strong heritage and marriage links to the neighbouring Tsonga (Shangaan).[3] She was born in Xigalo,[4] a predominantly Tsonga area which was later incorporated into the Gazankulu homeland, and she married a Tsonga. After returning from the city she stayed in Vuwani, a Venda area, but moved between the two regions. Despite her marriage her Venda identity remained dominant, and that gave her access to a particular tradition; at the same time her association with the Tsonga led to a more complex sense of self which arguably allowed her, supported by the imperative of her dreams, to behave in an unconventional way for a traditional woman. She was not subservient, as other women were, to the rural order of things.

Mabasa's work does come out of a local Venda women's craft/art tradition. Clay is their medium, and their work is focused on transforming mud into cooking and container vessels and figures for female initiation ceremonies. When Mabasa sought to appease the spirit that was troubling her, she turned to clay. Many of these early figures are images of women in traditional dress and in ritual poses. In a sense they are therapeutic,

Page 71: Noria Mabasa poses with the male guardian figure at the gate leading to her home.

70

and represent her place in and relationship to local social systems. She seems to be making some connection between healing and health through the representation of ritual practices, although they are not ritual figures.[5] Similar, painted figures were used in her commission for the Venda Development Corporation. But it was not these that charmed Burnett when he 'discovered' her work; it was rather her free-standing, single figures.

Characteristically, the latter stand facing forwards, hands at their sides or close to their bodies, making some small gesture; this is a limitation of the medium of coarse, rough clay from which they are made. Clearly recognisable, though not quite right, the proportions are not naturalistic. Although they seem repetitive and formulaic, as though they had been made from a mould, they nevertheless have an appeal which falls somewhere between doll and icon. Words like 'quaint' and 'naïve' have been used to describe the figures.

Mabasa made these figures in the same way that pots are made: by coiling and firing in an open pit, after which she applied enamel paint to the surface to add detail. Men and women are dressed differently, echoing the relationship first explored in the guardian figures at the entrance to her homestead courtyard. Women are dressed in traditional costume, while the men generally wear Western clothing in a variety of styles, and are labelled by what they wear: they are policemen, soldiers, old men and young men in T-shirts, smoking cigarettes. These outward signs reflect the reality of gender behaviour in the rural areas; the men travelled, went to the city, encountered other cultures, and bought things, while the women remained at home, culture-bound. Women, the works seem to say, have only one kind of life, while men have many. However there are exceptions; some figures of women are in Western dress. Their clothes act as signs indicating that they are women who operate outside of the conventions or

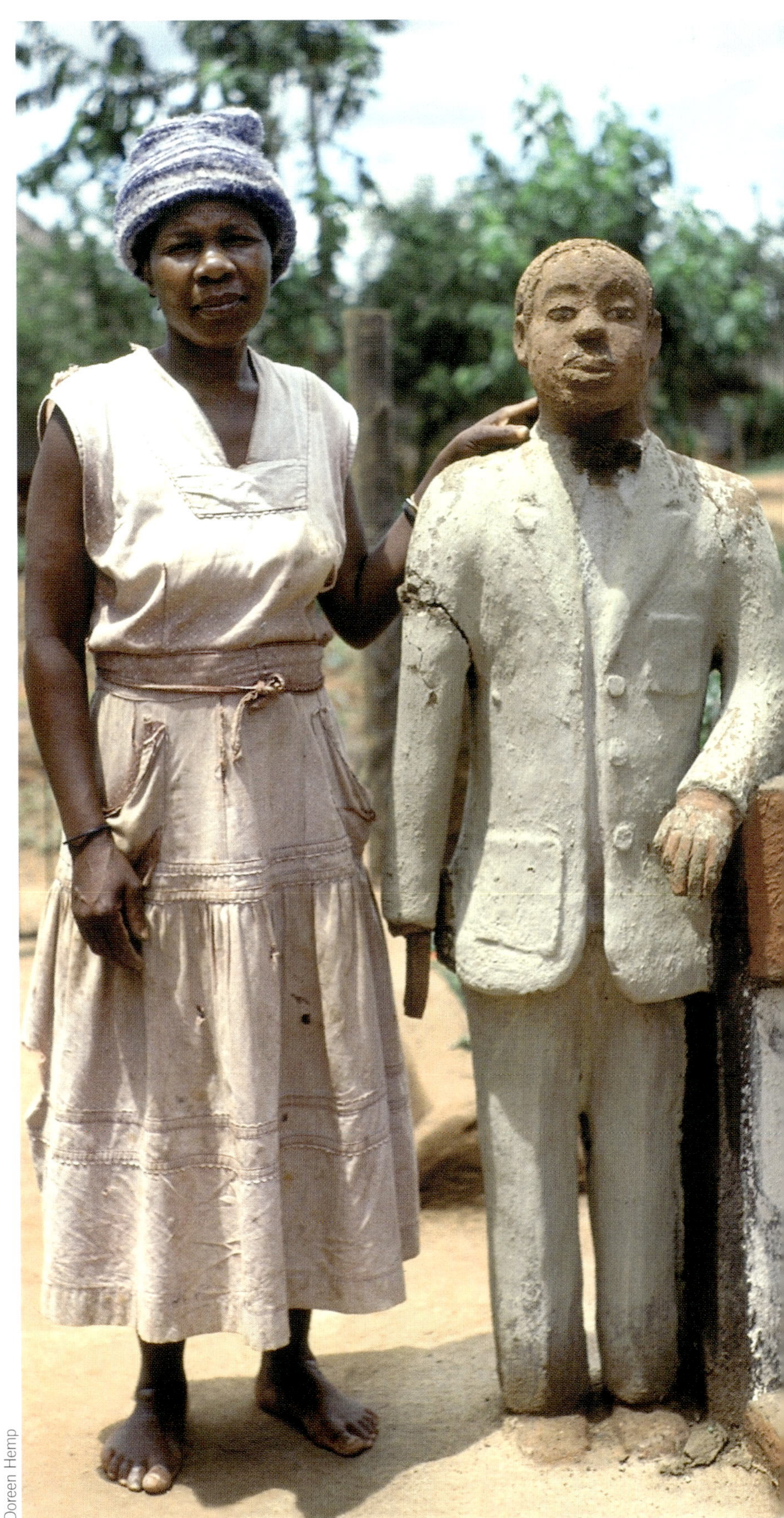

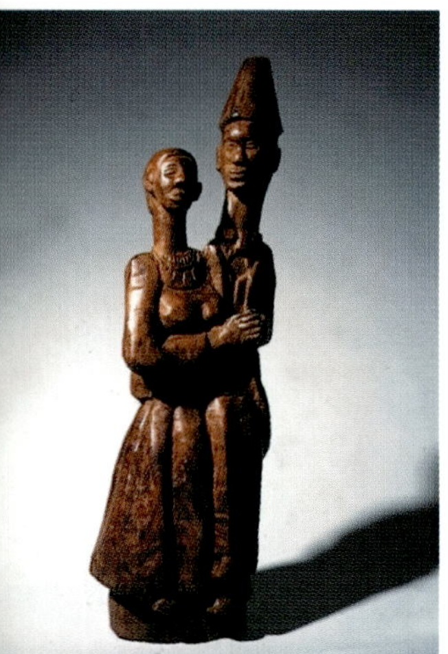

50

who are outsiders to the rural world: they are nurses, prostitutes and white women. Most of the figures are generic types, although a few are meant to be portraits. Named as individuals, they are identified by a particular token, gesture or feature. The figure of Mphephu, for example, is Mphephu because Mabasa made the sculpture with the particular man in mind, named him and added his trademark glasses. Two of the *Priest/Preacher/ Clergyman/Mufandisi* series are different because they begin to address a technical problem concerning the fragility of clay. Breakages in the production and transport stages were proving time-consuming and expensive to replace, and Mabasa was keen to find a more durable alternative. However, the bronzes did not provide a permanent solution and only a few were made in a workshop organised by David Rousseau in 1989. Without the resources and skills provided by Rousseau as intermediary, she could not continue. In any case, the quality of the finished object was substantially different from the clay versions.

The big change in Mabasa's work came with a change in medium, when she started to carve wood. She provides two not necessarily contradictory explanations for this move. The first is found in her dreams (she presents this version in her interview with Straughan) and the second focuses on the practical considerations referred to above. She has said that she prefers working in wood because it does not break so easily. But wood offered other opportunities: firstly to earn more money and secondly to develop artistically. Mukhuba, she admits, trained her to carve, which by implication suggests that carving was something she learned whereas working in clay was not.

One of the reasons that Mabasa could, in the late 1980s, even contemplate a move to wood, a non-traditional medium for women in so-called traditional societies, was that she was already operating outside of that traditional context. She was functioning in two of the many worlds that make up South Africa. She had negotiated a relationship with the urban art market, and was marginalised within her own Venda context through her familial relationships with the Tsonga, and through the fact that her involvement with the art market had afforded her a degree of economic independence from her local community. The community had in fact begun to react to this independence by ostracising her for her work.

From the outset the iconography of the wood pieces differed from the works in clay. They were large, complex, and narrative. Their sources were multiple, lying in the news media, mythology and history and, interestingly, not in dreams. Three of these works make the point about their sources explicitly, and all use dramatic moments to highlight and focus the narrative. The first, *Carnage II (Natal Flood Disaster)* is based on a news event reported on television. The circle of swirling, submerged figures and animals captures something of the drama of the event. The second, *Ngoma Lungundu* concerns the sacred drum of legend and records the epic journey of the Senzi people as they migrated south from Zimbabwe to settle in the Soutpansberg in South Africa. The sacred drum could not touch the ground and the carved figures are represented as supporting the drum. The drum forms the apex of

50. Untitled, tambotie wood, c. 1988, 92 x 30.5 x 32 cm, University of South Africa collection, Pretoria.

Photograph: Robbie Robinson

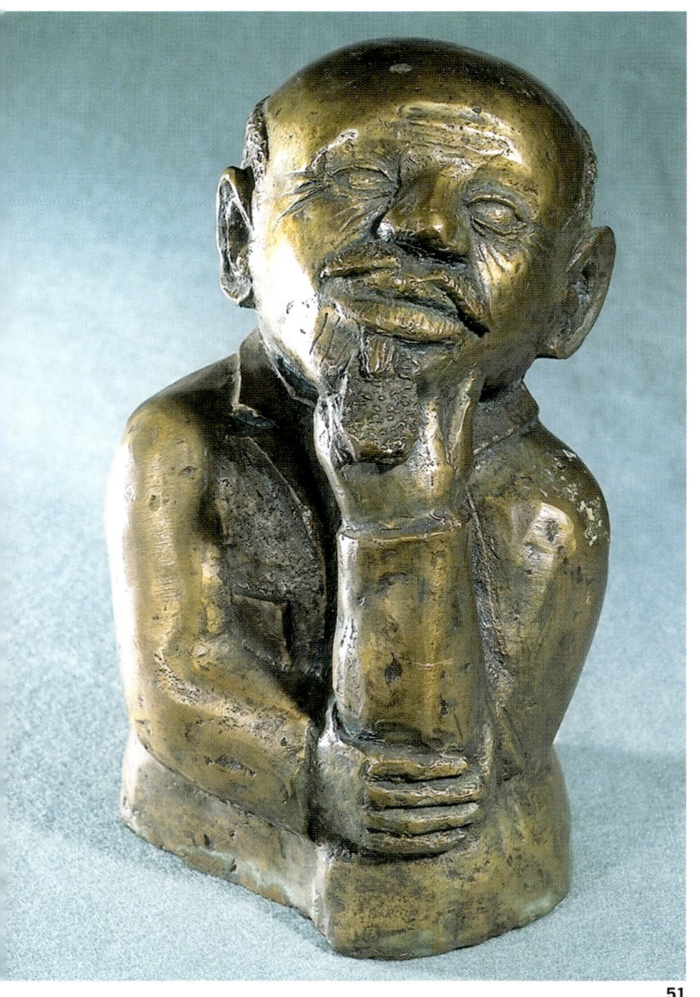
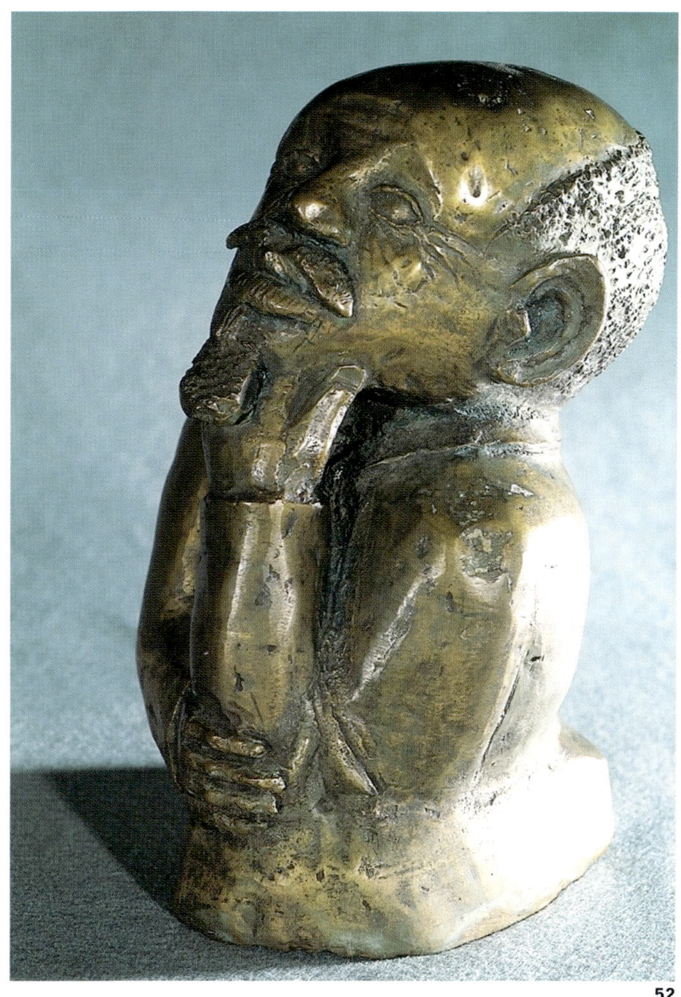

51   52

the composition; it is not a representation but a real drum with hide and pegs. The movement and placing of the figures, some below the drum, suggests another dramatic moment, in this case perhaps when crossing the Limpopo River, or perhaps, as Nettleton suggests, the figures are overcome by the power of the drum.[6] The third work, *Union Buildings*, records an important event in women's struggle and resistance history in South Africa. It shows an episode from the famous march to the Union Buildings in Pretoria in August 1956 to protest against the implementation of the legislation that would compel all black women to carry passes. The moment selected is when Prime Minister Strijdom fled after refusing to accept the thousands of letters of protest that the women had brought with them. It is possible that Mabasa was influenced by the brochure and publicity surrounding the competition in 1999 for a women's monument for the Union Buildings, to commemorate the march. In all three of these works the titles provide the entry point into reading the works, and only *Carnage* moves into a more expressive realm. (This was not a title provided by Mabasa.[7])

The wood retains its shape as a found form and sets the terms and limits of the compositions. Mabasa neither alters the form radically nor changes the colour. Taking her cues from the found form, she crowds and covers the

51–52.
Preacher, c. 1994, bronze, Wits Art Galleries collection.

Photographs: Theresa Collins

73

available surfaces with masses of figures. There are no backgrounds, no additional or unnecessary detail; everything is on the surface in a kind of relief sculpture that works its way around the form. The holes in the wood are natural and Mabasa leaves them to function as open form. Developments and explorations in her carving work have subsequently fed back into later clay works such as those produced for Lesheba.

PUBLIC RECEPTION

The question now is how to evaluate Mabasa in the light of these new works, which have not been accorded the same response as was given to the early works that accompanied her 'discovery' at *Tributaries*. Given that this essay began with a discussion of Mabasa's reception in the public sphere, it seems appropriate to end with a return to these considerations by looking briefly at the inclusions and exclusions of Mabasa's work in major public exhibitions and recent publications in the 1990s. The context now is the new South Africa, where the local art world has re-engaged with international discourses that have set new ground rules for contemporary art.

Mabasa's work was included in the first Johannesburg Biennale in 1994, where she formed part of a rather haphazard and last-minute exhibition of Venda artists, but she was not included in the second Biennale in 1997. For the latter the Nigerian-born curator, Okui Enwezor, sought to display and interrogate the theme of trade routes through international works and trends rather than through a focus on local works, following the prescription that Biennales are celebrations of international contemporary art. Mabasa's work did not fit this theme; nor did it explore the techniques and technologies of contemporary international, and now South African, art. Her work was too local, too object-based, and seemed to be caught in a time warp. Related reasons may explain Mabasa's exclusion from the publication *Grey Areas* whose editors, Brenda Atkinson and Candice Breitz, wrote that they sought to bring to the fore 'contemporary South African art and related issues of representation – particularly as these issues had started to become more contentious in the early years of post-apartheid SouthAfrica' (Atkinson and Breitz 1999: 13). Authors and commentators in the book grappled with cross-race representation, the issue of white artists/black subjects. In broad terms Mabasa's work, like all art, can be seen in terms of representation, but her work does not self-consciously interrogate the issue; or at least, no one who wrote on the subject for *Grey Areas* thought that it did. In any event, the fact that she was a black artist meant that her example was not a useful one in any attempt to illustrate cross-race representation.

Her inclusion in Marion Arnold's *Women and Art in South Africa* and Nettleton's 'Home is where the art is' would suggest that Mabasa's relevance is seen to lie within local frameworks. Arnold's book is not a feminist, political or contemporary art tract but a series of essays which, the author explains in the opening sentence of the Preface, deal with 'women and art'(Arnold 1996). Within such broad parameters, Mabasa's inclusion is obligatory as she is one of very few black women artists in this country. Nettleton's article for *African*

Arts begins to challenge the earlier observation that Mabasa has little international relevance, since it is published in the United States. However, as the journal is not a cutting-edge contemporary art journal, Mabasa's inclusion must be seen within another framework. Significantly, Nettleton notes that the exclusion of black rural artists from contemporary art discourses is due to other kinds of exclusions. She argues that they have had little access to modern art in all its guises, techniques and theories and have been further disadvantaged by language, as most only speak rudimentary English (Nettleton 2000: 30). The inheritance of the past still lingers now as explanation. Mabasa and the other artists are valued only as African makers, and this begs the question of whether contemporary African art is contemporary art in the international sense, or still something different and other, which requires another kind of classification.

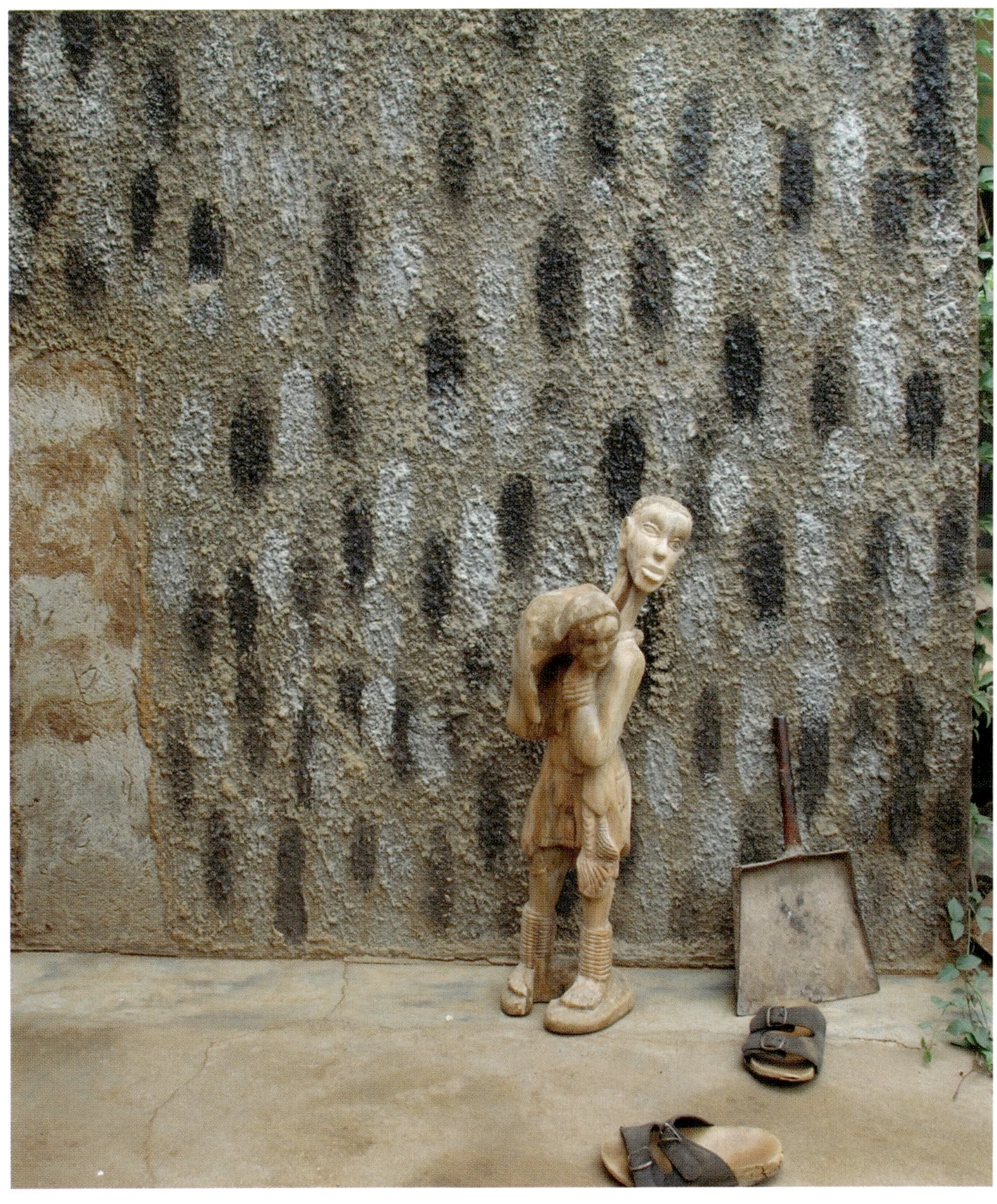

Wooden sculpture at Mabasa's home in Tshino village.

Notes

1 Interpreting dreams purely in the Western or European sense misses the point of what dreams may or could mean in a southern Africa society, where they are understood as a means of communicating with an ancestor. Nor are they quite the equivalent of imagination, as Marion Arnold suggests (Arnold 1996: 142).

2 Interview with Mabasa at her house in August 1989.

3 Tsonga and Shangaan are used inter-changeably, although these names and groupings have different histories. Shangaan generally refers to those Tsonga who came under the influence of Soshangana and the Gaza kings during the 19th century in Mozambique, and who fled to the Transvaal after the wars in Mozambique in 1895-6. Correctly speaking, the term should only be used in connection with Tsonga who have a Zulu heritage. Shangaan has, however, become the more popular name for all people of the region and is used, for example, in the media more often than Tsonga. A number of artists from Limpopo Province, including Jackson Hlungwani, define themselves as Shangaan although that heritage may be fictional. The reasons are complex, but one suggestion is that Shangaan provides associations with the military prowess of the Shangaan in the 19th century; another is that the ascription is inherited from the gold mines, where all men from the East Coast were called Shangaan, whatever their heritage.

4 The orthography of Tsonga names is still not settled. The number of different spellings on road signs around Xigalo can be quite confusing. The X in Tsonga is pronounced 'sh' from the Portuguese (hence Xigalo would be pronounced as Shigalo and spelt alternatively as Tshigalo).

5 The association between art and healing in Mabasa's work is interesting. She has undertaken a number of commissions for clinics on AIDS and on the theme of feeding children. The idea of using sculpture as a didactic tool has its origins in the initiation ceremonies.

6 Nettleton wrote that *Ngoma Lungudu* literally translates as the 'drum of thunder' and invokes the concept of chiefship as well as being the most sacred symbol of Venda cosmology. Nettleton, 'Home is where the art is', pp. 32-33.

7 See Nettleton, 'Home is where the art is' p. 32, and the interview with Kathryn Straughan in this volume.

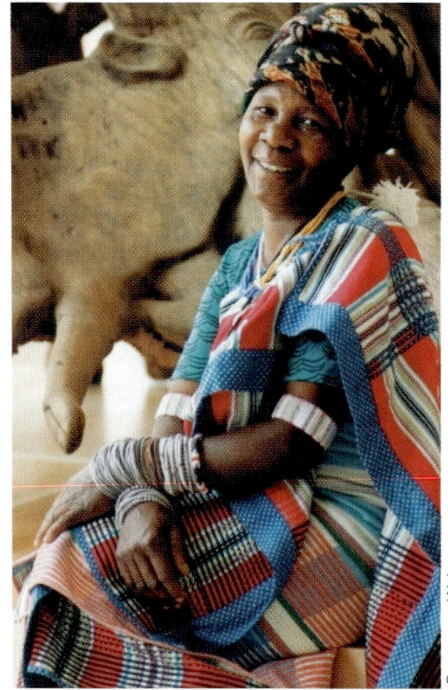

Bibliography

Arnold, Marion. 1996. *Women and Art in South Africa.* Cape Town: David Philip.

Atkinson, Brenda and Breitz, Candice (eds). 1999. *Grey Areas: Representation, Identity and Politics in Contemporary South African Art.* Johannesburg: Chalkham.

Hammond-Tooke, David and Nettleton, Anitra. 1989. *Ten Years of Collecting (1979-1989).* Johannesburg: University of the Witwatersrand Art Galleries.

Nettleton, Anitra. 2000. 'Home is where the art is: Six South African rural artists.' *African Arts,* Winter, Vol. XXII, pp 25-36.

Powell, Ivor J. 1986. 'Bad faith makes bad art.' *The Weekly Mail,* 10 January.

Rankin, Elizabeth. 1991. 'Training and trading: the influence of tuition and the art market in the work of some South Africa artists'. *De Arte* 43, p 23.

Sack, Steven. 1988. *The Neglected Tradition: Towards a New History of South African Art (1930-1988).* Johannesburg: Johannesburg Art Gallery.

Williamson, Sue. 1989. *Resistance Art in South Africa.* Cape Town: David Philip.

Younge, Gavin. 1988. *Art of the South African Townships.* London: Thames and Hudson.

NORIA MABASA

En juin 2002, Kathryn Staughan a interviewé Noria Mabasa pour lui demander comment elle avait décidé de consacrer sa vie à la sculpture, et comment elle plaçait l'art qu'elle pratique par rapport aux traditions culturelles de la société venda. Le texte qui suit est un extrait de leurs entretiens.

Voyage en pays Venda

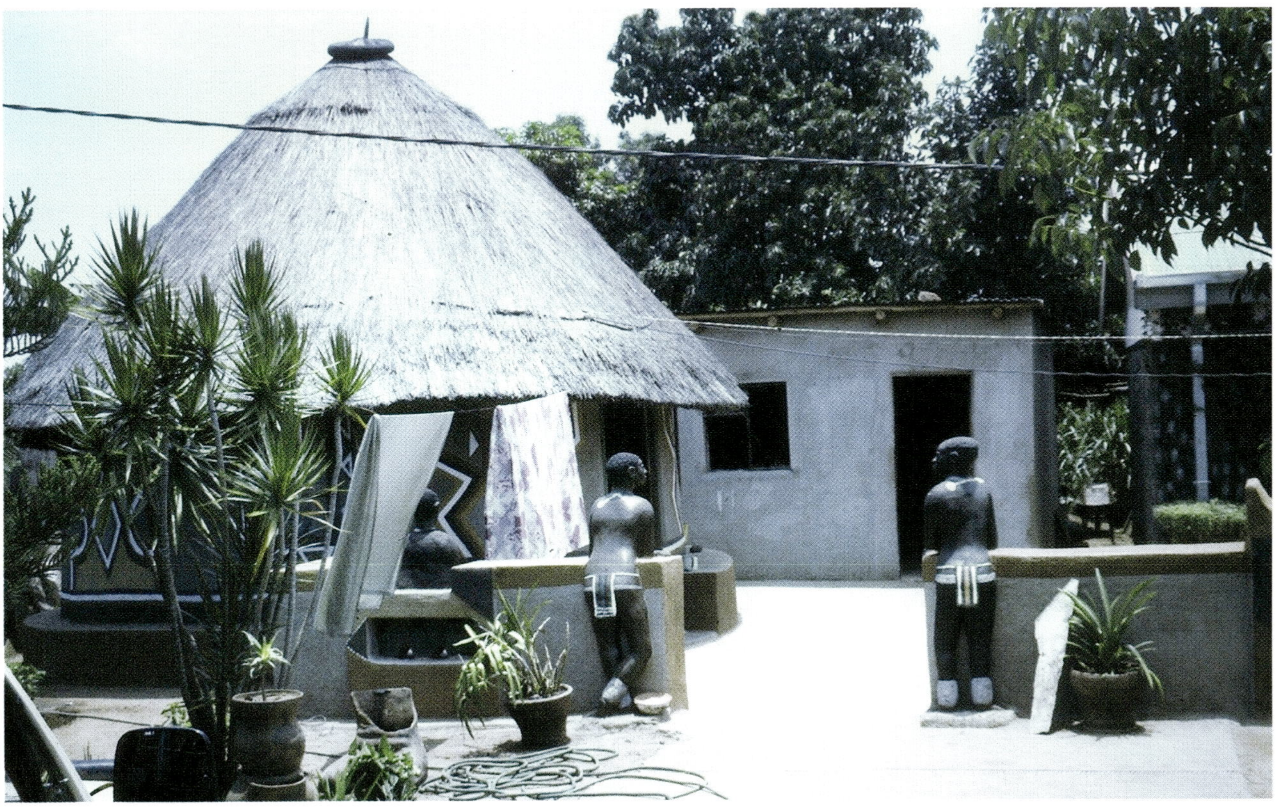

NORIA MABASA habite au Venda, région située au nord-est de l'Afrique du Sud, où la plupart des gens demeurent dans des vallées, entre de hautes montagnes noyées dans la brume. Il existe maintes légendes et bien des contes sur les Vendas et sur leur origine, ainsi que sur le pays lui-même. Noria habite le village de Tshino qui, comme les autres villages, se compose d'habitations regroupées - les *midi* - où chaque logis est entouré de haies et de murs bas faits de boue séchée. Les huttes sont couvertes de chaume et certaines sont ornées de motifs traditionnels. Le chef, le *khasi*

du village, a sa hutte sur la partie la plus élevée du *midi*, et ses femmes et sa famille habitent en contrebas. Le reste des habitants est réparti alentour sur les parties basses du terrain. Dans la société venda, un mudi est constitué d'une ou plusieurs familles qui appartiennent en général au même clan. Les membres du *mudi* vivent ensemble dans un groupe de huttes proches les unes des autres, et chacune est entourée de sa cour, la *muta*. Chaque foyer du *mudi* s'appelle un *khoro*. A Tshino, parmi les habitations traditionnelles, des huttes rondes, s'élèvent des maisons modernes en brique. Le

" **Les huttes sont couvertes de chaume et certaines sont décorées de motifs traditionnels."**

village est plein de monde et d'animation: des femmes vont et viennent avec leurs enfants sur le dos, maintenus par des couvertures de couleurs vives, des hommes assis à l'ombre des arbres fument et boivent la bière artisanale *marula*, des chiens bâtards se glissent entre les pieds des gens à la recherche de quelque chose à manger et les poules grattent ici et là et s'affairent à picorer.

Un grand portail métallique couleur rouille, flanqué de deux piliers sculptés, une haute clôture, surprenante dans ce cadre rural, voilà ce qui démarque la propriété où Noria vit et travaille. Son studio "en plein air" se trouve sous un vieux mûrier où *Union Buildings*, sa dernière œuvre en date, repose sous des bâches de plastique jaune. On remarque aussi d'autres œuvres de grande dimension auxquelles elle travaille. Autour du studio s'étendent ses champs de maïs, son verger et son potager.

C'est sur les berges du Luvuvhu, où les femmes viennent laver le linge sur des rochers et où s'ébattent les enfants qui jouent à s'éclabousser, que Noria a construit sa maison, dans laquelle se mêlent culture venda traditionnelle et influence occidentale. Autour d'une cour centrale sont disposées des huttes aux toits de chaume ornées de motifs traditionnels, et une maison banale, rectang-ulaire, avec des cadres de fenêtre métalliques. Un mur bas forme une enceinte, teintée d'un oxyde rouge et décorée de sièges pareils à des trônes et de statues de terre cuite. L'une des huttes est destinée à accueillir des gens de passage qui y dorment et prennent le petit-déjeuner, une autre fait office d'atelier où elle crée ses figures d'argile et où elle les entrepose. Il y a aussi dans cet ensemble une modeste galerie d'exposition et un magasin sous un toit de tôle ondulée, où Noria entrepose certaines de ces œuvres et les ouvrages de perles de sa fille. Avec sa famille, elle habite la maison de style occidental avec eau courante et électricité, symboles de luxe dans ce village.

Deux figures de terre cuite, une femme et un homme, se tiennent à l'entrée de la cour. Noria refait chaque année ces sculptures en bas-relief. Elle vit entourée de ses œuvres d'art: des jeunes filles nubiles allongées dans la position qui indique le respect, *vha a losha*, des croco-diles sacrés qui paressent au soleil, des lions qui montent la garde, et ici et là des succulents dans des pots de fleur en forme de corps de femme. Voilà l'espace de sa vie quotidienne, le cœur de sa vie privée.

"Quand je me mets à travailler l'argile ou le bois, d'abord, je ne vois rien. Puis, peu à peu, cela me vient - du doigt elle montre son front - ça vient doucement, je ne sais comment, mais c'est merveilleux de voir l'objet que je façonne prendre forme."

Voici la belle Noria, la maman aux dreadlocks, grand-mère, potière et sculptrice, et qui aussi enseigne son art. L'on est surpris, lorsqu'on contemple ses créations, de son humilité et de sa joie à observer les réactions qu'elles suscitent, car elle est la première à s'étonner de ce qu'elle a produit. Noria fait grande impression à ceux qui la rencontrent pour la première fois. Elle n'a pas coupé ses cheveux depuis 1989 ; elle les porte longs et se couvre la tête d'un foulard ou d'un bonnet de laine. Dans un rêve, on lui a dit que chaque fois qu'elle se coupait les cheveux, elle coupait son pouvoir de création. Elle y croit dur comme fer, et si l'une de ses tresses vient à casser, elle la rattache à sa chevelure. "Si je coupe mes cheveux, l'art m'abandonne et je tombe malade," dit-elle.

Pour comprendre les sculptures de Noria, il faut l'entendre expliquer d'où elle vient, parce que sa culture, ses croyances et sa vie spirituelle tiennent une place essentielle dans ses œuvres. Elle n'est jamais allée à l'école, ne sait ni lire, ni écrire, sauf son nom dont elle signe ses œuvres. Elle n'a reçu aucune formation artistique.

A quatorze ans, en 1952, Noria est partie habiter à White City, un quartier de Soweto, à Johannesburg. La femme de l'un de ses frères venait d'accoucher et avait perdu la vue. Noria est allée aider la jeune mère. Elle faisait la lessive, le ménage et la cuisine, et s'occupait du nourrisson. Au bout d'un an, la jeune femme a recouvré la vue et Noria est allée habiter chez une de ses cousines à Alexandra, un township plus petit dans la banlieue nord de Johannes-burg.

C'est à Johannesburg que Noria a commencé à avoir les rêves qui jouent un rôle si important dans sa vie. Les rêves n'ont pas cessé durant toute cette période de sa vie. Ses visions étaient parfois prophétiques: une fois, elle a vu que l'un des jumeaux d'une voisine allait mourir ; ou elle a vu encore une lettre adressée à une amie. En 1965, une vieille dame lui est apparue en rêve, et lui a dit qu'elle devait se mettre à travailler l'argile. A cette époque-là, elle ne connaissait aucune femme qui façonnait des figures d'argile, et pourtant cette vision lui intimait l'ordre de sculpter.

D'abord Noria n'a pas prêté attention à ses rêves, mais peu à peu elle est tombée malade. Dans son sommeil, la vieille femme, qu'elle appelle aujourd'hui *Tshidzeuli*, qui signifie "ruminer le passé" ou "doux souvenirs", ne cessait de lui apparaître en rêve. Cette vieille était rongée par la lèpre, il ne restait que quelques doigts à ses mains mutilées, elle n'avait plus de nez, il lui manquait une partie de la bouche. Elle se couvrait de peaux de bête, sa peau était très noire, ses cheveux courts, noirs aussi, elle laissait voir ses seins tombants, elle était vieille et toute ridée. Son apparence terrifiait tellement Noria qu'elle avait peur de dormir. Et puis, une nuit, elle a rêvé de son père. Elle était debout à ses côtés dans une mare, de l'eau jusqu'à la taille. D'une voix forte il a prononcé son nom en Venda, "Muelelwa", et lui a posé cette question: "Pourquoi donc, lorsque la vieille femme te dit comment devenir riche, lui dis-tu non?"

Noria a haussé les épaules, a tourné le dos à son père. C'est alors qu'elle s'est éveillée, tremblante de frayeur. Avant qu'elle ne se détourne de son père, il l'avait frappée sur l'épaule avec une poignée de roseaux. Elle était saisie de frissons. Le rêve s'était dissipé, la vieille et son père avaient disparu, mais elle ne pouvait se rendormir. Elle a continué à trembler toute une semaine, et puis, le vendredi suivant, son père a reparu et lui a crié: "Muelelwa, réveille-toi tout de suite! Va voir Muthewana (la sœur de Noria) et dis-lui qu'il te faut aller prier les ancêtres."

Noria s'est réveillée et sa peur terrible avait disparu.

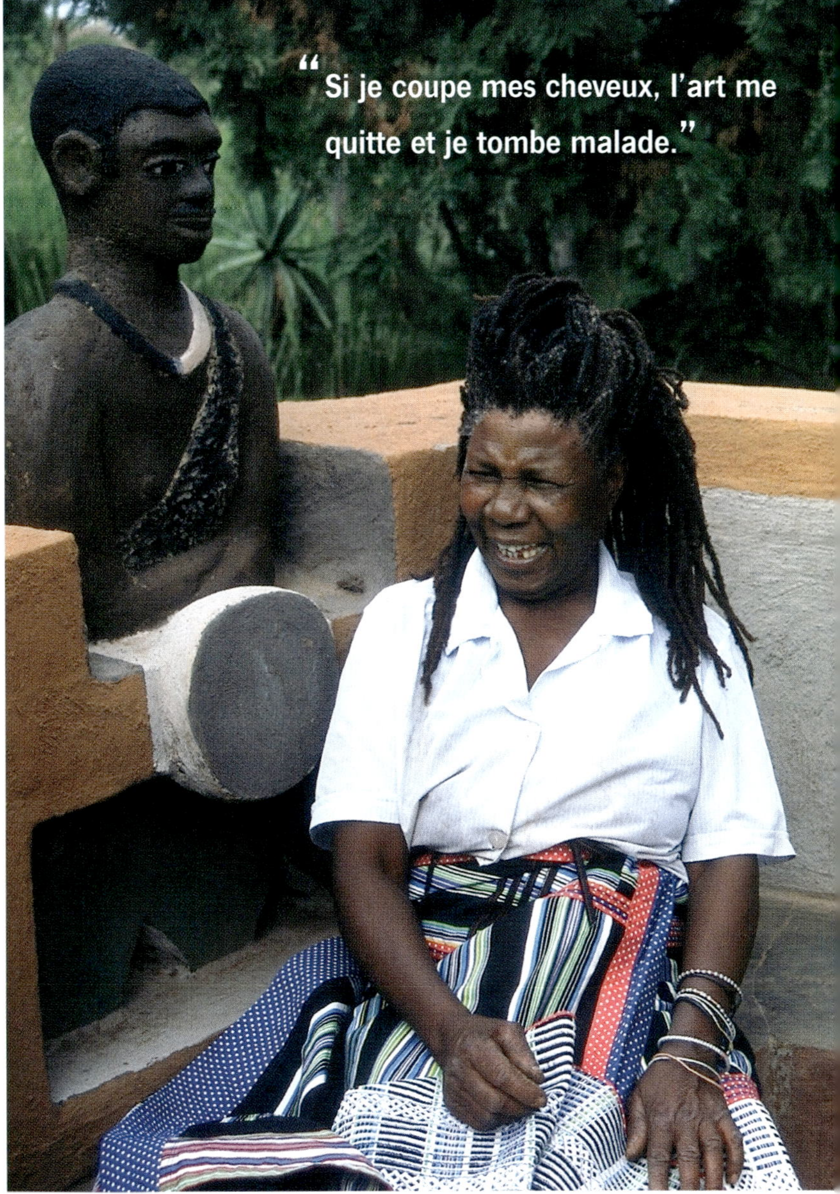

Le matin suivant, on est allé chercher de la glaise dans la rivière, on l'a foulée aux pieds et on a allumé le feu dans la maison. Ce soir-là, Noria s'est mise à façonner une figurine à la lumière du feu. Son premier modelage de terre glaise était une petite figure de femme. Elle s'est immédiatement sentie mieux. Ce soir-là elle a modelé trois figurines et le lendemain trois ou quatre de plus. Elle a continué à modeler ainsi pendant quelques jours, puis elle est allée ramasser du bois et de l'herbe sèche et a creusé un trou dans la cour. Durant cette première semaine, Noria a cuit sa première fournée de figurines d'argile.

L'ARGILE

Le travail de l'argile à la campagne présente un véritable défi à l'artiste. Noria se rend dans un endroit bien précis près de chez elle pour extraire de la glaise des berges de la rivière. C'est un travail dur et pénible et elle emploie des jeunes gens pour l'aider. Elle choisit la glaise avec le plus grand soin, recherchant la texture, la couleur et la consistance idéales. Elle préfère la glaise noire qui tourne au brun rouille à la cuisson. Noria recouvre la glaise recueillie de plastique et la laisse reposer un jour ou deux. Puis elle pilonne la glaise avec un gros bâton, la pétrit et la façonne en une sculpture. Noria travaille l'argile en enroulant des bandes qu'elle superpose et lisse ensuite. Elle ne dispose pas de tour de potier, d'outils de spécialiste, de produits chimiques pour émailler les poteries, ni de four électrique. Tout est fait selon les méthodes traditionnelles. Elle laisse les objets sécher lentement sous des couvertures ou des bâches en plastique. Au cours du séchage, Noria teinte les poteries en utilisant du *luvhundi* (de la terre d'un ocre rouge) et du graphite.

La cuisson est toute une affaire. On creuse un trou vaste et peu profond. Une mince couche de pierres est posée sur le fond, recouverte à son tour de bois. Les sculptures sont ensuites disposées avec soin et recouvertes d'une épaisse couche d'herbes sèches, comme de la paille. Noria place parfois de la tôle ondulée autour du feu pour réfléchir et augmenter la température de cuisson. On entretient le feu pendant longtemps. La cuisson d'une série de poteries peut prendre toute une journée.Noria s'est mise à produire des sculptures beaucoup plus grandes et de bien meilleure qualité qu'à ses débuts, preuve de ses progrès techniques dans le traitement de l'argile. Ses sculptures sont de plus en plus expressionnistes. Elle ne

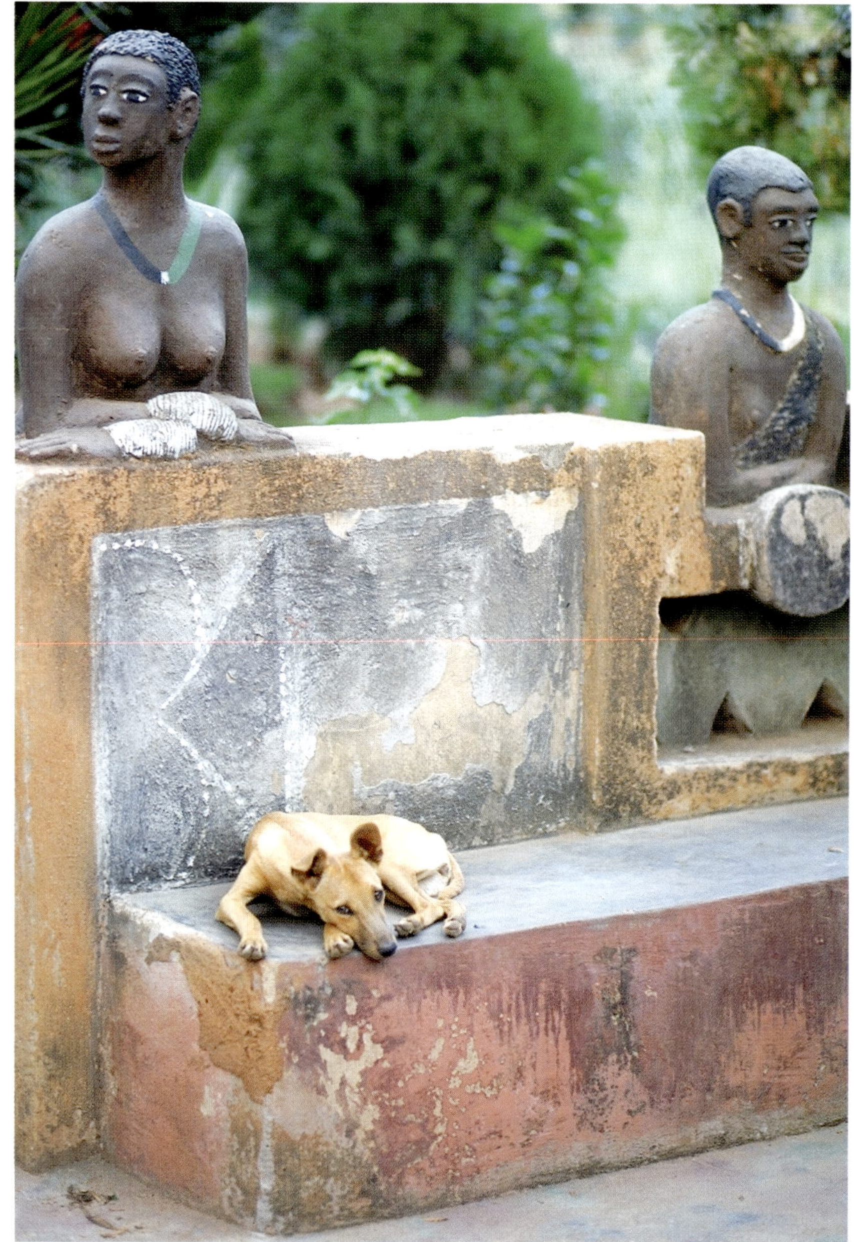

cesse d'expérimenter et de chercher à exploiter les possibilités du matériau avec lequel elle travaille.

LE BOIS

En 1976, Noria a fait un rêve. " Un matin, je dormais. Dans mon rêve, j'ai vu la rivière Luvuvhu qui coule en contrebas de ma maison. J'ai vu un gros morceau de bois coincé sous le pont. J'ai demandé à une femme qui passait si cette bûche était à elle. Elle m'a répondu: « Il n'y a pas de bûche. » "

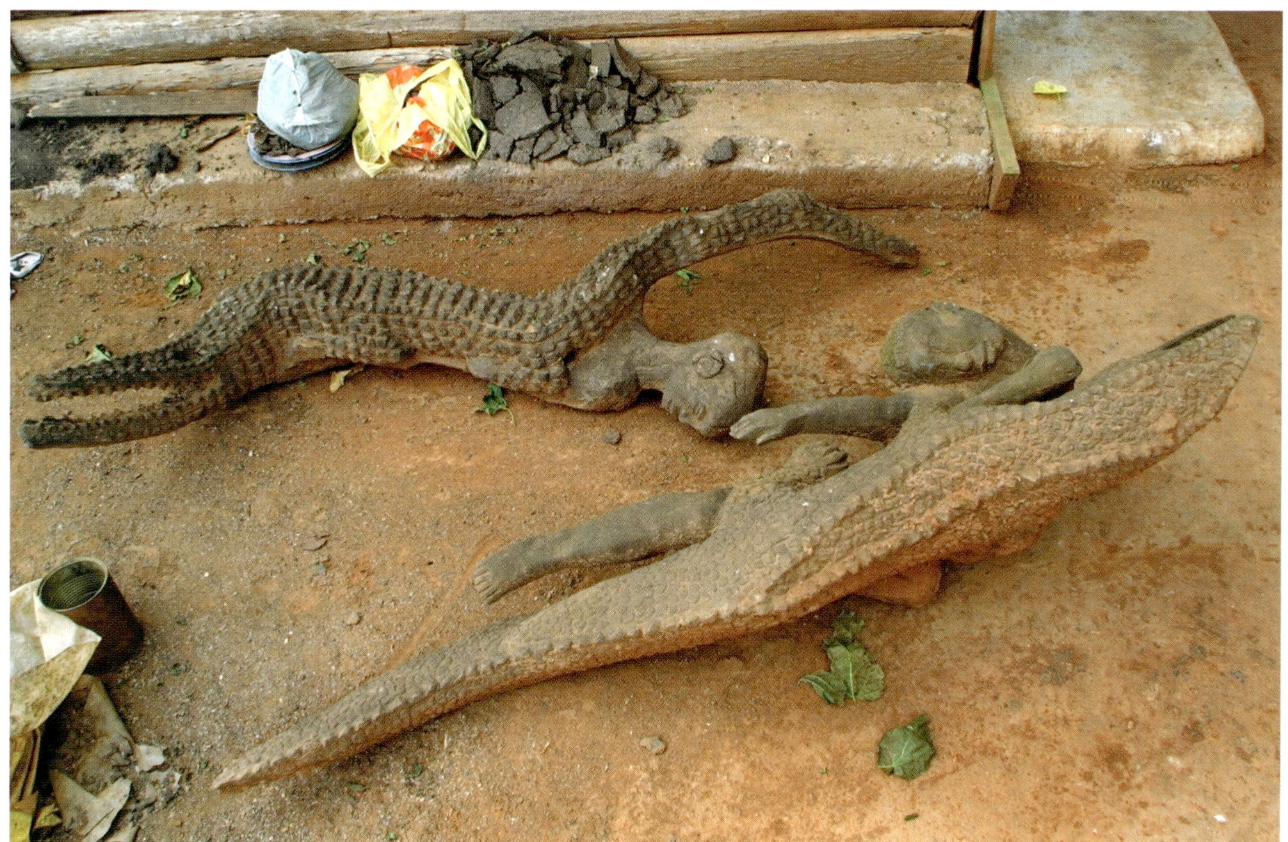

Quand elle s'est réveillée, Noria est descendue à la rivière, et, à sa grande surprise, elle a trouvé la bûche qu'elle avait vue en rêve. Prise d'une inspiration, elle l'a rapportée chez elle. Comme elle n'avait pas d'outil pour la sculpter, elle l'a laissée dans un coin et a continué à travailler sur la sculpture d'argile qu'elle avait en chantier. Mais le bois continuait à l'appeler et pour finir, elle n'a pu s'empêcher de répondre à son appel. Un vieillard de ses voisins lui a donné une hache, et, à l'aide de ce seul outil, elle a réalisé sa première sculpture sur bois - une figure de femme qu'elle a appelée *Sangwani.* Elle a mis cette œuvre de côté et n'a pas retravaillé le bois jusqu'en 1981. Elle a fini par offrir *Sangwani* à sa belle-sœur.

Au cours de ces années-là, Noria a produit de nombreuses poteries de terre cuite et a beaucoup exposé. Elle a commencé à modeler de plus en plus de figures de femmes dans des postures traditionnelles: femmes portant des récipients, femmes dans des attitudes de respect, femmes donnant le sein à un nourrisson. Puis, un jour où elle ramassait du bois pour cuire ses figures, elle s'est mise à chercher du bois qu'elle pourrait sculpter. Cette fois, elle s'est débrouillée pour se procurer un ciseau et elle a repris son travail du bois. Elle laissait ses sculptures dehors, exposées à la pluie, et ne s'en souciait guère. Elle les montrait à ceux qui venaient la voir, mais sans y attacher d'importance et n'attendait pas qu'on y prête grand intérêt. Elle les vendait pour trois fois rien.

C'est ainsi que Noria est devenue la première femme noire à sculpter le bois. Ce matériau l'a libérée, car avec le bois elle pouvait produire des œuvres de beaucoup plus grande taille qu'avec l'argile. Parmi ses premières grandes œuvres en bois, nous citerons *Bushman* et *Carnage (Natal Flood Disaster)*.

De l'argile au bois: Noria s'attire les critiques et les menaces des tenants de la tradition.

"Certains disaient que mes ancêtres allaient me punir pour avoir fait fi de la tradition. Ces menaces ne m'inquiétaient guère parce que c'étaient justement mes ancêtres qui

81

m'avaient dit de sculpter le bois." Noria ne s'est pas laissé intimider.

Les devins, les herboristes et autres invoquent leurs rêves pour expliquer qu'ils répondent à l'appel des ancêtres. Certains sculpteurs prétendent que ce sont les ancêtres qui leur ont intimé l'ordre d'obéir à une vocation d'artiste. Leur inspiration et leur art proviennent des rêves que leur envoient les ancêtres.

Dans la culture venda, les traditions culturelles jouent un rôle essentiel et l'on dit qu'elles sont transmises par les ancêtres. Ces traditions dictent une division des tâches bien définie entre les hommes et les femmes. Les femmes venda pratiqueront poterie et tissage, alors que les hommes sculpteront. Une femme venda se consacrera aux soins du ménage, et, dans les campagnes, les femmes apprendront de leurs aînées comment travailler la terre glaise pour façonner des objets utilitaires pour la cuisine.

En choisissant de sculpter le bois, Noria s'oppose à cette conception du rôle traditionnel de la femme dans la société venda et se pose en anticonformiste: elle aime sculpter le bois et ne se laisse pas démonter par les critiques.

CULTURE ET TRADITIONS VENDA

Noria attache beaucoup d'importance à ses racines et à la culture à laquelle elle appartient. Elle reconnaît les rôles traditionnels des hommes et des femmes et ne croit pas que les femmes et les hommes soient égaux, ni d'ailleurs qu'ils devraient l'être. Cela ne veut cependant pas dire qu'un des deux sexes vaille mieux que l'autre, mais qu'ils tiennent des rôles différents dans la société. Quand on lui demande si elle pense qu'il est important que les hommes sachent cuisiner, afin de soulager les femmes de la préparation de tous les repas, elle répond: "Les femmes doivent faire la cuisine pour leur mari. Il n'est pas bon qu'un homme soit au fourneau pendant que la femme se prélasse, et de toute façon, les femmes cuisinent mieux!"

Ses poteries de terre cuite et ses sculptures sur bois expriment les rituels et les traditions du peuple VhaVenda, ainsi que les traditions shangaan et zouloue, aussi présentes dans les communautés de la région. De nombreuses œuvres représentent des femmes en costume traditionnel, et les détails du costume, les perles et autres décorations, ont leur signification: ils montrent le statut du personnage représenté. Dans la culture VhaVenda, certains éléments du costume comme le shedo sont liés aux écoles initiatiques. Noria nous a expliqué l'importance qu'ont pour elle les écoles initiatiques. C'est la seule école qu'elle ait fréquentée et l'influence qu'elle a eue sur elle se trouve reflétée dans ses œuvres. 1938, année de naissance de Noria, est aussi la dernière année où les jeunes filles ont quitté la maison pour l'école initiatique, où elles passaient six mois. Par la suite, les écoles étaient plus proches, et les jeunes filles s'y rendaient pour des périodes plus courtes. Il est essentiel de connaître les rites initiatiques pour comprendre Noria et interpréter son œuvre.

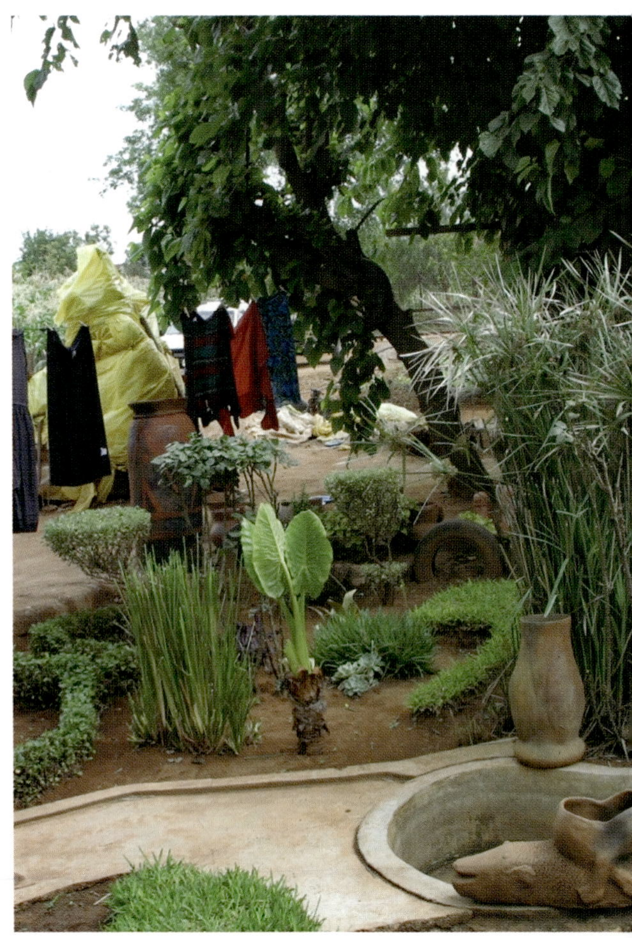

ECOLES D'INITIATION

Dans les cultures traditionnelles indigènes d'Afrique du Sud, les femmes sont généralement considérées comme subalternes. Ce n'est toutefois pas nécessairement le cas au Venda. Dans sa cour, la *muta*, c'est la femme qui commande. Une femme peut être propriétaire. Sa propriété lui aura été donnée par son père ou bien elle en aura hérité s'il n'avait pas d'héritier mâle. Noria est à la tête de son foyer, elle est propriétaire et elle est respectée par sa famille et par la communauté du village.

Cependant il reste certains domaines de la vie quotidienne dans lesquels une femme venda est inférieure à l'homme. Aidées de leurs filles, les femmes doivent s'acquitter des tâches domestiques, comme la cuisine et le ménage, et c'est à elles d'aller chercher l'eau.

Noria m'a raconté un souvenir d'enfance. L'une des femmes de son père rentrait avec une cruche d'eau sur la tête et une calebasse pleine à la main. Son père s'est mis à la houspiller et à la battre parce qu'elle ne travaillait pas assez dur. Mais l'épouse n'a pas bronché et n'a pas renversé une seule goutte d'eau. Une femme savait rester à sa place. Noria ajoute: *"Aujourd'hui les femmes sont plus fortes."*

Selon la tradition, chez les VhaVenda, une fille doit fréquenter trois écoles d'initiation avant de se marier: la vhusha, lors de la puberté ; la tshikanda, école intermédiaire où l'on consolide ce qui a été enseigné dans la précédente, et la domba, où les jeunes femmes se préparent au mariage.

Le développement de l'individu est considéré comme une série d'étapes bien distinctes: la puberté et le mariage marquent deux moments importants de la vie. Le passage de l'une à l'autre se fait sous l'influence de forces extérieures, comme les ancêtres, les bons et les mauvais esprits, les sorciers et les sorcières. Ces forces peuvent avoir une influence faste ou néfaste sur la vie des gens. La fonction des

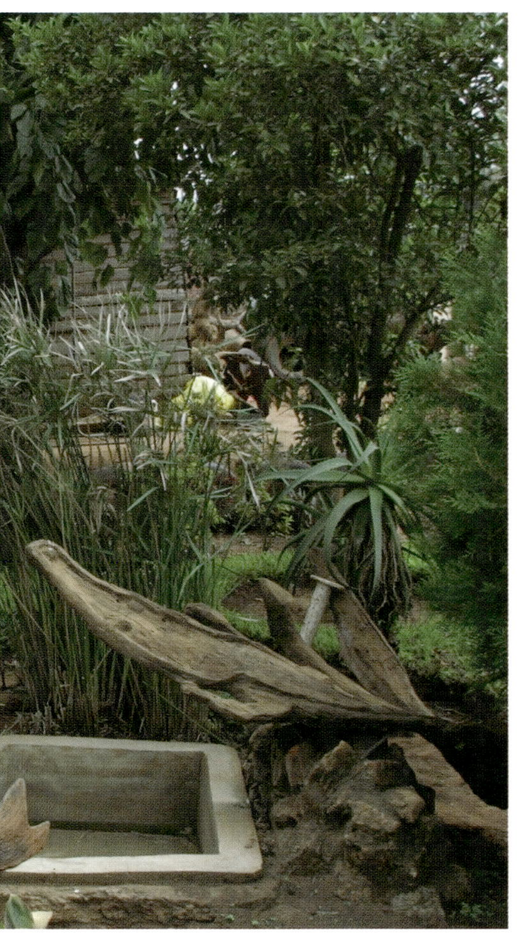

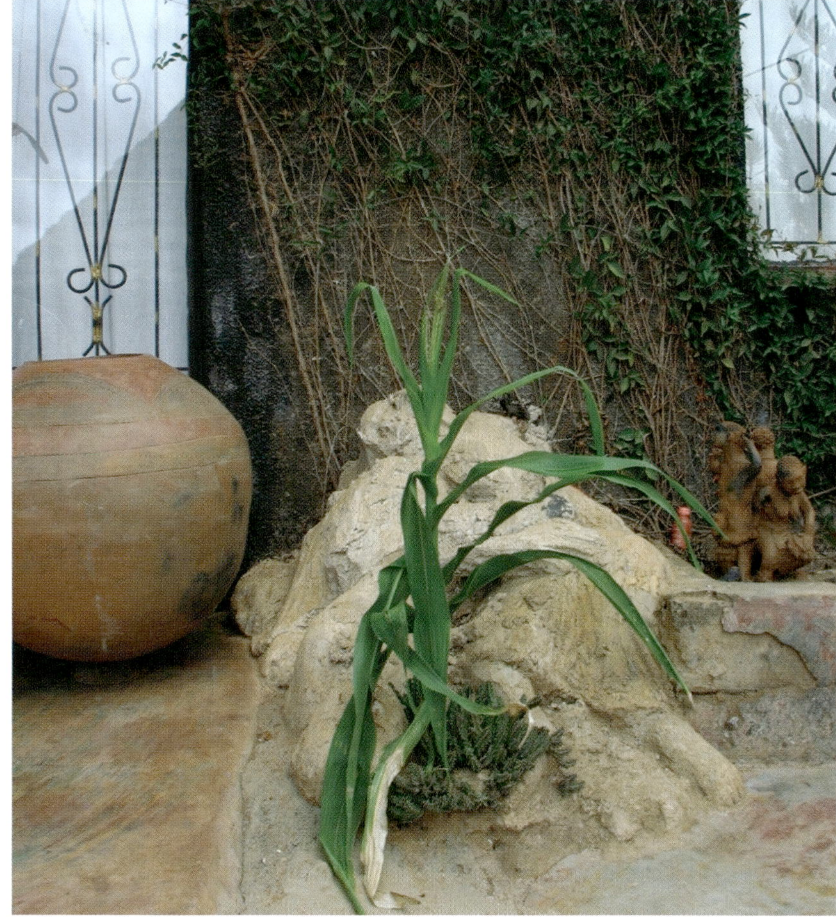

écoles initiatiques est d'enseigner aux novices ce qu'on doit attendre de la vie et comment il convient de se comporter dans le stade suivant du développement de chaque individu: par diverses cérémonies et par des danses, les novices apprennent à éviter les erreurs du passé et à faire face aux défis de l'avenir. Lors de ces cérémonies, on invoque les ancêtres pour qu'ils accordent leur soutien et qu'ils confèrent par la magie de la force aux novices. De nombreuses figures sculptées par Noria représentent l'enseignement symbolique de la *domba* et montrent bien l'importance de ces traditions pour l'artiste.

La vhusha est un enseignement de huit jours qui se fait dans une cabane d'initiation où les filles sont isolées et où on leur apprend que l'essence de la féminité pour une Venda est l'humilité. Elles doivent garder la tête baissée, les épaules basses et les bras croisés, ou les mains tenues en coupe sous le menton dans une attitude de totale servilité. On leur impose diverses tâches serviles comme de porter de grosses pierres d'un bout à l'autre de la cabane, ou porter sur le dos ou sur la tête de lourds fardeaux. Parfois on leur fait faire le tour de la cour en rampant, ou elles doivent se tortiller sur le ventre comme des serpents, ou encore tenir dans leurs mains des braises brûlantes. Les novices reçoivent une instruction approfondie en matière de sexualité, de comportement sexuel, de fiançailles et de mariage. On insiste sur la nécessité d'éviter les grossesses en dehors du mariage.

On enseigne aux novices à chanter et à danser et elles apprennent le *milayo*, qui allie des leçons sur la vie quotidienne et un symbolisme culturel ésotérique. Noria explique que sa connaissance du *milayo* la dote d'un savoir particulier qui lui donne le droit de participer à certaines cérémonies et réunions réservées aux femmes.

L'école du deuxième degré, la *tshikanda* reçoit les novices trois ou quatre ans plus tard, juste avant qu'elles n'entrent dans la dernière école, la *domba*.

La domba constitue l'apogée du processus initiatique. Durant neuf mois environ les novices se préparent au mariage. On commence par sonner la *phala phala*, une corne de kudu, la grande antilope. Un grand feu est allumé dans le village du roi, que l'on entretient pendant toute la durée de la *domba*. Une fois le feu allumé, les novices reçoivent d'un spécialiste des rites diverses médecines, et tous les objet utilisés dans la domba sont aspergés de médecines pour tenir les mauvaises influences à l'écart. On rase les néophytes et il leur est interdit de laver aucune partie de leur corps pendant la durée de la domba. On leur enseigne des chants secrets et des danses. Elles reçoivent une instruction sexuelle, observent et participent à des activités de mime porteuses d'enseignements, et on leur montre des objets secrets de la tribu. L'objectif de la domba est de familiariser les jeunes filles avec tous les aspects du mariage, ainsi qu'avec les mœurs et coutumes de la culture venda. Les VhaVenda considèrent la domba comme un événement national.

Noria nous décrit la danse de la domba qui est un élément important de la cérémonie. Les novices dansent autour d'un feu sacré dans le khoro du roi. Elles forment une file, chaque participante tenant le coude de celle qui la précède, constituant ainsi une chaîne ininterrompue qui serpente autour du feu sacré au rythme des tambours ngoma et mirumba. A l'origine, les filles dansaient nues, mais aujourd'hui elles portent le shedo qui leur passe entre les jambes et dont un pan retombe sur les fesses. Elles ont aux poignets et aux chevilles des bracelets métalliques qui scintillent dans la lumière du feu et accompagnent leur danse d'un cliquetis. Cette danse symbolise un python, animal associé à la fertilité et considéré comme un symbole sacré. Le symbolisme de la domba identifie le mur du khoro au corps du dieu python, et la cour au lac Fundudzi, le lieu des origines, le ventre primordial. Les novices sont alors dans le ventre du python, prêtes à renaître, à passer à l'âge adulte, aptes au mariage, pour devenir des membres de la société, respectueuses des traditions.

REIS NAAR VENDA

In juni 2002 had Kathryn Straughan een interview met Noria Mabasa over het ontstaan en de ontwikkeling van haar betrokkenheid bij de beeldhouwkunst als haar levenswerk, en de manier waarop zij haar kunst heeft gesitueerd in relatie tot de culturele tradities van de Venda maatschappij. De tekst die hieronder volgt, is een samenvattende weergave van deze gesprekken.

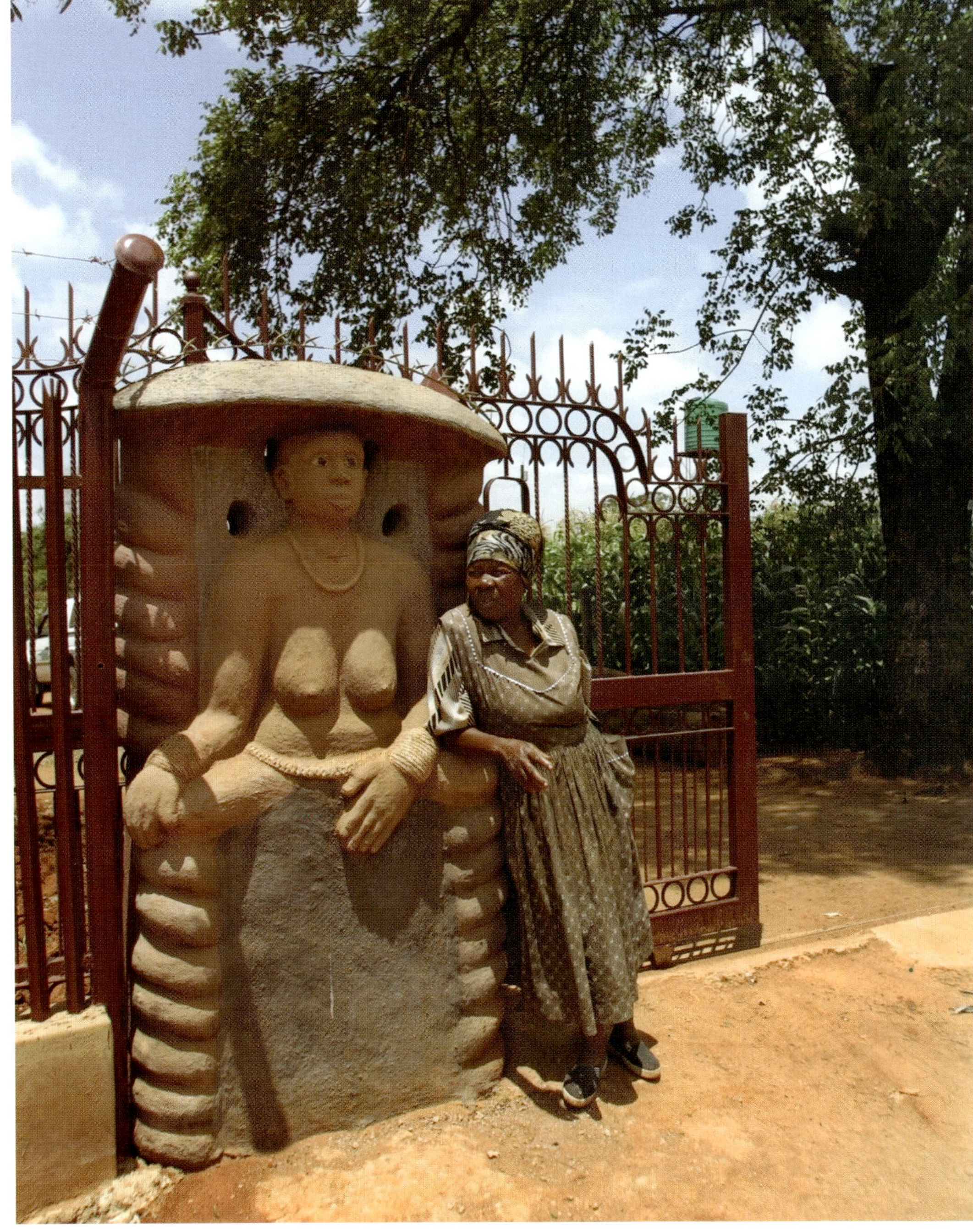

Een hoog hek, ongebruikelijk in deze landelijke omgeving, omgeven het terrein waar Noria Mabasa woont en werkt.

In gesprek met Noria Mabasa

NORIA MABASA'S huis staat in Venda, een streek in het noordoostelijke gedeelte van Zuid-Afrika waar de meeste inwoners in valeien tussen hoge, met mist beklede bergen wonen. Ze kunnen veel verhalen en legenden vertellen over hun mensen en hun afkomst, evenals over het land zelf. Noria woont in het dorp Tshino dat, zoals de andere dorpen in de streek, vol staat met woningen (*midi*) waar ieder huis door heggen en lage moddermuren omgeven is. De hutten zijn met riet bedekt en sommige zijn met traditionele ontwerpen beschilderd. Het huis van de hoofdman (*khasi*) van het dorp staat op de hoogstgelegen plek, en zijn vrouwen en familie wonen beneden hem. De rest van de dorpelingen bezetten de lagergelegen gebieden.

In de Venda maatschappij bestaat een huishouden (*mudi*) of uit een enkel gezin of een verzameling van gezinnen, die gewoonlijk allemaal tot dezelfde stam behoren. De inwoners van de mudi wonen samen in een dicht op elkaar gelegen verzameling hutten, ieder met zijn eigen erf (*muta*). Ieder individueel huishouden staat bekend als een khoro. Tussen de traditionele ronde huizen in Tshino staan ook moderne bakstenen huizen. Er hangen mensen rond – vrouwen met baby's in kleurrijke dekens op hun rug gebonden, mannen zittend onder de schaduw van de bomen, tabak rokend en eigengemaakt marula bier drinkend, bastaardhonden met de staart tussen hun benen op zoek naar afval en rondscharrelende kippen.

Een groot roestig metalen poort, geflankeerd door twee gebeeldhouwde pilaren, en een hoog hek, ongebruikelijk in deze landelijke omgeving, omgeven het terrein waar Noria woont en werkt. Haar openlucht 'studio' ligt onder een oude moerbeiboom waar Union Buildings (Uniegebouwen), haar laatste werk, onder geel plastic ingepakt staat. Op de grond liggen andere grote werken die nog niet af zijn. Het studioterrein is omgeven door maisvelden, boomgaarden en een moestuin.

Op de oevers van de Luvuvhurivier, waar de vrouwen hun kleren op de rotsen wassen en de kinderen in het water spelen, heeft Noria haar huis gebouwd. Haar erf is een mengeling van traditionele Vendacultuur en Westerse invloeden. Ronde, met riet bedekte hutten, beschilderd in traditionele patronen en een conventioneel rechthoekig huis met ramen met metalen kozijnen omgeven een centrale binnenplaats. Een lage muur, met vlekkerige en ingewikkelde troonachtige zetels en kleien beelden, omcirkelt dit terrein. Een van de hutten doet dienst als bed-and-breakfast en een andere als werkruimte waar ze haar kleibeelden maakt en bewaart. Er is ook een galerie met een winkeltje met een zinkplaten dak buiten het complex, waar Noria een gedeelte van haar voltooide werken en de kralenstukken die haar dochter maakt, heeft ondergebracht. Zij woont samen met haar gezin in een Westers huis met stromend water en elektriciteit, een luxe in deze gemeenschap.

Twee figuren van klei, een man en een vrouw, staan bij de ingang naar het erf. Noria maakt ieder jaar weer opnieuw dit soort bas-relief werken. Haar kunst staat overal. Huwbare jonge meisjes liggen in een respectvolle houding, *vha a losha*, heilige krokodillen bakken in de zon, leeuwen houden de wacht en plantenpotten in de vorm van vrouwenlijven staan vol met vetplanten. Dit is haar eigen thuisruimte, het centrum van haar privé-leven.

'Als ik met klei of hout begin te werken, zie ik niets. Maar zodra ik begonnen ben, komt het hier naar binnen [wijst op haar hoofd] en dan komt het en komt het en ik weet niet hoe het gaat, maar het is geweldig en het stuk wordt iets ...'

Dit is Noria, de mooie moeder met gevlochten haar, grootmoeder, houstsnijder, pottenbakker en leraar. Wanneer men haar werk ziet, is men verbaasd over haar nederigheid en haar vreugde over de respons die haar stukken opwekken, want zij is net zo verbaasd over wat ze gemaakt heeft. Noria maakt een grote indruk op degenen die haar voor het eerst ontmoeten. Ze heeft haar haar sind 1989 niet meer geknipt en draagt het lang, op haar hoofd

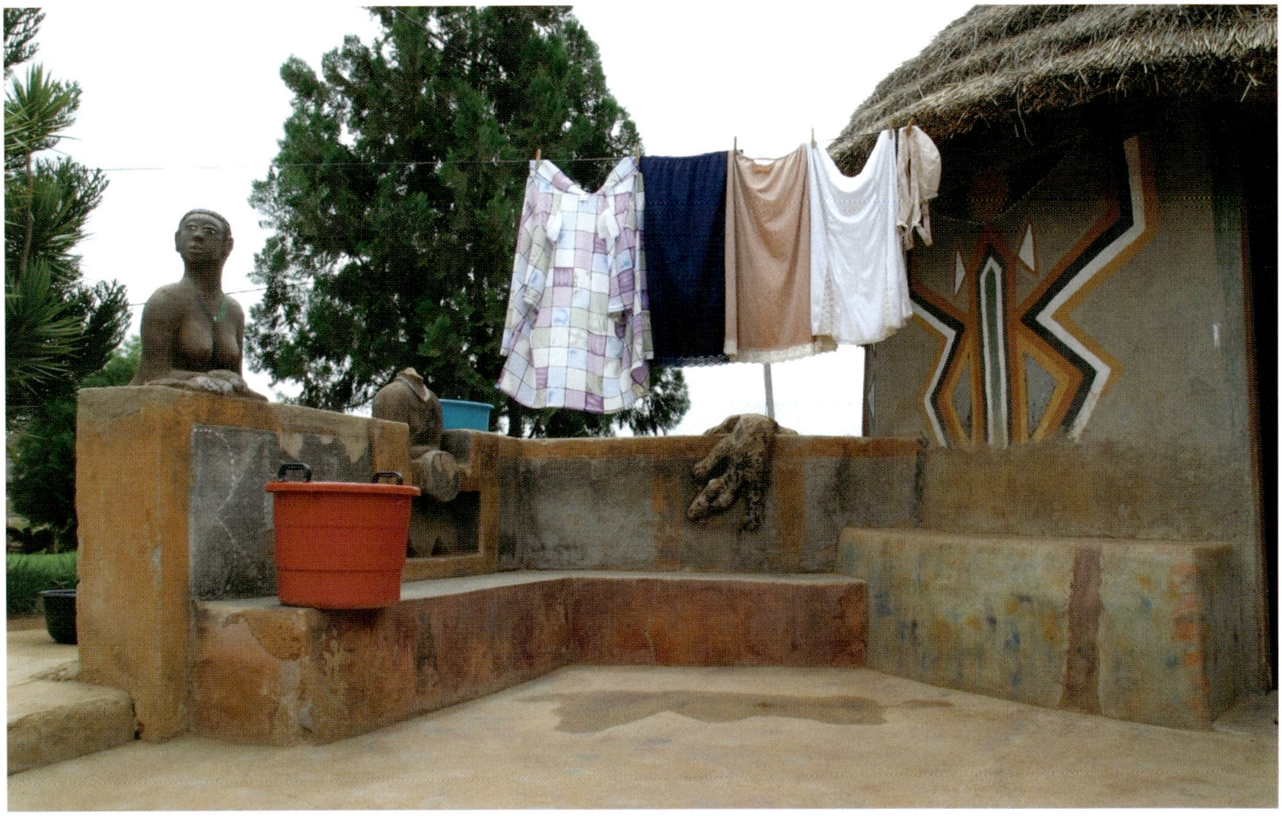

een sjaal of wollen pet. In een droom kreeg ze
te horen dat iedere keer als ze haar haar zou
knippen, ze hiermee haar creativiteit zou
wegknippen. Ze gelooft hier heilig in en als er
een vlecht afbreekt, knoopt ze deze weer vast.
'Als ik mijn haar afknip, verdwijnt de kunst en
word ik ziek ...', zegt ze.

Om Noria's sculpturen te kunnen begrijpen
moet men haar horen praten over waar ze
vandaan komt, omdat haar cultuur en
spirituele geloof de voornaamste plaats in
haar werken innemen. Ze heeft nooit een
formele opleiding gehad en heeft nooit leren
lezen of schrijven, behalve haar naam, die ze
op haar werken zet. Ze heeft ook geen
kunstopleiding ontvangen.

In 1952 ging Noria op veertien-jarige leeftijd
in White City wonen, een gedeelte van Soweto,
Johannesburg. De vrouw van een van haar
broers had een kind gebaard en was daarbij
blind geworden. Noria ging de jonge moeder
helpen. Ze deed de was, maakte schoon, zorgde
voor het eten en verzorgde de baby. Toen er een
jaar voorbij was, kon de vrouw van haar broer
weer zien en ging Noria bij een van haar

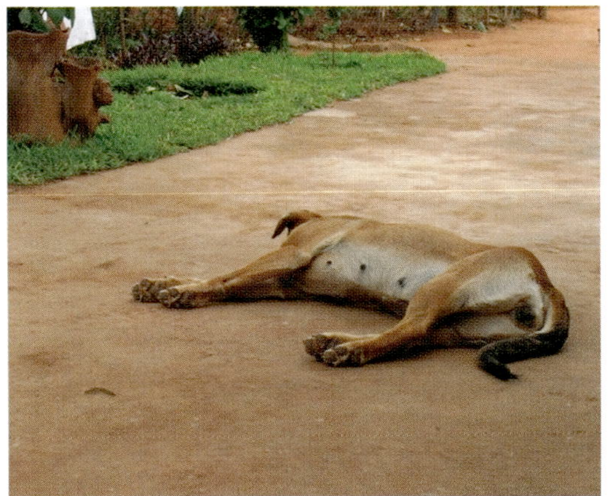

nichten in Alexandra wonen, een kleinere
township in het noordelijke gedeelte van
Johannesburg.

Het was in Johannesburg dat Noria voor het
eerst dromen begon te krijgen die zo'n
belangrijke rol in haar leven zouden gaan
spelen. In deze periode bleven de dromen maar
komen. Haar visie was soms profetisch: in een
van haar dromen zag ze dat een van de
tweeling van de buren zou sterven en in een
andere kon ze een brief zien die aan een vriend
geschreven was. In 1965 had ze een droom

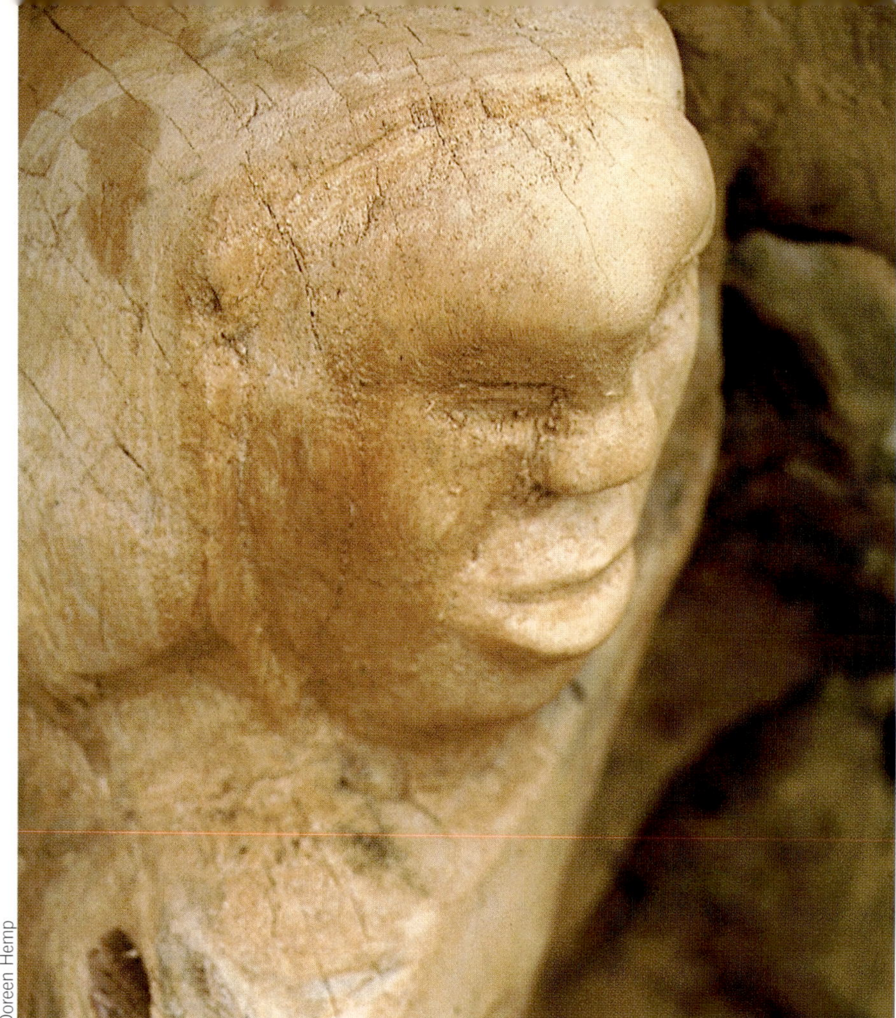

Doreen Hemp

53

waarin een oude vrouw aan haar verscheen die haar liet zien dat ze met klei moest gaan werken. In die tijde kende ze geen enkele andere vrouw die kleien figuren maakte, en toch had haar droom haar opgedragen te gaan boetseren.

Noria liet de dromen voor wat ze waren en begon geleidelijk aan ziek te worden. Toen ze sliep, kwam de oude vrouw die ze nu Tshidzeuli noemt, wat 'herkauwen' of 'een goede herinnering' betekent, terug in haar dromen. Deze oude vrouw, krom van de melaatsheid, had zwaar beschadigde handen met maar een paar vingers, geen neus en er waren stukken van haar mond verdwenen. Ze droeg dierenvellen, had een hele donkere huid, kort zwart haar, slappe loshangende borsten en zag er oud en gerimpeld uit. De verschijning van deze vrouw maakte Noria zo bang dat ze angst had te gaan slapen. Op een gegeven moment sprak deze oude vrouw haar in een droom aan en zei: 'Je begrijpt het niet omdat ik jou aan het leren bent en je luistert niet.' Toen droomde ze op een gegeven moment van haar vader. Ze stond naast hem, tot het middel in een poel water. Hij riep 'Muelelwa' (Noria's Venda naam) en vroeg: 'Waarom zeg je nee als de oude vrouw jou les geeft hoe je rijk kunt worden?'

Noria haalde haar schouders op en draaide zich om. Toen werd ze wakker, ze was bang en beefde. Voordat ze zich in haar droom had omgedraaid, had haar vader haar met een roede van riet op haar schouder geslagen. Ze beefde. De oude vrouw en haar vader waren allebei uit haar droom vertrokken, maar ze kon niet meer in slaap vallen. Ze bleef nog een week beven, en op vrijdag kwam haar vader terug en schreeuwde, 'Muelelwa, nu wakker worden! Ga naar Muthewana (Noria's zusje) en vertel haar dat je aan de voorouders moet gaan bidden.'

Noria werd wakker en haar vreselijke angst was verdwenen.

's Ochtends werd er wat klei uit de rivier gehaald. De klei werd aangestampt en er werd een vuur in huis gemaakt. Die avond begon

53. Detail from *Union Buildings.*

54. Detail of a wall at Ditike, a craft centre near Thohoyandou.

Noria bij het licht van het vuur een kleifiguur te boetseren. Haar eerste beeld was erg klein, een vrouwenfiguurtje. Ze begon zich onmiddellijk beter te voelen. Die nacht maakte ze nog drie figuren en de volgende dag drie of vier meer. Dit duurde een paar dagen tot ze hout begon te verzamelen en gras en een oven op haar erf maakte. In die eerste week had Noria haar eerste lading kleistukken gebakken.

KLEI

Het werken met klei onder plattelandsomstandigheden is een enorme uitdaging. Noria gaat naar een speciaal gebied vlak bij haar huis waar zij de klei uit de rivieroever graaft. Het is zwaar werk, waarbij ze hulp krijgt van jonge mannen die ze in dienst heeft genomen om haar te helpen. Ze is heel precies wat de klei aangaat die ze uitkiest: het moet de juiste tekstuur, kleur en samenstelling hebben. De zwarte klei is de beste; wanneer deze in de oven gebakken wordt, wordt het roodachtig bruin van kleur. Zodra de klei verzameld is, bedekt Noria dit met plastic en laat ze het een dag of twee liggen. Dan pakt ze een lange, zware houten stok en begint op de klei te beuken. Zo wordt de klei gekneed en geboetseerd. Ze gebruikt de vlechtmethode bij het maken van haar kunstwerken van klei. Ze heeft geen pottenbakkerswiel, speciaal gereedschap, chemisch glazuur of een elektrische potten-bakkersoven. Alles wordt op de traditionele manier gedaan. De werken moeten langzaam drogen onder dekens of stukken plastic. Gedurende dit droogproces brengt Noria vlekken aan op de sculpturen met luvhundi (rode okerkleurige grond) en grafiet.

Het bakken van de klei is een grote gebeurtenis. Een groot gedeelte van de aarde wordt uitgegraven tot een grote, maar niet al te diepe kuil. Een dunne laag stenen langs de bodem, met hout er bovenop. De beelden worden vervolgens zorgvuldig gearrangeerd en bedekt met een dikke laag stro-achtig gras. Noria gebruikt vaak ijzeren golfplaten aan de rand van het vuur om zo door middel van reflectie grotere hitte op te wekken. Het vuur wordt lange tijd brandend gehouden. Het kan wel een hele dag duren om een lading te bakken.

Noria is begonnen veel grotere sculpturen te

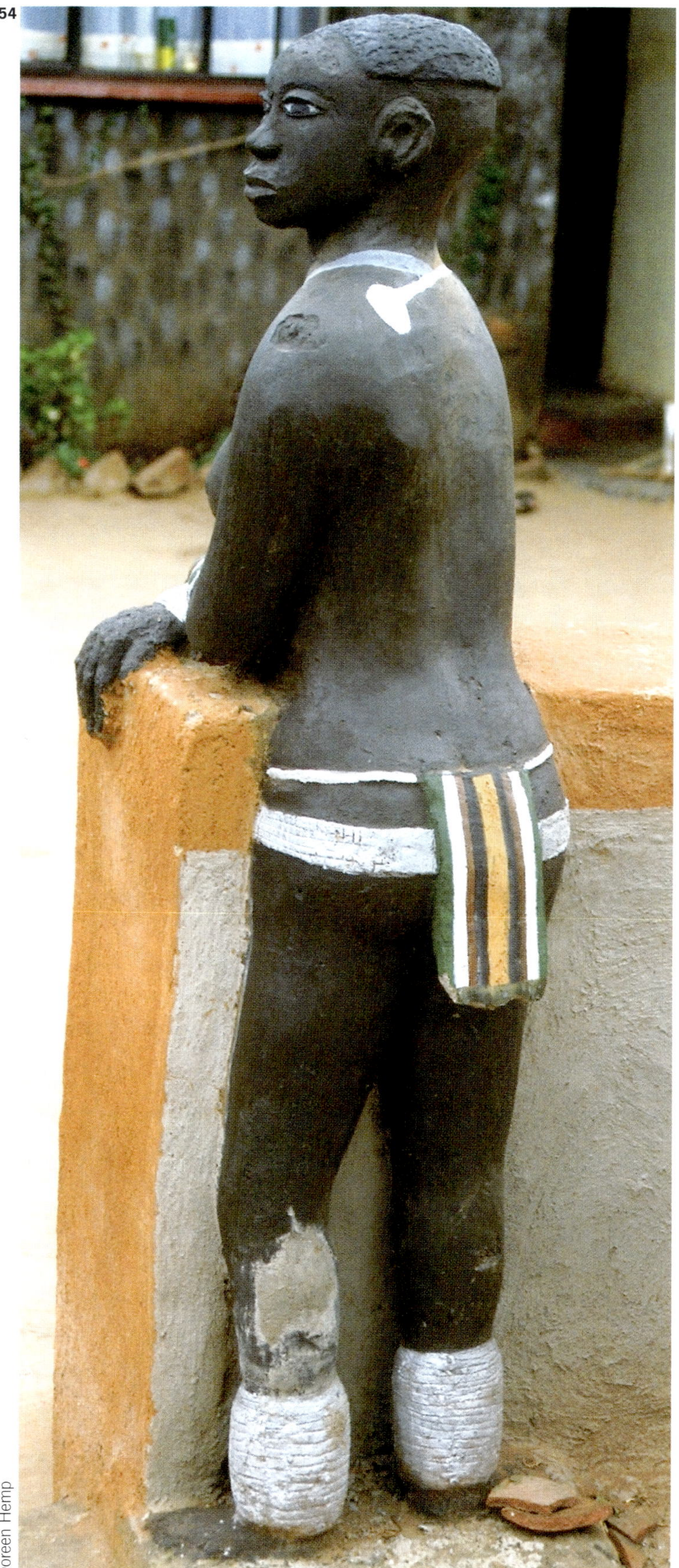

maken die een betere kwaliteit hebben dan haar eerdere werken. Dit getuigt van haar toenemende technische kennis en beheersing van het materiaal. Haar beelden worden steeds expressionistischer. Ze is een kunstenaar die constant met het door haar uitgekozen medium speelt en daar de mogelijkheden van onderzoekt.

HOUT

In 1976 had Noria een droom. 'Ik sliep 's ochtends. Ik zag de Luvuvhurivier beneden mijn huis. Ik zag hoe een groot stuk hout onder de brug bleef vastzitten. Ik vroeg aan iemand: "Is dit van jou?" Ze antwoordde: "Nee, ik zie geen hout."'

Toen ze wakker werd, ging Noria beneden naar de rivier en tot haar verbazing lag daar het hout dat ze in haar droom gezien had. Vol inspiratie nam ze het mee naar huis. Maar omdat ze geen gereedschap had om het hout te bewerken, liet ze het links liggen en ging ze door met het boetseren van het kleibeeld waar ze al aan begonnen was. Maar het hout bleef naar haar lonken en ze kon er geen weerstand aan bieden. Een oude man gaf haar een bijl en met dit enige stuk gereedschap maakte ze haar eerste houtsnijwerk – een vrouwenfiguur, die ze Sangwani noemde. Ze legde het stuk terzijde en tot 1981 werkte ze niet meer met hout. Uiteindelijk gaf ze Sangwani weg aan haar schoonzusje.

In deze tijd maakte Noria veel kleiwerken en had ze een aantal tentoonstellingen. Ze begon meer traditionele vrouwen te maken – met potten op hun hoofd, respect betonend, borstvoeding gevend. Toen op een gegeven dag was ze brandhout aan het verzamelen en betrapte ze zichzelf erop dat ze op zoek was naar hout dat ze kon snijden. Deze keer slaagde ze erin een beitel te pakken te krijgen en zo begon ze opnieuw hout te bewerken. Haar houten beelden bleven buiten in de regen staan en ze besteedde er geen aandacht aan. Als er mensen op bezoek kwamen wees ze achteloos naar deze beelden en verwachtte er nooit veel aandacht voor, en meestal verkocht ze ze voor weinig geld.

Noria was de eerste zwarte vrouw in Zuid-Afrika die hout bewerkte, en door middel van dit nieuwe materiaal raakte ze plotseling bevrijd van alle beperkingen van het maken van kleine beelden, omdat hout de gelegenheid bood veel grotere werken te maken dan ze tot nu toe met klei had kunnen bereiken. Haar eerste grote werken in hout waren onder andere Bushman (Bosjesman), Inkhata (Vrijheid) en Natal Flood Disaster (Overstromingsramp in Natal).

'Noria's overgang van het boetseren van klei naar houtsnijwerk zorgde voor controverses en bedreigingen.

'Er waren sommige mensen die zeiden dat mijn voorouders me gingen straffen omdat ik tegen de traditie in zou gaan. Ik was niet bang omdat mijn voorouders mij verteld haddden hout te gaan bewerken,' zegt Noria.

Waarzeggers, kruidendokters en anderen gebruiken dromen om hun 'roeping' door voorouderlijke krachten te rechtvaardigen. Sommige houtsnijders claimen ook dat ze in hun dromen door hun voorouders opgeroepen zijn kunstenaar te worden. Ze ontvangen training en inspiratie voor hun stukken middels de dromen die hun door de voorouders worden toegezonden.

In de Venda cultuur spelen tradities een grote rol, en er wordt wel beweerd dat deze door de voorouders worden doorgegeven. Deze tradities houden een duidelijke taakverdeling tussen mannen en vrouwen in. Venda vrouwen worden verondersteld pottenbakkers en wevers te zijn, terwijl van de mannen verwacht wordt dat ze houtsnijders zijn. Van een Venda vrouw wordt verwacht dat ze een huiselijke rol in deze maatschappij vervult en vrouwen in plattelandsgemeenschappen worden door hun oudere vrouwelijke familieleden verteld hoe ze klei moeten gebruiken om functionele gebruiksvoorwerpen te maken, zoals kookpotten.

Noria vormt een uitdaging voor deze manier van denken door te kiezen voor het beeldhouwen in hout, en daardoor weigert ze zich te voegen in de conventionele rol die Venda vrouwen is toebedeeld. Ze houdt van houtsnijden en laat zich niet door haar critici uit het veld slaan.

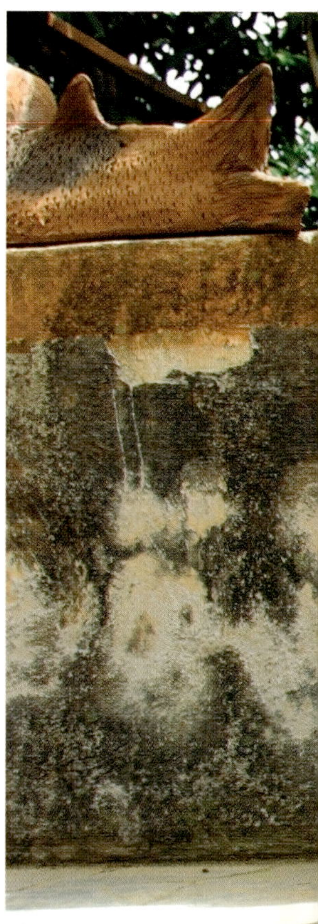

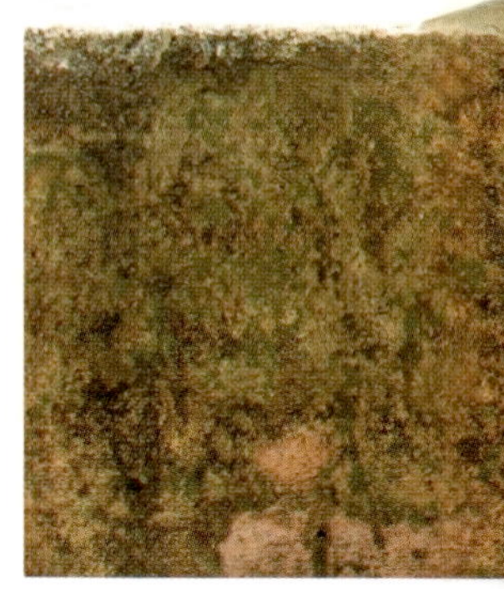

VENDA CULTUUR EN TRADITIE

Wortels en cultuur zijn erg belangrijk voor Noria. Ze erkent de traditionele rollen die door mannen en vrouwen gespeeld worden, en gelooft niet dat mannen en vrouwen gelijk zijn noch dat dit het geval zou moeten zijn. Dit impliceert echter niet dat het ene geslacht beter is dan het andere, alleen maar dat ze verschillende rollen in de maatschappij spelen. Op de vraag of ze het belangrijk vond dat mannen ook kunnen koken zodat vrouwen niet altijd de maaltijd hoeven te bereiden, antwoordde ze: 'Vrouwen moeten voor hun echtgenoten koken. Het is niet goed als een man kookt terwijl de vrouw neerzit, en in ieder geval koken vrouwen beter dan mannen!'

Haar kleistukken en houtsnijwerk weerspiegelen de rituelen en tradities van het VhaVenda volk, evenals de culturele tradities van de Shangaan en Zoeloes die ook aanwezig zijn in de gemeenschappen in haar streek. Veel van haar werken laten vrouwen gehuld in traditionele kleding zien, en de details in de stijl van kleden, kralen en andere versierselen die zijn gebruikt, zijn belangrijk. Deze fijne nuances laten de status van de persoon zien die zij uitbeeldt. In VhaVenda cultuur hebben

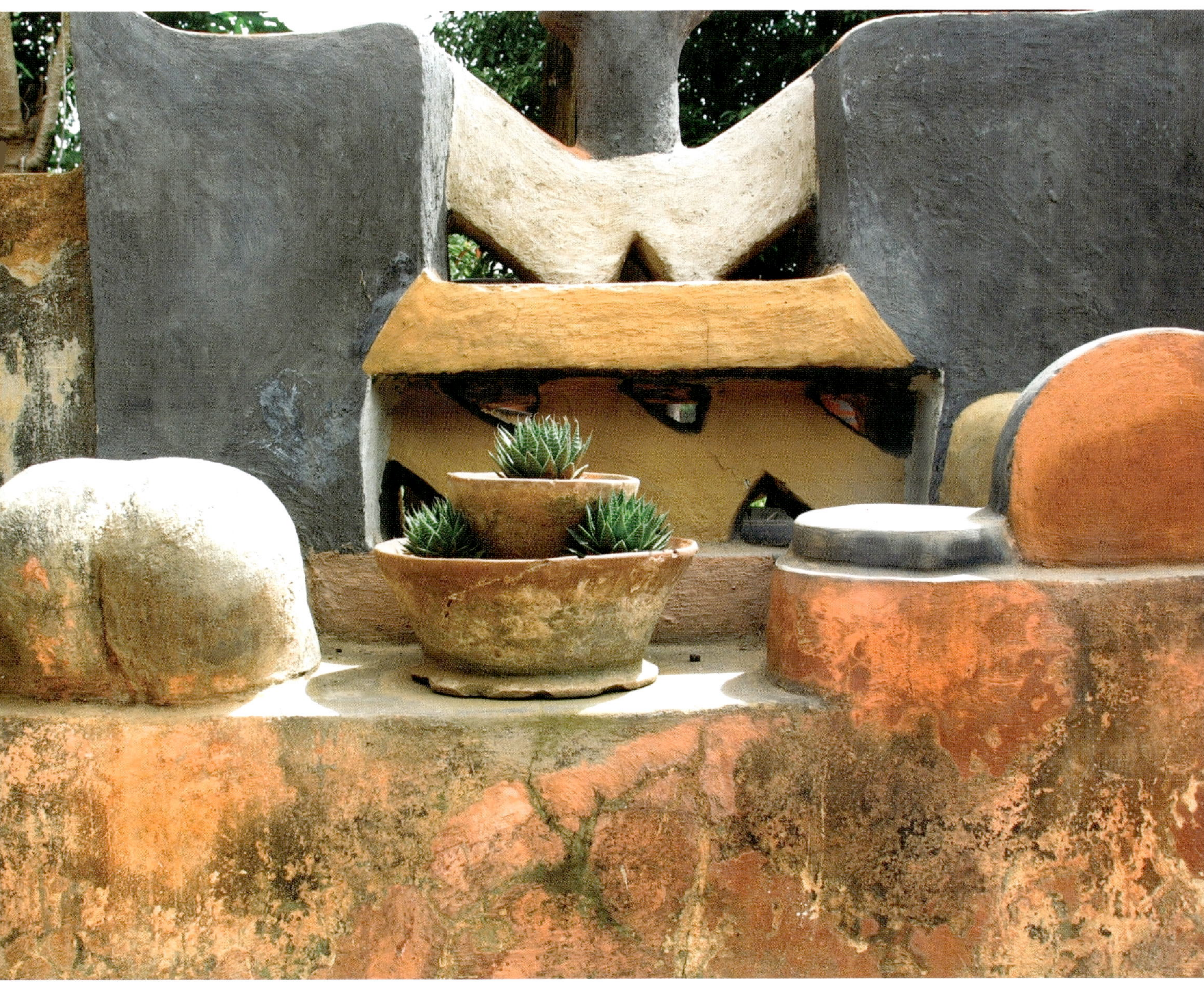

bepaalde kledingstukken, zoals de *shedo* , betrekking op de initiatiescholen. Noria legde uit hoe belangrijk inwijdingsscholen voor haar zijn. Dit was de enige scholing die zij ontvangen heeft en de invloed daarvan wordt in haar werk weerspiegeld. 1938, het jaar waarin Noria geboren is, was de laatste keer dat de meisjes het huis verlieten om zes maanden lang initiatie-onderricht te volgen. Daarna waren de scholen dichterbij en ging een meisje gedurende kortere perioden. Om haar werk te kunnen interpreteren en om Noria zelf te kunnen begrijpen, is kennis van de inwijdingsriten van groot belang.

DE INWIJDINGSSCHOLEN

In inheemse culturele tradities in zuidelijk Afrika worden vrouwen over het algemeen als ondergeschikt aan mannen beschouwd. In de Venda maatschappij delen vrouwen deze minderwaardigheid echter niet noodzakelijkerwijs. Op haar eigen erf is de vrouw de baas. Vrouwen mogen onroerend goed in eigendom hebben, dat hun gewoonlijk door hun vaders gegeven is of dat ze geërfd hebben bij gebrek aan een mannelijke erfgenaam. Noria is het hoofd van haar huishouden, eigenaar van haar onroerend goed en wordt door zowel haar familie als de gemeenschap gerespecteerd.

Toch zijn er nog terreinen in het dagelijks leven waarbij de positie van een Venda vrouw ondergeschikt is aan die van een man. Van vrouwen, geholpen door hun dochters, worden nog steeds verwacht dat ze elementaire huishoudelijke klussen zoals koken, schoonmaken en water halen, verrichten.

Noria vertelde me een ervaring uit haar jeugd. Een van haar vaders vrouwen keerde terug met een pot water op haar hoofd en een volle kalebas in haar hand. Haar vader begon tegen de vrouw te schreeuwen en begon haar te slaan omdat ze niet hard genoeg zou werken. Maar ze gaf geen krimp, en verspilde niet een druppel water. Een vrouw kende haar plaats.

Noria zegt: 'Vandaag de dag zijn de vrouwen sterker.'

Traditioneel gezien wordt van een Venda meisje verwacht dat zij de drie voornaamste inwijdingsscholen voor haar huwelijk doorloopt: de vhusha, het geen tijdens de puberteit plaats vindt; de tshikanda, een middelbare school bedoeld om de lessen van de puberteitsschool te herhalen, en de domba, een voorhuwelijkse school voor jonge vrouwen.

De ontwikkeling van het individu wordt gezien als een serie apart onderscheiden fasen: de puberteit markeert een belangrijke fase en het huwelijk een andere. De overgang van de ene fase naar de volgende wordt mogelijk door externe krachten (zoals de voorouders, goede zowel als kwade geesten en heksen die mannelijk zowel als vrouwelijk kunnen zijn). De rol van de inwijdingsscholen is om beginnelingen te onderwijzen in wat ze kunnen verwachten en hoe ze zich moeten gedragen in de volgende fase van hun ontwikkeling: door ceremonies en dansen uit te voeren worden ze in staat gesteld met fouten uit het verleden te breken en de uitdagingen van de toekomst aan te gaan. Deze ceremonies roepen ook de hulp van de voorouders in en versterken de initiates door middel van magie.

Vhusha is een achtdaagse training die bij een inwijdingshut gehouden wordt waar de meisjes in afzondering worden gehouden en waar ze geleerd wordt dat het belangrijkste onderdeel van het Venda vrouwzijn nederigheid is. Ze moeten hun hoofd gebogen, hun schouders naar beneden en hun armen gevouwen houden, of op een onderdanige manier hun handen onder de kin vouwen. Ze moeten huishoudelijke taken uitvoeren, grote stenen van de ene kant van de hut naar de andere kant sjouwen, of zware ladingen op hun ruggen of hoofden dragen. Soms moeten ze rond het erf kruipen, of als slangen met hun buik schudden, of gloeiende kooltjes in hun hand houden. Degene die ingewijd worden krijgen uitgebreid onderricht in zaken die met seks te maken hebben, en seksueel gedrag, verloving en huwelijk, met nadruk op het vermijden van zwangerschap buiten het huwelijk.

De inwijdelingen worden onderricht in zingen, dansen en ze leren de milayo, een combinatie van alledaagse lessen en obscuur en cultureel symbolisme. Noria legde uit dat het kennen van de milayo haar speciale kennis heeft gegeven en haar het recht geeft deel te nemen aan speciale vrouwenbijeenkomsten en ceremonies.

De middenschool, de tshikanda, vindt iedere drie tot vier jaar plaats, net voordat de school ter voltooiing van de opvoeding, de domba, plaats vindt.

De domba markeert de culminatie van het inwijdingsproces. Hier krijgt men het laatste onderricht voor het huwelijk en de school duurt ongeveer negen maanden. Het begint met het blazen van de phala phala, een koedoehoorn. Er wort een heilig vuur aangestoken in het dorp van de koning dat gedurende de domba aan de gang wordt gehouden. Zodra het vuur aangestoken is, worden de inwijdelingen door een ritueeldeskundige met geneesmiddelen behandeld, en alles dat in de domba gebruikt wordt, is besprenkeld met geneesmiddelen om de invloed van boze geesten af te weren. Er worden dansen geleerd en geheime liederen. Ze ontvangen seksuele voorlichting, kijken naar en nemen deel aan het onderwijzen van mime en krijgen geheime 'tribale' objecten te zien. Het doel van de domba is om jongeren met alle aspecten van het huwelijk vertrouwd te maken, evenals met de zeden en gewoonten van de Venda cultuur. De domba wordt door de VhaVenda als een nationale gebeurtenis gezien.

Noria beschreef de domba dans, een belangrijk onderdeel van de ceremonie. De dans wordt door de meisjes rond een heilig vuur in de khoro van de koning uitgevoerd. De dansers vormen een lange rij, waarbij iedere inwijdeling de elleboog van het meisje voor haar vasthoudt zodat ze allemaal naadloos in een grote ketting passen, die zich op het ritme van de ngoma en mirumba drums ritmisch rond het domba vuur slingert. Oorspronkelijk dansten de meisjes naakt, maar vandaag de dag dragen ze de shedo doek, die tussen de benen door wordt gehaald en zo van voren een schort vormt met een flap achter op de rug. Ze dragen ook metalen arm- en beenbanden die in het licht van het vuur glinsteren en rammelen als ze dansen. De dans stelt een python voor, die met vruchtbaarheid wordt geassocieerd en als een heilig symbool wordt beschouwd.

'Domba symboliek identificeert de muur van de khoro als het lichaam van de python god, en het erf als het Fundudzimeer, de plaats van oorsprong, de cosmologische baarmoeder. De inwijdelingen bevinden zich aldus in de baarmoeder van de python, klaar om herboren te worden, als volwassenen, huwbare en eerbiedige leden van de maatschappij af te studeren.'

Veel van Noria's figuren laten de symbolische leer van de domba zien en ook hoe belangrijk deze traditie voor haar zijn.

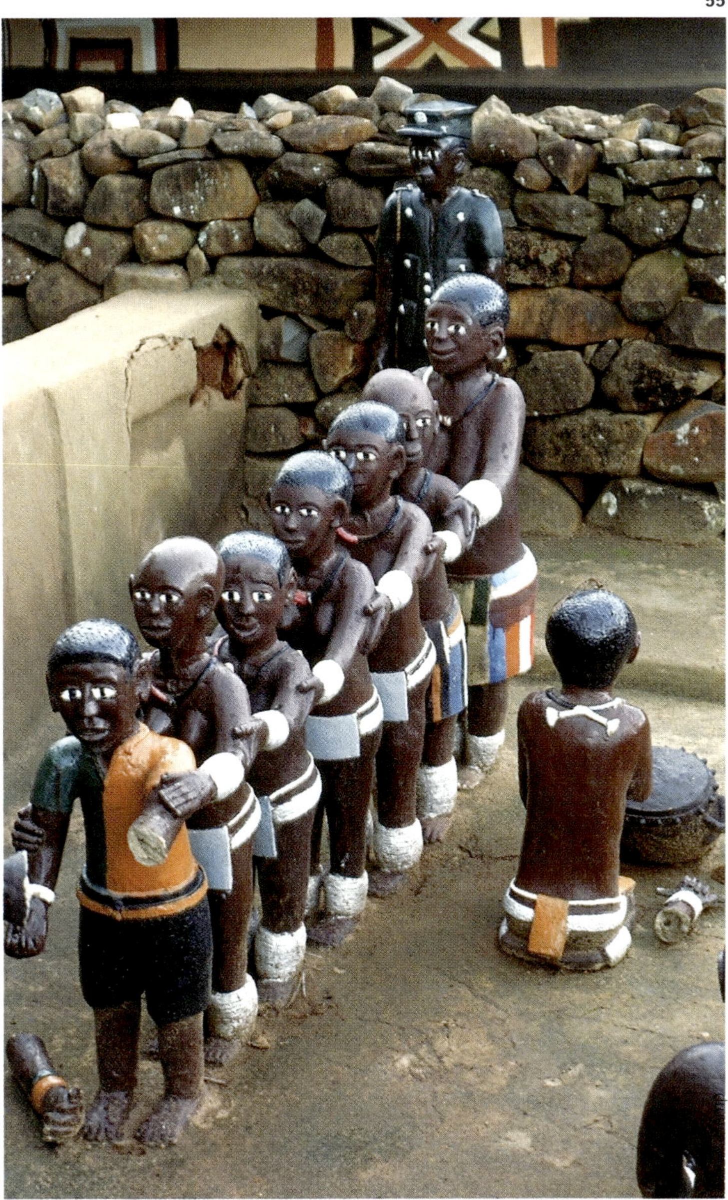

55. *Domba dancers,* clay and paint, at Ditike.

NORIA MABASA – EXHIBITION HISTORY

1984 *VhaVenda Art Exhibition*, group exhibition, Venda Sun Hotel, Thohoyandou, South Africa

1985 *Tributaries*, group exhibition, Africana Museum in Progress, Johannesburg and West Germany

1986 *Parade*, solo exhibition, Goodman Gallery, Johannesburg

Group exhibition, University of the Witwatersrand, Johannesburg

1987 *Vita Art Now*, group exhibition, Johannesburg Art Gallery, Johannesburg

Figurative Ceramics and Decorated Textiles, group exhibition, South African National Gallery, Cape Town

Cape Town Triennial, group exhibition, toured the major centres in South Africa

VhaVenda Sculpture Exhibition, group exhibition, Standard Bank National Arts Festival, Grahamstown, South Africa

1988 *VhaVenda/Shangaan Wood Sculpture Exhibition*, group exhibition, South African Association of the Arts, Pretoria

Clay+, group exhibition, University of South Africa, Pretoria

Neglected Tradition, group exhibition, Johannesburg Art Gallery

1989 *Group exhibition*, South African Association of the Arts, Pretoria

Images of Wood, group exhibition, Johannesburg Art Gallery, Johannesburg

Group exhibition, Sanderling Gallery, Johannesburg

Ten Years of Collecting, University of the Witwatersrand, Johannesburg

1990 *Group exhibition*, South African Association of the Arts, Pretoria

Afrika Now, group exhibition, Sanderling Gallery, Johannesburg

Art from South Africa, Museum of Modern Art, Oxford, United Kingdom

1991 *Group exhibition*, South African Association of the Arts, Pretoria

Town Country, group exhibition, Everard Read Gallery, Johannesburg

1992 *Ceramics in South Africa*, Tatham Art Gallery, Pietermaritzburg. Group exhibition to coincide with the launch of the book of the same name.

1992 *New Acquisitions*, South African National Gallery, group exhibition

1993 *Emhlabini. From the Earth: Pottery and Clay Sculpture from Southern Africa*, group exhibition, Standard Bank Gallery, Johannesburg.

1993 *Three person show* with Lucky Sibiya and Helen Sebidi, Everard Read Gallery, Johannesburg

Southern Cross Exhibition, Stedelijke Museum, Amsterdam, Holland

Incroci del Sud, Venice Biennale, Italy

1994 *Venda Exhibition*, group exhibition, First Johannesburg Biennale

1995 *Panoramas of Passage: Changing Landscapes from South Africa*, group exhibition, toured the United States for three years. Exhibited at the University of the Witwatersrand Art Galleries, Johannesburg, on its return in 1999.

1995 *Siyawela: Love, Loss and Liberty in South African Art*, group exhibition, Birmingham, United Kingdom, as part of the Africa 95 Festival. Exhibited at the University of the Witwatersrand Art Galleries, Johannesburg, on its return in 1996.

1998 *Rhythms of Africa*, group exhibition, Mukondeni Fine Arts, Johannesburg.

1999 Sandton Convention Centre, Johannesburg, group exhibition on permanent display

2000 *Artworks,* group exhibition, Mukondeni Fine Arts, Johannesburg.

2001–2003

Motho ke motho ka batho (A person is a person because of other people), group exhibition organised by the University of the Witwatersrand for the Department of Arts and Culture. Exhibited in Polokwane (Pietersburg), Limpopo, from June 2001 to March 2002, and at African Window, Pretoria, from September 2002 to November 2003.

2002 Awarded the Silver Level of the Order of the Baobab by President Mbeki.

PUBLIC COLLECTIONS

Among collections that include works by Noria Mabasa are those of::

Department of Arts and Culture

Guilford College, USA

Johannesburg Art Gallery, Johannesburg

Lesheba Wilderness, Limpopo Province

Museum of Modern Art, Oxford, UK

Pretoria Art Museum, Pretoria

South African Broadcasting Corporation collection (SABC), Johannesburg

Sandton Convention Centre, Johannesburg

South African National Gallery, Cape Town

Standard Bank Collection, University of the Witwatersrand

Tatham Art Gallery, Pietermaritzburg

University of Fort Hare, Alice

University of South Africa, Pretoria

University of the Witwatersrand, Johannesburg

University of the Western Cape, Belville

William Humphreys Art Gallery, Kimberley

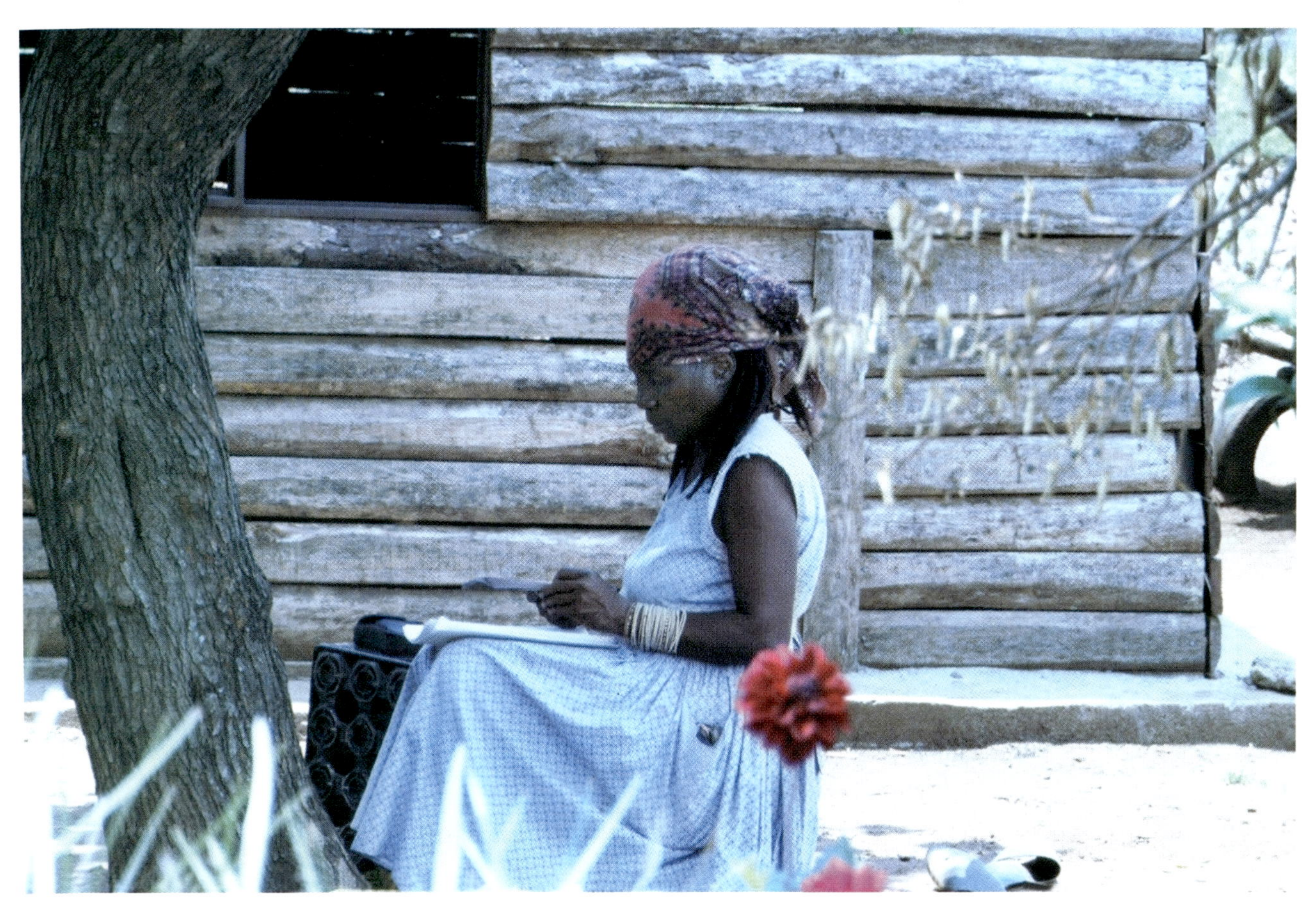

" The Venda people have always made everything themselves. This is why they know art. Venda is the number one place for art and I like the style of the Venda. I am proud to be Venda. I am also proud of myself because I am 'big', even if a man is carving, me, I am not a man, I am a woman and it makes me happy!"